D1453210

Now the War is Over

Now the War is Over

Britain 1919–1920

Simon Fowler and Daniel Weinbren

Pen & Sword

MILITARY

AN IMPRINT OF PEN & SWORD BOOKS LTD.
YORKSHIRE - PHILADELPHIA

First published in Great Britain in 2018 by
PEN & SWORD MILITARY
An imprint of
Pen & Sword Books Ltd
Yorkshire – Philadelphia

ISBN 9781473885974

A CIP catalogue record for this book is available from the British Library

Typeset in INDIA by Geniies IT & Services Private Limited

Printed by TJ International Ltd, Padstow, Cornwall

Pen & Sword Books Ltd incorporates the Imprints of Aviation, Atlas, Family History, Fiction, Maritime, Military, Discovery, Politics, History, Archaeology, Select, Wharncliffe Local History, Wharncliffe True Crime, Military Classics, Wharncliffe Transport, Leo Cooper, The Praetorian Press, Remember When, White Owl, Seaforth Publishing and Frontline Publishing.

For a complete list of Pen & Sword titles please contact

PEN & SWORD BOOKS LTD
47 Church Street, Barnsley, South Yorkshire, S70 2AS, England
E-mail: enquiries@pen-and-sword.co.uk
Website: www.pen-and-sword.co.uk

Or

PEN & SWORD BOOKS
1950 Lawrence Rd, Havertown, PA 19083, USA
E-mail: Uspen-and-sword@casematepublishers.com
Website: www.penandswordbooks.com

Contents

When the War was Over, Why was There No Revolution?

In the months following the Armistice on 11 November 1918, Britain sought to come to terms with the loss of life, the transformation of the economy to war work, and the resulting disruption of society as a whole. Nearly ¾ million British men died during the course of the war and more than 1½ million were severely wounded during the conflict.[1] Few people escaped the grief of losing a husband, father, son, fiancé, uncle, cousin or friend. There was a recognition that the war had destroyed the comforting certainties of Europe.[2] In 1921 Stephen Graham, who wrote accounts of his travels around Europe, concluded that he had witnessed the end of 'the pride of Christian culture, the greatest achievement in human history'.[3]

In the face of this severe disruption some people strove to build a better world, inspired by the Revolution in Russia. Most, however, did not wish to risk the prosperity or security they had acquired. Having stared into the chasm of the war, they sought a quiet life. When proposing a way forwards, they made sense of the world by looking backwards. In the City of London, there was reassertion of ideas of economic orthodoxy which would have been familiar to Peel and Disraeli. The powerful trade-union movement sought both to consolidate its wartime gains, but also to return to the pre-war situation wherever possible. In south-east London, the campaign for the conversion of Woolwich Arsenal to the production of locomotives, not munitions, reflected an enthusiasm for a return to the pre-war status of the skilled men.[4] In Skye and Lewis there were frequent attempts by local people to claim and work the land but these were not, historian Ewen Cameron argued, expressions of radicalism but 'demonstrations of loyalty to the orthodoxy'.[5] People wanted to retain a way of life, not create a new order. Elsewhere, people sought out mediums who, through claiming to have links to the dead, offered reassurance to the families of the fallen that their sons were indeed in a better place. By 1919 there were an estimated 250,000 bereaved members of the Spiritualists' National Union. Cults were formed. Mabel Barlthrop, a widow whose son had been killed in action, satisfied the yearning of 2,000 followers seeking a saviour and an explanation for suffering and death. She established a Commune of the Holy Ghost, in Bedford, telling people that she was Shiloh, the divine daughter of God and the female

Messiah. After the devastation of war, people found a future in which the past was ever present.

The disruptions seen in 1919 and 1920 were rarely unified, concerted or charismatically led. There was no single dominant vision of pre-war practices or how to restore them, rather a widespread nostalgia for a peaceful antebellum Eden that was expressed in many ways. When a community was threatened, its members got angry but their demands were largely for redress, not revolution. They used the weapons of strikes, bombings, land seizures and mutinies, but once minor adjustments had been made, small-scale concessions realized, anger quickly dissipated. It was only in the sense of a spot on a wheel travelling through 360 degrees and then returning to make contact with the ground, that there was an interest in revolution. As Adrian Gregory noted, the 'wars after the war were brief in duration and low intensity'.[6]

The revolutions in Russia in 1917 provided a model for rapid change. Echoing events there, soviets (committees of soldiers and workers) were established in several German cities. Short-lived Soviet Republics were created in Bavaria and in Hungary. Of more concern to imperialists there was a general strike in Winnipeg. This was presented by Scotland Yard's Director of Intelligence, Basil Thomson, as being 'not an industrial dispute but really an attempt to overthrow the constitutional government and to replace it by a form of Soviet government'. However, even in Glasgow, the most radical city in Britain, there was no effective attempt to establish a soviet.[7]

But this must not have seemed to have been the case to respectable citizens. In the United Kingdom in an eighteen-month period there were at least 422 Irish Republican Army (IRA) operations in mainland Britain, while in 1919 alone the actions of 2.4 million people led to 35 million days lost to strikes, compared with 6 million in 1918 and 11.5 million in 1913.[8] Servicemen mutinied and veterans, angered by their lack of pensions or work and their poor treatment by the State, protested, sometimes violently. The Home Office reported that 'in the event of rioting, for the first time in history, the rioters will be better trained than the troops'.[9] In Scotland and Ireland, land was seized. More subtly servants began to demonstrate new attitudes towards those who might have been seen as their social superiors. In her memoirs Vera Brittain noted that her maid was 'clearly an amateur prostitute who painted her face ten years before lipstick began to acquire its present fashionable respectability', while Virginia Woolf claimed that cooks were picking up the left-wing *Daily Herald* and entering the drawing room for a chat.[10] There was also an influenza epidemic from which 250,000 died in Britain alone – civilians and service personnel alike. Hospitals had little room as thousands of soldiers were still being treated there. Cities and towns in England and Wales experienced 30–40 per cent higher death rates as a result of the epidemic compared with rural areas. War production was affected as, unusually for such an illness, men and women living in urban areas and aged 15 to 40 were the most susceptible.[11]

These stresses and distresses seemed to threaten the stability of the country. When in August 1918, 10,000 of London's 19,000 policemen went on strike, the Prime Minister, Lloyd George, felt that Britain 'was closer to Bolshevism that day than any other time since'.[12] In January 1919 Conservative Minister Walter Long told Lloyd George that: 'I believe that there will be some sort of Revolution in this country and that before 12 months are past.'[13] The Duke of Northumberland concluded that: 'We are now faced with precisely the same position in regard to Labour as that with which we were faced before this war in regard to Germany.'[14] The suffrage campaigner Millicent Garrett Fawcett announced, somewhat optimistically, that: 'the war revolutionised the industrial position of women. It found them serfs and left them free.'[15] *Saturday Review* feared: 'crushing taxation, [an] impossible cost of living and an unseemly scuffle for jobs'.[16]

In January 1919 communists organized a general strike and took part in an armed battle in Germany which became known as the 'Spartacus' rising. The *Glasgow Herald* felt that the authorities 'actually believed a Spartacus coup was planned to start in Glasgow' and the chairman of the Clyde Workers' Committee, Willie Gallacher, later wrote 'This is correct. A rising was expected. A rising should have taken place.'[17] In *Red Terror and Green; the Sinn-Fein-bolshevist movement* (1920), Richard Dawson suggested that the Irish republican party, Sinn Fein, had 'entered into relations with John Maclean, the Bolshevik Consul-General in Glasgow', that 'Sinn Féin and Labour must be regarded as a single entity for the purpose of its revolutionary enterprise against Great Britain' and that 'the Irish republicans are in receipt of money from Russia'.[18] The idea that a revolution might well occur was widely discussed in the press.

On the Hebridian island of Uist, there was a sense, claimed businessman Tom Sandison shortly before the Armistice, that: 'We are all, consciously or unconsciously, heavily mortgaging "when-the-war-is-over". And I fear, most of our expectations will be unfulfilled, or claims unpaid.' A few months later he felt 'it's a topsy-turvy world, and no mistake, in this year of God 1919'.[19] Even in remote Lerwick, the *Shetland News* declared: 'Conditions in almost every phase of life have profoundly and fundamentally changed . . . it is utterly impossible to go back and live as if the war had never been'.[20] The *Shetland Times* averred: 'We are living in a period of unrest and desire for change . . . the underlying and compelling force of life . . . is . . . a determination that old things must pass away, and all things become new'. Yet, it saw no sign of the 'new heaven and new earth' promised after the war.[21]

The deputy leader of the Labour Party, Arthur Henderson, felt that: 'We have entered upon a new world with the coming of peace the world will enter upon a new era of revolutionary change to which there is no parallel in history.'[22] In 1919 he argued that Britain was: 'on the verge of industrial revolt'.[23] Another Labour MP, G.H. Roberts, felt that across the country 'there are large groups preparing for Soviet government'.[24] Similar sentiments were expressed by the Socialist Beatrice Webb and the Liberal Edward Grey.[25] The Deputy Secretary to the Cabinet, Thomas Jones, and even Lloyd George the Prime Minister echoed these ideas. They argued that the threatened coal strike of April 1919 could lead to the establishment of 'a Soviet Republic', while the national railway strike in September 1919 heralded: 'the most serious labour war the country has ever seen'.[26]

It was not only contemporary observers. Radical scholars have also seen this as a period when a revolutionary transformation seemed likely. The French historian Élie Halévy argued that 'in the spring of 1919 it was difficult to resist the impression that England was on the edge of a social revolution' and Walter Kendall called 1919 'the greatest revolutionary opportunity in generations'.[27] Subsequently Stuart Hall and Bill Schwarz have identified 'a profound crisis of the British state which became acute from 1910 to 1926'.[28] It has also been claimed that Britain was 'on the brink of revolution'.[29] Jay Winter pointed to the sense of rupture and discontinuity.[30]

The talk of revolution was overblown, yet there was a subtle but important transformation of society, although it was not for another generation and another world war that its full effects were to be felt. Arthur Marwick and Bentley Gilbert, two widely respected historians, agreed with contemporary observers that the war hastened change.[31] George Lansbury, the editor of the *Daily Herald*, wrote in the week after the 1918 General Election result, which had resulted in the overwhelming electoral victory of the Conservative coalition: 'It is a simple and dazzling fact that 1919 can be, and must be, the beginning of a veritable New Order, a radiant point of time to which our children's children will look back as a Renaissance, a Resurrection, decisively marking the workers' passing out of slavery to freedom, their progression from death to life.'[32]

Keith Jeffrey and Peter Hennessy concluded that on many occasions trade unions offered a challenge to the State which was 'often more subtle and to some more insidious' than armed insurrection.[33] Moreover, some of the talk of revolution disguised an enthusiasm for reform. Some press reports presented the miners' leaders and their associates as eloquent and adept tribunes of the people, fighting and winning the class war, by proxy. *Labour Leader* concluded that: 'The Revolution is evolving . . . The rugged figure of Robert Smillie, the miners' intrepid leader in that gilded setting is symbolic of the day that is yet to dawn – but will dawn – when Labour shall enter its full inheritance.'[34] When Labour won a majority on a county council for the first time, in March 1919, George Lansbury concluded that 'This is indeed a revolution.'[35]

Much of the disruption was localized. It did little to challenge the national order. Different trades and different localities tended to emphasis their independence.[36] Although there was some national welfare provision, much of what people received was arranged locally, administered by local committees, or paid for by local charitable or mutual aid organisations.[37] There was genuine anger but protesters disagreed as to the cause of their problems and how to resolve them. The historian Joan Smith points out that: 'was still 'a "local" society in the sense that each conurbation's industrial and social structure could have a profound influence on the political life of the town. Not until the late 1920s/1930s were local differences overwhelmed …workers' beliefs develop[ed] in relation to the 'common sense' of their towns as well as their own class interests'.[38]

During the war agreements in the munitions industries were often reached on a plant-by-plant basis and after the war people focused on the local.[39] A former serviceman in Bristol who smashed tram windows, attacked the police and called for ex-servicemen to replace the 'conductresses' recalled how: 'You was feeling revolutionary. I know I did nearly go off the deep end. Only those who went through it knows. That's when we nearly had a revolution in Bristol, smashed the tram cars up.'[40]

Willie Gallacher, a union activist on Clydebank in 1919, also looked largely to his own locality when he argued that: 'had there been an experienced revolutionary leadership of these great and heroic masses . . . we could easily have persuaded the soldiers to come out and Glasgow would have been in our hands'.[41] According to the historian of the movement, Peter Hart, even the IRA activists in England and Scotland had 'internalised a very British sense of localism'.[42]

When, in March 1919, a Nottinghamshire Miners' Association strike leader, Charles Bunfield, raised the issue of the nationalization of the mines at a meeting about local concerns in the pits, he was heckled with cries of 'We don't want to hear about that, this is a local programme.'[43] In the same month the elections for Nottinghamshire County Council were reported as being 'very quiet . . . It is impossible to get the people generally to take an interest in the contests and the polls were lamentably low.'[44] The focus was on local industrial struggles. Militant miners were often organized through ad hoc networks rather than formally constituted bodies. While there were a few local newspapers, notably the *Merthyr Pioneer* in South Wales and the *Worker* on the Clyde, there was no national newspaper that connected the different campaigns.[45] There were numerous localized, episodic and parochial actions but little national co-ordination across the industry. Against national policy, 150,000 miners in Yorkshire went on strike for four weeks.

Nottinghamshire miners had no coherent theory or organization but instead, concluded historian Martin Ives, 'parochialism' and 'semi-developed ideas and contradictions', while the Yorkshire Miners Association has been characterized in terms of 'parochial solidarity' and in South Wales the strikes were 'brief, sectional and uncoordinated'.[46]

Communities defined themselves in terms of those who were excluded as well as those who were included. Around the country, in 1919 black people, Chinese, Arabs and Asians were attacked by white people anxious to defend and protect communities based on race. And German residents were deported to Germany.

In addition to the continued importance of locality and community, a further factor which accounts for the relative quiescence of the country was the determination of those in control to ensure that, while there was some broadening as to who would be permitted to engage with the levers of power, those levers would remain in safe hands. Lloyd George's government was prepared, in the event of a miners' strike, to 'use all the resources of the state without the smallest hesitation', as the Lord Privy Seal, Andrew Bonar Law, promised in March 1919. He presented the miners as an existential threat, adding 'if such a struggle comes it can have only one end or there is an end of government in this country'.[47] He was supported by the coal owners, the press and, because they were as nervous of victory as well as defeat, many trade unionists. In March 1919, the rail workers union leader, Jimmy Thomas, argued that: 'victory for either side may be purchased at too great a price', that an industrial dispute could have consequences 'almost as dangerous as defeat by Germany'.[48] In July 1919 he told a conference that the government was 'making preparations to crush' the Triple Alliance of unions and was prepared to call out 'the military to shoot down our people'.[49] When the government offered a commission on the mines, most of the miners voted to accept this rather than take strike action.

The Bolshevik coup in Russia could not be mimicked in Britain because groups such as the Socialist Labour Party and the British Socialist Party had few members, were sectarian and had little influence. The Independent Labour Party, No Conscription Fellowship, Fellowship of Reconciliation, Union of Democratic Control and the Women's International League agreed in their opposition to the war but on little else. The radical Soldiers', Sailors' and Airmen's Union, which was formed in late 1918, ran a campaign for men to demobilize themselves, was raided by the police and swiftly disappeared.[50] The communist A.L. Morton, who lived through the period, claimed that the ruling class 'was saved only by the absence of a determined centralised leadership to coordinate the separate streams of turbulent popular revolt'.[51] *The Times* argued that striking engineers were 'the unconscious instruments of a planned campaign drawn up by "intellectuals" in the background who desire to emulate Lenin and Trotsky'.[52] It later referred to manipulation by Russian leaders 'using their 'clear logical Jewish brains to undermine Christianity'.[53] These fantasies have been dismissed by historian Chris Wrigley who concluded that 'there does not appear to have been a potentially revolutionary situation.'[54]

There was widespread acceptance of the constitutional framework among all sections of society. Labour's strategy of gradual state intervention was popular. The widened franchise revitalized interest in parliamentary democracy. As in Germany and many other European countries, there were also populist activists on the extreme right. However, in Britain they lacked support let alone effective leadership. Historian Adrian Gregory concluded that:

> All of the poisonous ingredients of extreme right-wing politics existed in Britain – particularly southern England by the end of 1918: middle-class grievance and resentment of big capital and big labour, xenophobia including anti-Semitism, disillusionment with parliamentary government, conspiracy theories and even perhaps a tendency to reluctantly condone violence. The soup was ready, but no one turned up the heat.[55]

Most people, including trained, armed mutinous soldiers, sought to ameliorate their conditions, not to topple the government.

Even if tiny left-wing organizations had been as dedicated as Morton desired, they would have been stymied by the fragmented and sectional trade unions. Some union leaders blocked militancy.[56] Under the guidance of the labour movement leadership, 'protesters and dissenters in England largely confined themselves to seeking ways to force the system to respond to their needs and demands'.[57] The government offered concessions, bought time and promoted divisions within the ranks of its opponents. Such options were not open to governments of the defeated nations of Germany, Russia and Hungary, where there were revolutions. Unions had gained a place within the new arrangements via the Labour Party. Analysis has shown how trade-union leaders, having challenged the State from below, were offered opportunities to work with employers in order to rebuild.[58] Ralph Miliband concluded that the unions favoured parliamentary government as the means of achieving the new society.[59] Employers, and trade unions, pledged themselves to the legal enforcement of a 48-hour week.[60] John Foster built on the view of the Russian revolutionary leader, Lenin, that 'the labour aristocracy had been "bribed out of imperialist super-profits and converted into watchdogs of capitalism, into corruptors of the labour movement"'.[61] Foster's explanation for the political quiescence was that working people were given 'a set of bribes that by-passed the market and went direct from the state or employers to (or through) the trade union leaders and politicians'.[62] Keith Middlemas also attributed significant powers to the labour movement leadership noting that the Trades Union Congress and the

National Conference of Employers' Organizations, 'crossed the political threshold and became part of the extended state' thus marginalizing the extremists and reducing the level of class conflict.[63]

Union leaders felt that the constitution gave them a platform and status. Labour had confidence in the neutrality and malleability of the State. It could be used to provide jobs, economic growth and goods. Perhaps because union leaders gained greater influence there was widespread acceptance of the constitutional framework. As a result people at all levels of society, sometimes through seemingly disruptive methods, sought stability.

Across the country there were other frustrations. Food was scarce, often of poor quality and expensive, jobs were hard to get or keep, the demobilization of the troops was slow and there was the threat that troops might be sent to Russia in order to defeat the Bolsheviks and, as we have seen, numerous strikes disrupted life. There was also the sense that the State had in some way deceived the people over the costs and direction of the war. This was a particularly strong feeling among veterans. However, when perceived problems were mitigated, notably once black sailors and Chinese workers were seen to return to the state of second class citizens and women were dispatched back to care for their families or into domestic service, the anger diminished. In Ireland, the demand for land was linked to national identity and focused on ownership, not the right to be tenants. Many of the 'soviets' formed in Ireland collapsed when the officially recognized managers and owners made concessions to the workers. Ross McKibbin noted that the rate of trade-union growth was less during the war than in the period between 1910 and 1913 and concluded that 'everything points to Labour's enduring *ante-bellum* character: continuity of leadership and personnel at all levels, effective continuity of policy and, above all, continuity of organisation'.[64] Simon Webb concluded that the government was not overthrown because people remained loyal to their own leaders.[65] The story of 1919 is the story not of a revolution which failed, though there were revolutionaries, but of uncoordinated anger which slowly dissipated.

The government did not seek to take on vast new functions after the war. Rather, it tried to present itself as eager to disengage from activity, especially the ownership of the means of production and distribution. This was not done in a systematic manner, there was no plan. The many policy papers of the Ministry of Reconstruction were largely ignored and the Ministry itself disappeared into obscurity. But then the government was not faced with a well-organized united opposition. Despite the upheaval and turmoil on every level the yearning for a settled community built on familiar notions of the State and the Empire prevailed. In 1919 *Punch* produced a strip cartoon about the war. It began and ended with the hero sitting by his range and included the line 'It's not as if we are a military nation.'[66] The British working man had reluctantly left his fireside, had fought gallantly but had long sought to return to his hearth and home. Such a notion of British civility which categorized strife, at home or abroad, as alien to the peaceable British psyche was adapted and adopted. Following the amelioration of a number of immediate concerns the country settled into grumbling stability.

Chapter 1

Demobilization and the Return to Civilian Life

One of the biggest crises to face the government in the immediate post-war period was the demobilization of the armed services. At the Armistice some 3.5 million men, and a few thousand women, were serving in the Army with another 415,000 in the Royal Navy and 290,000 in the Royal Air Force. The experience of demobilization after previous wars, particularly after the Napoleonic War a century before, suggested that rapidly reducing the Army might lead to economic depression and mass unemployment as tens of thousands of men entered the labour market at the same time. This was something the government wanted to avoid.

For many, the return to 'civvy street' was long-winded and complicated. Although the government wanted to release men from the armed forces, it also wanted to maintain the services at a reasonable level to meet any emergencies. Delays caused frustration among the troops awaiting discharge, and this occasionally turned to violence and in Whitehall there were concerns over unrest among angry men trained to kill. While many men were delighted to return, life in peacetime Britain could be distressing, challenging and confusing. Many veterans had physical wounds and some had psychological scars. The effects of these frequently remained for many years, as did bitterness at the paucity of the pension or appropriate acknowledgement of their service. Relationships between those who had remained at home and those who had fought and found limited opportunities on their return became strained.

In 1917 and 1918 detailed plans for demobilization were drawn up by the Minister of Reconstruction, Edwin Montagu. His intention was that skilled workers, and those with confirmed jobs to go to, would be discharged first. This would minimise the shock to the economy and the released men could begin the work of returning Britain to a peacetime economy. To do otherwise might 'flood British industry with man power without reference to its fitness, much of it would be worthless in the initial stages of reconstruction and, which for that reason would provide an added problem of unemployment'.[1] In addition, it was thought that soldiers would continue to be needed in case of further hostilities with Germany. The only real problem, it was believed, would be finding enough shipping to bring discharged men back from France and the other theatres of war.[2] It turned out that shipping was the least of the problems, although the Channel ports proved to be a frustrating bottleneck.

Even if they had ever thought about it, decision-makers at the Ministry of Reconstruction had forgotten that the British Army was no longer simply a professional elite. It had become a civilian army, increasingly representative of the nation as a whole. Professor John Bourne has noted that: 'The British soldier . . . was essentially the British working man in uniform'.[3] It had become largely an army drawn: 'from an urbanised, disciplined and deferential society, enjoying a popular culture that made light of hardship and with an experience, a sense of community and a sense of values different to our own'.[4] This had given the Army real strength during the war. Despite constant grumbling, morale had remained high among the troops. There had not been the mutinies and other disciplinary problems that had occurred in the French and German armies.[5] But when the war was over the soldiers naturally wanted to return home. They could not see any reason to remain in uniform just in case an obviously broken Germany restarted the war, let alone become involved with a new war in Russia.

It seemed only fair that the men who had served longest should be discharged first. But under the original scheme it was quite likely, if they had no job to return to, they might end up being some of the last discharged. The perceived gross unfairness of the plan led to mutinies and protests throughout the Army. In February 1919, Winston Churchill, then Secretary for War, called it a 'complicated artificial system open at every point to suspicion of jobbery and humbug'.[6] Demobilization was open to abuse, as it was fairly easy to obtain a form or 'slip' that allowed early discharge. Major Richard of the Royal Field Artillery remembered that at his demobilization centre at Dieppe:

> a boy of about eighteen turned up at the battery – and I'm damned if he didn't get a white paper! Apparently his father was a miller and he was considered indispensable to his father's business. That really was too much. I knew that if I let this chap off before all the other lads who had been out at the Front for years, I'd be asking for trouble. I was angry about the injustice of it – obviously he had nobbled an MP to get his white paper. There was no other possible reason for it. So I did the only thing possible and I tore up his paper and forgot about it.[7]

General James Whitehead, who was Assistant Adjutant at the General Headquarters, British Expeditionary Force, came across release forms for the 'mace-bearer of a mayor and . . . someone's butler'.[8]

As a miner, Private Frank Richards was one of the first men to be discharged from his regiment, the Royal Welch Fusiliers. At the base in Cambrai he and other miners had to answer a few questions about mining in an attempt to weed out malingers: 'One man admitted to me before he left the Battalion that he had never been on top of a coal pit in his life. I gave him a few particulars and he passed the mining officers all right. No doubt he had saved himself six or twelve months' soldiering. I expect many more did the same.'[9] There were further grumblings about the inflexible nature of the plans and their slow implementation. As early as 7 December 1918, the *Daily Herald* complained:

> Send the boys home. Why in the world the delay? The war is not officially 'over', but everybody knows that in fact it is over. Munition making has stopped; motorists can joy ride; the King has had a drink; society has had its victory ball and is settling down to its old job of pleasure making . . . Danger of too rapid demobilisation? Bunkum? There are thousands of men for whom jobs are waiting, but the Army won't let them go. And – even if a man hasn't a job – why not let him go home at once?[10]

Lieutenant George Thomas, Sherwood Foresters, wrote to his parents, just before Christmas 1918, that:

> The job is finished and one put up with a great deal of things when there was a necessity to help beat the Boche [Germans], but now a lot of things simply irritate me. Nobody has as yet been demobilised except coalminers and they are going as fast as the authorities can print new forms. There are extremely few men who have any desire to remain in the Army – all are anxious to discard their khaki now the job is finished.[11]

Employers too protested about the scheme. Birmingham City Council spoke of the 'incapacity, circumlocution and general disorder with which the question of demobilisation is being dealt with by government departments, leading to general dislocation of business and great disadvantages to the men'.[12] More seriously a flood of protests erupted across the Army. In France, Sergeant Guy Buckeridge remembered that: 'It seemed as though the whole Army had become imbued with a spirit of revolt against the system which had held the individual for so long.'[13]

The months between the Armistice and the demobilization of the armed forces were strange and difficult ones for both the Army, the men themselves and their officers. Discipline and routine, which once seemed so important, lost their significance. It was, as Philip Gibbs, the pre-eminent journalist of the day, suggested, as if an unwritten contract between ordinary soldiers and the Army had been broken, that the men would serve loyally for the 'duration of the war'. In return, their military service would cease once the war had been won. 'It was now for the War Office to fulfil its pledges.'[14] Brigadier General Frank Crozier wrote that in France: 'impatient men burn their camps and huts, assault their officers, imprison their generals and the staffs, and hold up demobilisation itself – the very thing their wish to speed up – by their mutinous conduct and the destruction of the demobilisation papers'.[15] There was little problem with the troops who moved into Germany to occupy the Rhineland under the terms of the Armistice, as they were fully engaged in their work.

The real difficulties for the British authorities lay not with the troops in Germany, but within the units in bases behind what had been the front line, where there was little to do and where officers were little respected or able to enforce discipline. To fill the gap in a soldier's day once occupied by the war many officers, particularly those few remaining pre-war regulars, tried to re-impose the strict discipline that had existed in the Army before 1914. In Frank Richards' battalion of the Royal Welch Fusiliers, the colonel commanding lectured the non-commissioned officers (corporal and sergeants) threatening to reduce to the ranks any man who fraternized with ordinary soldiers. But it had little effect, because, as Richards' pointed out, most in the audience: 'had joined up for the duration of the War and did not care a damn whether they were reduced or not'. Another idea to keep men busy was for them to parade with their steel helmets burnished. This meant scraping off dark green camouflage paint, which took hours: 'There was more swearing over this order than I had heard for some time . . . the only good [the order] had done was to improve the praying language of the men'. More positively the battalion launched an education scheme, although perhaps more through boredom rather than real attempt to teach anything useful. As Richards concluded: 'The bulk of the men were quite indifferent: to get home, not to prepare for a nebulous job on getting there, was all they cared about.'[16] Over the next few months, men left the Royal Welch Fusiliers in dribs and drabs, with Richards being one of the first to leave. The battalion finally departed for England on 29 May 1919, when just five officers, under Captain William Fox, who had been one of the first men from the regiment to step ashore in France in August 1914, and seventy-five other ranks embarked at Le Havre. Their departure was enlivened by a wrangle over whether the regimental goat had the right papers to be allowed into England.[17]

Elsewhere, officers organized sports and other activities to keep their men busy. Gunner Leonard Ounsworth, Royal Garrison Artillery, and his comrades: 'were kept occupied while we were waiting to be demobilised – we were playing football several times a week, and we had the horses to look after and exercise every morning. There were other activities – including a boxing tournament once a week.' Even so they took their revenge on a group of military policemen (MPs), who had been responsible for maintaining military discipline, in a brawl at Leeds station: 'I just sat and watched – and in less time than it takes to tell, there were all these MPs stretched out unconscious on the platform.'[18]

Many officers found it hard to motivate the men. Major Richard Russell of the Royal Field Artillery admitted that it 'was still very hard to keep the chaps amused when all they wanted to do was to go home. But they just had to wait.'[19] In such circumstances, the men often turned to drink and to women, both of which were in short supply in France and Belgium. In Brussels, Frank Crozier found: 'an orgy of vice in which many British soldiers joined'. He warned his officers that: 'The men have evidently gone woman-mad.'[20]

In such atmosphere, it was easy for emotions to get out of hand and difficult for discipline to be maintained. In the backwater of Salonika, Major Alfred Bundy had to talk to a group of men who had been:

> disgracefully abusive to their officers . . . My remarks were greeted by catcalls and rude noises, but I knew that there must be a large proportion of the men who were anxious to assist me in the performance of my duty and in facilitating their return to England, so I announced that if there was obstruction I should have the offenders arrested and kept back. There was then almost complete silence, and I had no further difficulty.[21]

Even so, Bundy later confided to his diary that: 'there seems to have been nothing exciting except reports of murder, robbery and rioting. If this is peace, war is better!'[22] But often it was not enough, Brigadier General Frank Crozier, advised that the 'majority of the men [were] savage for freedom. Tactful handling of the situation is required, and when this is the rule, the British soldier is, as usual, sensible.'[23] Alf Drury recalled a situation where tact appears to have triumphed over discipline:

> The lads who'd been in the Army weren't going to put up with anything. I was stationed in Biggleswade in 1918; I'd had to stop in for 12 months extra, had malaria and been in hospital. I was in civvy lodgings and I'd got a side of bacon for the landlady, so I was cock lodger, you see. But the young lads in camp only had biscuits for breakfast [. . .] these lads at Biggleswade came to me and asked what they should do. So I said 'Tomorrow morning, when the whistle blows, don't fall in'. Sure enough when the whistle blew, not man moved.

The complaints were noted and the men were not punished for as Colonel told Alf, 'If it goes no further, I'll forget what happened'.[24] Ginger Byrne remembered that when he reached Le Havre he was stopped by the military police and taken to the Rail Transport Officer:

When we got there we let Ross do the talking because he'd got the MM [Military Medal] up and all. He gave the officer the full strength: told him all our little troubles. He listened. Then he turned to the red cap [military police] and said he didn't think it was necessary to take us up to the dispersal camp and would the red cap please take us down to the jetty. 'Yes' he says, a bit grim, 'I'll see them down to the jetty, Sir'. Nothing can stop Ross, once he got started. He turned round. 'You take us down to the jetty and put us on the leave boat', he says . . . We 'ad a right quiet walk down to the jetty, I can tell you.[25]

During 1919 servicemen mutinied in at least twenty places across the country as well as at Calais and camps elsewhere in France and Flanders. Men demanded to be demobilized as soon as possible and called for an improvement in their conditions while they waited. The authorities were in two minds about how to respond. If their response was too harsh, it risked inflaming and perhaps politicizing the situation, but to cave in risked the spread of mutinies.[26] At Calais, Field Marshal Haig wanted the mutineers shot in order to maintain Army discipline, but the Secretary for War Winston Churchill refused to allow this to happen.

The worst riots took place in North Wales in March 1919. Almost 15,000 Canadians soldiers were held at Kinmel Park waiting to go home. The place was overcrowded and a sea of mud. Strikes had held up the delivery of both fuel and food supplies. Men were on half rations and many had received no pay for weeks. Several delegations were sent to the senior officers, protesting about conditions and the way the men felt they were being treated. Nothing was done. Troop ships allocated to Canadians were re-allocated to the US forces, who had only been fighting since 1917. On 1 March, there were rumours that tempers had boiled over and that one of the canteens had been looted. Then some of the soldiers refused to go on a route march. In the early hours of the morning of the 4th, with tempers growing more and more frayed by the second, discontent finally spilled over into direct action. As some of the groups moved off to raid and loot the camp stores the call 'Come on the Bolsheviks' was heard. There was a large, privately run canteen just outside the military camp but its goods were too expensive for most soldiers. It was set on fire and the officers' and sergeants' messes were looted. When twenty mutineers were seized by loyal troops the rest simply charged the guardroom and set them free. Three rioters and two guards were killed in the affair. Many others had been wounded or injured. There was, however, no great conspiracy to mutiny at Kinmel. Following the riots priority was given to repatriating the men. By the end of month, they had all returned to Canada.[27]

At Shoreham, there was a mutiny of Guards in March 1919. According to Robert Graves and Alan Hodge: 'they marched into Brighton, amid friendly cheers from the crowds along the roads, to lodge a protest with the Mayor, who received them so gracefully that they returned to camp feeling that something had been done'.[28] There were naval mutinies in January 1919. Although a red flag was raised on HMS *Kilbride*, the disputes were largely over pay, tardy demobilization and the threat of deployment against the former ally, Russia. Folkestone harbour was seized so that for a few days vessels could not take soldiers to France or Russia. The unrest soon died away after many men were granted leave or demobilized, a few were imprisoned or had fire hoses turned upon them. Following the removal of soldiers who had been arrested to local police cells the police stations in Bow Street and at Epsom were besieged. Soldiers of the 6th Battalion, Royal Marine Light Infantry and regiments based in Yorkshire and Hampshire mutinied rather than be sent to face the Bolsheviks in Russia.

The National Federation of Discharged and Demobilized Sailors and Soldiers organized a march to the Houses of Parliament in January 1919. Former soldiers appeared on lorries with signs reading 'We won the war, Give us our tickets', 'No more red tape', 'More beer' and 'Promises are not pie crust'. *The Times* reported that the demonstrators received a 'distinctly cool' reception from passers-by.[29]

Alarm Within the Authorities

Scotland Yard's Special Branch had been gathering information about labour unrest since at least 1917. By 1919 its head, Basil Thomson, was focused on a possible link between working class unrest and Bolshevik subversion. He was particularly concerned about Bolshevism in the armed forces. In January 1919, he reported to the Home Secretary that revolutionaries were 'snatching at the opportunity offered by the unrest in the Army' and that the left-wing press was reporting on mutinous activities in Folkestone while others on the left opposed the use of British troops in a war against Russia and promoted strike action. He added that, 'It would be foolish to make light of the serious effect of the recent demonstrations by soldiers, particularly in France' and went on to claim that 'The trouble may largely be ascribed to the action of a few newspapers'. The *Daily Mail* had an edition printed in Paris. This was one of the few sources of news for those in the services on the Continent. It carried articles on demobilization, ran a labour column and according to Thomson had a 'bad effect on the troops'. However, he concluded that 'the heart of the Army is sound, the recent demonstrations and the Police strike show how a determined minority of Extremists can stampede the quiet men into subordination'. The report added:

The wildest rumours are being circulated, In Sheffield they are saying that at a recent meeting of naval ratings at the Crystal Palace eight officers were shot and all the men discharged and that the trouble began by some men being shot for refusing to go to Russia.

Soldiers on leave talking in railway carriages are doing harm by declaring that there is no discipline left in the Army, as for instance at Brussels a battery refused to clean the guns and went unpunished. They are even boasting of getting home with property 'looted' from the officers.

Another rumour is to the effect that at Havre the ASC [Army Service Corps] refused to shoot at men of the RGA [Royal Garrison Artillery], that the officers opened fire, the men replied and many casualties ensued. . . . There has been, unfortunately, a decline in the morale of all the Allied troops during the past fortnight.

Thomson also noted: 'The queues that have already begun in Birmingham outside the butcher's shops and at the out-of-work Pay Offices are solid ground for the Extremists. In Birmingham, the people are already grumbling at the continuance of the 50% rise in rail fares'.[30] He later wrote that: 'February 1919 was the high-water mark of revolutionary danger in Great Britain. Many of the soldiers were impatient at the delay in demobilization. Russia had shown how apparently easy it was for a determined minority to seize the reins of power.'[31]

Not every unit suffered disciplinary difficulties, let alone mutiny, but there was enough of this to worry the authorities, which may explain the contradictory messages offered the mutineers, initially there was rapid acceptance of their demands, and then eventually the Army tried to take tough action against the mutineers to prevent things getting out of hand. One wonders, however, what would have happened had hostilities been resumed, but fortunately the Germans had their own, rather more severe, problems with mutineers and ill-discipline soldiers. The British were lucky that, unlike the Germans, there was no organized political movement among their mutineers. The radical historian Walter Kendall suggested that: 'If socialist influence had existed within any of the services, if there had been, for example, a common front between soldiers and sailors in 1918–19, if the soldiers had launched a co-ordinated movement or established links with any of the trade union struggles pending, then the whole future of the state might well have been called into question.'[32] The mutineers, however, really had only one demand and one demand alone, that was to be released from the services as soon as possible. And to this demand the Army had little choice but to agree. And as demobilization gathered pace, the mutinies faded away.

On receiving notification of demobilization men would be sent to a camp at one of the French ports to await transport across to England. Initially men were sent individually, but by the spring of 1919 companies and even whole battalions would cross together. The delay might be a few days or a few weeks of tedium, with basically nothing to do but mooch around the town, play cards with other men, and wait for the call. Conditions on the troops ships crossing the Channel were cramped. Colonel Rowland Feilding of the Coldstream Guards left France with men from his battalion on 11 May 1919. He wrote to his wife that:

> We crossed from Havre in a crowded transport, on which we passed the night. Besides ourselves there was about 1500 Canadian troops. I had, or rather shared, a cabin, but the men had scarcely room to breathe. We hung about all yesterday and got away about quarter to five in the evening.
>
> I might describe our journey from Southampton to beyond London – in fact till it became too dark to see – almost as a triumphant progress. The long train of transport never failed to draw attention to us as troops returning from France, and in the good old English way, the people turned out of their houses and thronged the streets as we passed and cheered and waved their handkerchiefs.
>
> Though they represented but a microscopic proportion of the fighting troops, it was nice to think that at last, after all the years of war, these men were getting some first-hand recognition from their fellow-countrymen.[33]

Feilding and his men ended up at Landguard Fort near Felixstowe, where the unit was discharged.

The initial demobilization plan was complicated and unfair. On becoming Secretary of State for War on 10 January 1919, Winston Churchill quickly abandoned the scheme. Instead of a system based on industry's ability to absorb discharged men, soldiers were now discharged by age, length of service and combat experience. Once the new plan was introduced demobilization began to go smoothly. Within weeks 50,000 men a day were passing through the dispersal centres. Lance Corporal A.J. Abraham was one of the men to be demobilised early, probably because he was discharged from a military hospital in Aldershot:

> On 30 January, I had my final medical board and was asked to sign a declaration that I was leaving the Army in a perfect state of health. I was

not, but at that time I think I would have signed a declaration saying that I was Lloyd George if that what it took to get my release – so I put my signature to the document without a qualm.[34]

By mid–April, over half the officers and three-quarters of ordinary soldiers had been discharged, with the vast majority of the rest having left by the end of the year, and by the first anniversary of the Armistice all but 125,000 of men who had enlisted for the duration of the war had been released. All but 900,000 men were discharged, most of whom who remained were to be volunteers or had been conscripted in 1918. According to Churchill: 'if anyone has to stay, it must be those who are not the oldest, not those who came the earliest, not those who suffered the most'.[35] Unemployment did not rise significantly and, in general, men were quickly absorbed into the booming economy, However, there were great regional variations and, as the economy faltered towards the end of 1920, many ex-soldiers found themselves out of work.[36]

Discharged men were given a suit, and allowed to keep their uniform, boots and underclothes, although they were expected to wear civilian clothes after a month. Each discharged man was issued with a bundle of papers: seven different certificates, including a voucher for a suit (or an allowance of 52s 6d) for clothing, a voucher for return of his Army greatcoat to the value of £1, a railway warrant to his home station and a protection certificate, which had to be kept in case the man was recalled to the colours. Inevitable the suits didn't always fit very well. The Revd Philip Clayton, universally known as Tubby because of his short physique, was issued with a suit that had been made for a guardsman 'as a final tribute from a grateful country'.[37] A man also had £2 to be charged against his account, a service gratuity of £1 for each year of service, and a war gratuity that was meant to 'compensate him for the loss of the ancient and honourable privilege of looting' together with a protection certificate. Private Ginger Byrne recalled going to the Machine Gun Corps Pay Office and then to Crystal Palace: 'I went in to the Crystal Palace a soldier with my rifle and equipment and everything on, and I come out the other end a civvy – civvy clothes, civvy suit. And I drew thirty-five quid blood money – that's me gratuity, see. Then I was on my own. Out of the Army and out of a job.'[38] In addition, a veteran was entitled to an 'out of work donation' of 29s for himself, 6s for his first child under 15 and 3s for each additional child to tide him over until he found work. Initially this payment was to be for twenty weeks, but it was eventually extended to a year. In May 1919, 360,000 ex-servicemen were drawing the donation. Because of fears of disturbances if it was withdrawn, the payment was eventually extended to March 1921.[39]

Adjusting to civilian life was undoubtedly difficult for men who had spent years at the front, many of whom would today be recognized as having Post-Traumatic

Stress Disorder (PTSD) or related disorders, that is shell shock or neurasthenia. Robert Graves and Alan Hodge thought that all veterans who had served in the trenches or been 'under two or three rolling artillery barrages' suffered shell shock to a 'greater or lesser degree'.[40] Philip Gibbs described how the men who returned:

> Put on civilian clothes again, looked to their mothers and wives very much like the young men who gone to business in the peaceful days before the August of 1914. But they had not come back the same men. Something had altered in them. They were subject to queer moods, queer tempers, fits of profound depression alternating with a restless desire for pleasure. Many of them were easily moved to passion when they lost control of themselves. Many were bitter in their speech, violent in opinion, frightening. For some time, while they drew their unemployment pensions, they did not make any effort to get work for the future. They said, 'That can wait. I've done my bit. The country can keep me for a while. I helped to save it . . . Let's go to the movies.'[41]

In their account of the 1920s and 1930 Graves and Hodge noted that those who had committed most to the war often seemed ill-served by the peace:

> The problem of re-absorption of these men into civil life was complicated by their unfitness for any kind of work that needed reliable judgement and steady application. They had been led to believe that the fact of having served honourably at the Front would be a safe coupon for employment, whereas on the contrary, the more exhausting their service had been, the smaller was the peacetime demand for them.[42]

The veterans missed the changes that had occurred in society between 1914 and 1918. They had returned to a different world, but they themselves, in an example of Einsteinian physics, had not changed as rapidly, or perhaps had changed in different ways than might have been expected. For most the family reunion was a happy occasion. Corporal Hawtin Mundy remembered his return to Newport Pagnell:

> When eventually I got home, I knocked on the back door and I heard my mother come down – then my dad, with my little brother – and we had a nice reunion. My mother got out a bottle of whisky – she said she had got it a long time ago, specially for when I came home. We sat chatting for a long time, then eventually my mother broke down and began praying and

giving thanks to God for bringing me home safely. How lovely it was to
be back at home after all those hardships!⁴³

However, the gaps were between men and women were hard to bridge. In her
memoir, in which she recorded that her brother, fiancé and two close male friends
were killed in the war, Vera Brittain concluded that the war had erected a 'barrier
of indescribable experience between men and the women they loved'.⁴⁴ In Edith
Wharton's novel *A Son at the Fron*t (1923), the father whose son has died of his
war wounds reflects on the 'unbridgeable abyss' between those who fought and
those who did not. Communication stalled, 'I was considering how the meaning
had evaporated out of lots of old words', one character remarks, 'as if the general
smash-up had broken their stoppers'.⁴⁵

Many veterans had become so accustomed to the regimented life in the Army
that initially it was hard to adjust to the freedom outside. Norman Ellison wrote
that after demobilization, it: 'was strange and unsettling to be my own master again
after four and a half years of discipline. I had to find 'diggings', buy a complete
rig-out of civilian clothing and get down to a job. But I was free at last and that was
all that mattered.'⁴⁶

Robert Graves had left school in 1914 in order to enlist. He found that
it was sometimes difficult to break habits gained in the Army: 'Other loose
habits of wartime survived, such as stopping cars for a lift, talking without
embarrassment to my fellow travellers in railway carriages and unbuttoning
by the roadside, without shame, whoever might be about . . . But at least I
modified my unrestrainedly foul language.'⁴⁷ Robert Roberts, who was ten
years Graves' junior in age, was more positive. He observed that veterans
who returned to Salford brought with them a less deferential attitude to their
betters together with a greater interest in events outside the narrow world they
normally occupied. This led to an increase in support for the Labour Party and
an interest in socialist ideas. And, oddly, in the area around Burnley returning
soldiers brought back a taste for Benedictine liqueur, which remains popular to
this day.⁴⁸

This divide was perhaps at its greatest in families, particularly those where there
were children who had grown up during the war. Ruth Armstrong remembered
that: 'My dad didn't like to come back and see us altered and growing up . . . He
still thought that he was going to come back and see two children.' Young children
hardly knew their fathers except through letters and the odd leave from the front.⁴⁹
Parents too might find it hard to accept that their sons who had gone away to war
had returned as men. On his discharge from the Welch Regiment Raynor Taylor
had returned home to Hollinwood near Manchester to join his brothers, both of
whom had also been soldiers. Their father took them to the pub for a drink: 'We

were three returning servicemen, and we got a pint and a half of beer and a shandy – that's all. He never got used to the fact that we had grown up.'[50]

More serious were the relations between husbands and wives who had been separated for so long. It could be hard for either partner to understand the wartime experiences of the other – the horrors of the trenches and the loneliness of the home front. Such strains could be exacerbated by uncertainty over the prospects for employment. Returning men sometimes feared that their wives had been unfaithful during their absence. This had been a common discussion topic in the trenches, but it seems to have been rare. But where it happened the effects were usually catastrophic for the family. In 1916 Mary Morton Hardie's mother had received a telegram to say that her husband was 'missing believed killed'. Assuming the worse, she took up with another man and was eight months pregnant by him, when she received a telegram to say her husband had just been released from a prisoner of war camp. When he got home, Mary's granny told him the news: 'He was very angry. His face was scarlet, and he said "I've heard about this happening to others, but I never thought it would happen to me."' Mary's parents divorced and the children were sent to live with her new stepmother, whom she loathed.[51]

There was an increase in divorces, which rose nearly fivefold from 801 in 1910 to 3,747 in 1920. Divorces were still hard to obtain – female petitioners had to prove cruelty as well as adultery – and expensive, which put them outside the reach of most couples. The result must have been many deeply unhappy families together with a large number of cohabiting couples and bigamous relationships.[52] Sue Palmer, describes a case in her own family tree:

> My father, William Scott rarely spoke of his family – it was a taboo subject. I did know, however, that he left home at around 14 years old when he found work on one of the many ships sailing from Tyne Docks. His mother was Ada Scott née Henderson, and that his father William Scott snr, was a Police Constable. From his records William snr was an alcoholic and violent man who was discharged from the Police for several offences including throwing a man off the top of a tram. According to family rumour Ada left her husband and three children (my father included) to live with a soldier who had been awarded a Victoria Cross.

Ada did indeed abandon her family in 1919 and left South Shields with James Whitbread Upton VC. By this time Ada was pregnant with James' child. It is likely that James was stationed at the local barracks, although he was originally from Lincoln – where he left a pregnant wife and two sons. The couple later lived in North London with their daughter Edna Upton. James and Ada married bigamously in Derbyshire in 1927.[53]

Some men enjoyed their time in the Army and were reluctant to be discharged. Bertram Neyland was stationed in Limerick, where he 'playing rugby for the Westmoreland and Cumberland Yeomanry and soccer for the Signals team, and it was a wonderful life'. He and three colleagues even volunteered for service in Russia: 'We'd had a wonderful respite in Ireland, and we knew what was waiting for us back in the Post Office. We knew it wasn't that much of a job, existing on about two pounds a week – and we knew that our postal service wouldn't be impaired by our remaining in the army, so four of us said we'd go.' Unfortunately, Post Officer engineers were required to leave the Army and return to their pre-war jobs. 'So my dream of going to Russia and having a few more months in the Army slipped away.'[54] For others, demobilization brought back memories happy, and otherwise, of their time in the forces. Lieutenant William Carr, of the Royal Artillery, left in tears: 'When it was time to go I slipped quietly away unable to face the gunners, for the memories of all that happened had come surging back in a great wave of emotion. The tears were streaming down my face.'[55]

Not all men returned home on their discharge. For some there was nothing for them there, others for various reasons remained drawn to the battlefields, while a happy few met and married local women and were absorbed into the local communities. Maude Onions, who was a member of the Women's Auxiliary Army Corps, remembered discussing the future with a soldier who gave her lift in his cart a few days after the Armistice. The cargo was a corpse of a soldier:

> 'Over?' the bitterness in his tone rings in my ears yet 'Over? Not for me Missy. The war – for me – is only just beginning.' We rode on for some minutes without a word, for I did not care to break the silence.
>
> 'The war is only just beginning for me.' He repeated at length. 'I've been out since 14 – been through Hell – and I am going back to worse. My wife has played me false. Home – as I knew it – no longer exists. Finished? For me. It's only just beginning. I'd change places with him gladly,' with a jerk of his head. 'He has the best of it.'[56]

Some ex-servicemen found work on what had once been the battlefields as guides to those coming from Britain to see where their loved ones had fought and fallen. Because of their personal knowledge such guides were much prized. The journalist H. V. Morton interviewed one old soldier at Ypres:

> It's a sad job we've got and at first I didn't like it. But now I know every inch of the town and I've learnt not to hurt people's feelings . . . The best thing to do is to lead them up to their grave and disappear. It hurts to see

the women who come here hoping to find graves, walking about reading other people's crosses and crying a bit.[57]

Mrs B. Brooke had been a volunteer in France since 1915. After the war, she joined the St Barnabas Mission, which helped widows and mothers who wanted to visit the war cemeteries.

> Part of my job was to hire taxis to pick these people up at the station – by this time the trains were running again – and then I had to take them to whichever hospital – or more generally the cemetery – they wanted to go to . . . It was just good that we were there, ready to help any English who looked a bit stranded.[58]

It was also possible to hire British drivers. A guidebook noted that in Ypres there was a 'garage run by British officers a half mile down the Dickebusch Road . . .The drivers know the country and will act as guides.'[59]

As the Commonwealth War Graves cemeteries were established, the Commission employed a number of British gardeners, generally ex-servicemen, who had no wish to return to England. At the cemetery in Etaples, Mrs Brooks befriended one of the gardeners: 'I felt he was too old for the work, but he went home once on leave and found that his wife had taken up with the lodger and he wasn't wanted any more, so when he returned he said "I'm here for life now. I am not going back to England."'[60]

Until well into 1919 in the more remote parts of the Western Front it was possible to come cross bands of deserters 'well hidden under the earth in holes and cellars and used strange means to gain a living'.[61] How many deserters there where and what happened to them remains a mystery, some must have been caught by the authorities, others returned home once travel restrictions were eased or merged into the local population. In October 1919, *The Times* reported the prosecution of a gang in London who had been stealing the necessary forms and selling them to deserters, who could then pass themselves as being properly discharged men.[62]

As men were demobilized they began to look for work. This was not often as easy as might seem on the surface. Veterans had demands and expectations that could not always be met. Some employers had got used to employing efficient women at lower rates than the returning serviceman wished to accept. According to Graves and Hodge: 'A million men found their old jobs had either disappeared or were held by somebody else – usually a woman, or a man who had escaped conscription.'[63] The historian Joanna Bourke also noted that men found the return to civilian life difficult.[64] In 1919 a third of the unemployed were ex-service personnel. By the winter of 1920 1½ million workers were unemployed, and 6 months later it was over 2 million. In Liverpool, Norman Ellison found that:

During the war too much money had been made too easily by those who had been classified as 'indispensable'. Mediocrity was now in power with money the god to be worshipped . . . The return of the ex-serviceman was vaguely resented. No doubt he could be fitted in somewhere, but . . . It took me some time to settle down to this new world of discontent and disillusionment.[65]

A lucky minority returned to their pre-war occupations because they had received a guarantee from their employer when they enlisted or because they had skills, such as mining, for which there was a crucial demand. Even so it must have been very difficult to adjust to the old routine after several years engaged in work of a totally different nature. However, the economic circumstances at the end of the war altered the situation at many companies and demobilized men seeking their old jobs back received varying kinds of treatment. Local government seemed especially good at keeping posts open for staff in the forces, possibly because the work they undertook had changed little. In Bedfordshire, George Herbert Fowler returned from the Admiralty where he had been engaged in secret intelligence work to run the muniment room (the precursor to the County Record Office). At a less exalted level, a Mr Bunn also returned from the Admiralty to teach at St Albans Technical Institute.[66]

Perhaps more typical was Bert Fearns who had worked in a gentlemen's outfitters in Southport before the war. He had enlisted, much to his employer's ire. When Fearns returned after his discharge, he that found his job no longer existed and was told in no uncertain terms that he had let his boss down when he had joined up. Two women were now doing his job for the same money. After many months of unemployment Fearns finally found work as a school caretaker, which he did for the rest of his life: 'too terrified', as he said himself, that he might not get another job.[67]

Some men, particularly those educated at public schools, had joined direct from school and so had had no workplace experience and knew nothing else other than the armed forces. They left as children and returned as men. Harold Clegg of the Liverpool Rifles wrote that he belonged to a generation of men: 'who even if they had escaped its shells were destroyed by the War. Youths of 18–20 were thrown back into civilisation whose only training had been that of musketry, bombing, killing and bloodshed: those who regarded carnage with complacency'.[68] On his return home Robert Graves looked for his civilian clothes: 'The one suit, other than the school uniform, which I found, no longer fitted.'[69] For Cecil Lewis, who had joined the Royal Flying Corps aged 16: 'the end of the war left me with no feeling of flatness: indeed the change was a stimulus . . . I was not going back to things previously known. Everything was shining new.'[70]

By 1918, most officers had been promoted from the ranks, rather than being directly commissioned into the Army. They were, as the phrase went, 'temporary gentlemen', no longer really working class nor properly middle class, so it was hard to categorize them in the inflexible class system of the time. When the War Office examined the previous occupations of officers demobilized up to May 1920, it discovered that 266 had been warehousemen and porters, 638 fishermen and there were well over a thousand former miners.[71] In addition, junior officers, having led their platoons and companies in countless actions and battles in no man's land and in enemy trenches, often were the ones who suffered most from neurasthenia and other war wounds. Philip Gibbs described one officer acquaintance of his: 'of good family and distinguished service, who hawked around a subscription work to private homes. It took him more courage than he had needed under shellfire to ring the bell and ask to see the lady of the house. He thanked God every time the maid handed back his card and said "not at home".'[72] In her 1928 novel, *Unpleasantness at the Bellona Club*, Dorothy L. Sayers' character Captain George Fentiman explained the lot of many ex-serviceman: 'Oh rotten as usual. Tummy all wrong and no money. What's the damn good of it, Wimsey? A man goes and fights for his country, gets his inside gassed out, and loses his job, and all they give him is the privilege of marching past the Cenotaph once a year and paying four shillings in the pound income-tax.'[73]

The personnel columns of *The Times* were full of appeals inserted by officers in the search for gainful employment, some were rather naive, many desperate:

Captain (Yeomanry) demobilised, aged 28, single, public school, excellent testimonials from pre-war business employers and the military authorities, of good county family, excels at all outdoor games and sports, and experience in the organisation of recreation for troops in France, desires appointment as Welfare Administrator to large firm . . .

Work is urgently wanted by invalided officer, who served in France 1914, has honour, single commercial experience, willing to do anything: have searched in vain . . .[74]

In February 1920, 'Ex-battery officer' wrote to *The Times* calling for action to provide work for officers:

there is a large balance owing to the credit of the ex-officer . . . When at last we came home, were demobilised and doffed our uniforms, we realised how much of our welcome had depended on the glamour of our clothes, with all that they implied. In mufti we were no longer heroes, we were simply 'unemployed' – an unpleasant problem.[75]

The employment position, for both officers and other ranks, was at its worse in the industrial districts, where firms began to lay off workers when orders from the government began to dry up. Private George Grunwell found no work in his home town of Bradford, and indeed was unemployed for three years before getting on a training course for tailors, but comforted himself that: 'I'd got away from the war, so even it wasn't good, it was far better than the mud fields of Flanders.'[76] Some had learned skills in the forces that were directly of use in the post-war world. A few ex-Army Service Corps drivers used their savings and the various war gratuities to buy war surplus lorries and set up small haulage or charabanc companies. But most had learnt no directly applicable skills or did not wish, or were unable, to look for similar work to that they had done pre-war. Over the four years they had been away the job market had changed.

Some thought had been given by the authorities to reintegrating soldiers back into the civilian workforce. Having made an election promise to offer allotments or small holdings to ex-servicemen, the English and Scottish boards of Agriculture issued a booklet, *Land Settlement in the Mother Country*. The Land Settlement (Facilities) Act provided £20 million to county councils for the purchase of land and equipment while the Land Settlement Act (Scotland) gave the Board of Agriculture for Scotland powers to break up farms into smallholdings. However, the prices of land and building materials were high and soon the money allocated had been spent with few seeing any benefit.[77] Those who set up poultry farms often failed as their owners did not have the skills to keep chickens in large numbers successfully. Robert Clothier described various schemes that were to be introduced for both officers and other ranks. Forms for 'officers and soldiers of like standing in civil life' and for 'soldiers of artisan standing in civil life' were completed and passed to the Ex-Officers Resettlement and Labour Resettlement committees established by the Ministry of Labour or direct to local employment exchanges.[78]

Within five months of the Armistice the number of unemployed in Lancashire and Cheshire was rising by 10,000 every week. In Bury the Lancashire and Cheshire Miners Federation threatened to bring the mines to a standstill if anyone was employed who hadn't been a trained skilled miner before the war. The union's position was that 'no man shall be employed in mining unless he had been brought up in the trade'. By 1921, as the economic turndown began to bite, appeals were made by the Ministry of Labour for firms to 'adopt' a man: 'everyone who succeeds in placing an ex-serviceman in a situation will feel he has done something towards paying off the national debt'. Many veterans and their families had to apply for support from regimental welfare funds, which once had never been used for this purpose.[79] Matters were little better in the prosperous market town of St Albans. Of the 1,000 men who had returned to the town by mid-February 1919, 486 had no work.[80]

Government plans for demobilization, let alone support for returned ex-servicemen, were neither efficient nor deemed to be fair. Protests led to changes in how and when men were discharged. Thereafter they were largely on their own. Most government provisions to help men readjust to civilian life, let alone find work, were either insufficient or plain inept. As a result, thousands of veterans became marginalized, and, in particular, those who were unemployed suffered most. Even a decade after the war's end, a third of those signing on each week had never found work after their discharge from the services.

Chapter 2

A Range of Struggles

There's no doubt that there was serious unrest in the immediate post-war period. The figures speak for themselves. There can have been very few areas in Britain or Ireland where there weren't disturbances. Most have long been forgotten. There were, for example, attacks on black seamen and their families in Cardiff and other ports. In Ireland about 100 'soviets' were established with land seizures in County Clare, in Ballyneety, in Broadford, County Limerick and of a fishery in Castleconnell.[1] When outdoor relief for single men was stopped there were disturbances around Britain.[2] *The Times* reported that 'for nearly five hours Sheffield was under mob rule'.[3] In April 1919 in Shetland, where drink was prohibited, drunken troops held a 'wild west show'.[4] A May Day rally in Manchester involved sports, games, food, the crowning of the May Queen and so much jeering of J.R. Clynes, the Chairman of the Parliamentary Labour Party, that he did not complete his speech.[5] Some protests were organized by unions, but some protesters blamed the unions. When 60,000 people demanded a 40-hour week and there was a strike across Glasgow based on the same demand *The Times* claimed that many of the instigators of unrest had almost 'as bitter a distrust and hatred of those trade union officials as they have of the "bosses" or the Government'.[6] In Belfast over 20,000 shipyard and engineering workers held a mass meeting at which 20,225 voted for a 44-hour week and an unofficial strike to get it.

In the face of these threats the authorities made some concessions. There were attempts made to ensure that those who mutinied or went on strike were not routinely given the harshest punishments and there were also efforts to encourage house-building and ensure that some citizens' rights improved. The government also organized labour to replace the work which would otherwise have been done by those on strike, dismissed many strikers and, in a set-piece standoff with the union leaders, made it clear that troops would be used to defend the status quo.

The most revolutionary situation was in Ireland, where the IRA with the broad support of people in the Catholic south of the island, fought a long and violent campaign against the British State. After the UK-wide General Election in December 1918, seventy-three MPs were returned for the Irish nationalist party, Sinn Fein, which boycotted the Westminster Parliament and instead established the Dáil Éireann in Dublin's Mansion House. Rates were collected but not passed to the British authorities and a war broke out between the British Army, the police and the Irish Republican Army (IRA). There were attacks on Royal Irish Constabulary stations. In April 1920 alone 400 abandoned Royal Irish Constabulary barracks and almost 100 income-tax offices were burnt down.

Workers at the mills and creameries at Quartertown, Ireland, seized the plants, formed themselves into a workers' council and ran production. At Mungret labourers demanded that a large estate's lands be divided among them.[7] In May 1920 workers in Knocklong creameries made deals with farmers and suppliers, declared a soviet and operated under the slogan: 'We make butter not profits'. They won a pay rise, shorter hours and the removal of an unpopular manager. The miners took over the Arigna coal mine in County Leitrim and ran it as a soviet for two months before the workers got a pay rise and handed back the mine to its owners. In Dublin and Drogheda 700 engineers took over their foundry and proclaimed a soviet which lasted six weeks. Two flour mills in Cork were seized by their employees. A gasworks in Waterford was run under workers' control for six weeks and the Tipperary gas workers created their own soviet. In Tipperary the town coachworks became a soviet, as did the Monaghan mental hospital. Unemployed workers took over and reopened a closed sawmill in Ballinacourty, Tipperary. A bakery and mills in Bruree, County Limerick were occupied for a month by employees. There was the appropriation of mills, creameries, factories and later railways and docks and land by workers in Cork. Following an attempt to increase the hours of railway staff, the workers took control and, for two days, ran the railways. When creamery owners attempted to cut wages by one-third, almost 100 creameries were turned into soviets. A dispute between a creamery and a supplier resulted in an attack with gelignite.[8] While these activities were short-lived and closely related to the struggle for independence, they had some impact on the rest of the United Kingdom.

The Irish War of Independence was also fought in other parts of the United Kingdom where murder and serious injury, theft, smuggling, arson and the destruction of communication cables, the burning of warehouses, farms and railway infrastructure caused what historian Gerald Noonan described as severe 'economic dislocation'.[9] The IRA had a branch in Liverpool from May 1919 and in London from October.[10] It soon operated in Tyneside and organized attacks in London, Cardiff, Swansea, Bristol and Manchester.[11] In September 1920 the Procurator Fiscal estimated that the IRA had 3,000 men in Glasgow and by 1921 almost every Scottish town with a sizable Irish presence had its own IRA company, which trained men and supplied small arms and explosives.[12] There was an attempt to blow up an oil pipeline along the Forth and Clyde canal but probably it was the flow of arms to Ireland that was the most tangible achievement of the IRA in Scotland.[13] Gelignite was obtained from pits and quarries and raids were carried out on Clyde shipyards engaged in munitions work and a gunboat being overhauled at Finnieston dockyard.[14] After two police officers were shot dead during the rescue of an Irish prisoner in Glasgow, a priest was arrested and rioting ensured.[15]

Holy War – Some Reflections from 1923

The Irish Republican Army could not hold the open field for an hour against ten thousand regular troops; they nevertheless succeeded in worrying an army of a hundred thousand out of the country [. . .] The nation was seized by a holy fire such as inflamed the first Crusaders at the call of Peter the Hermit. The Republican Army into which the young men flocked was not more truly an army than a great religious Confraternity as fanatical as the processions of the White Penitents which traversed Europe in the Middle Ages [. . .] The Black-and-Tans for their part, if they were less resourceful in wit, made up for their inferiority by a brutality run mad.[16]

William O'Brien (1852–1928). A Nationalist journalist, he proposed that tenants withhold their rents, was imprisoned by the British and later served as an MP for much of the period 1883–1918.

It was not only in Ireland that land was a matter of dispute. In the Western Highlands and Islands historian Leah Leneman showed how 'land raiding was endemic' with buildings erected and cultivation initiated on the seized property.[17] As a result many districts were reduced to what another scholar, James Hunter, described as 'chaos'.[18] In November 1918 a petition from fifty-seven people from North Tolsta, demanded the Board of Agriculture for Scotland purchase a farm near the township on Lewis and divide it into crofts for local landless families. 'We ourselves and our sons', wrote the petitioners, 'have fought in defence of our king and country and we shall also fight [. . .] if steps are not taken to see us settled on the land of our ancestors which we consider is ours by right'. Four months later eighty-four crofts had been delineated on the land. Few raiders were arrested.[19] In Glendale, South Uist, those who seized the land eventually came to own it. When the Board of Agriculture proved to be ineffective, other raids occurred. In 1920 applicants for land from Rona wrote to the Board of Agriculture to argue that 'there is great unrest prevailing among us here, owing to the slowness of your

Board in dealing with our applications, and granting us access to the Land . . . we are now determined to fight and shed our last drops of blood . . . for our liberties at home'.[20] Men on Tiree wrote to the Board of Agriculture: 'When there was fighting to be done we had first chance to be shot; not your precious crofters. Likewise, when the land is set out [. . .] we shall have first share of it, or there will be trouble'.[21] While there was bitterness in the Highlands, the struggles were focused on local events, not on making a challenge to the parliamentary system of government.

In England, there were claims that soviets had been formed. One of the incidents which got the most publicity rather reflected the fact that the works was destined to close, rather than any serious effort to create an alternative power structure. There was what was claimed to be a 'soviet' at the government-run Motor Transport Depot in Slough. Wal Hannington described how in October 1919 several militant left-wingers applied to work at the plant. Unemployed toolmaker and member of the British Socialist Party (precursor to the Communist Party) Hannington started work there and, with other activists, started to run dinner hour lectures. Soon elected as union officials, the militants organized a series of strikes, including a three-day one which led to negotiations in Whitehall. Feeling victorious Hannington returned to Slough where:

> A tremendous mass meeting was called in the chassis shop and, from a lorry used as a platform, we reported our negotiations in Whitehall. The terms of settlement were unanimously endorsed by the men, and that night as an expression of their solidarity they formed up in marching formation and marched in a body to the railway siding and the depot exits. Next morning work was resumed.[22]

The depot handled old lorries from the war. In April 1920, it was deemed to no longer be necessary, that it was a 'white elephant'. On the last day of work a huge wooden elephant, made on the site, was ceremonially buried with a mock funeral service. Hannington recalled:

> the funeral with its 5,000 mourners moved slowly down the roads of the works towards the big space in front of the main offices. The clergyman mounted a dais, the choir boys with their candlesticks gathered at his feet, and the congregation formed a huge semi-circle. The grave-diggers were ordered to dig the grave; it measured twelve feet long by twelve feet wide. The clergy-man read the funeral oration – it was an oration over the body of capitalism, ending with a call for the workers of the world to unite to end the system which had created the 'white elephant' . . .

The great mock funeral ended by all singing the 'Red Flag' – the workers' battle-hymn.

The Home Secretary was asked in Parliament by the Conservative MP for Newcastle upon Tyne North, Nicholas Grattan-Doyle, 'whether he is in a position to give the number of Soviet committees established in South Wales, in Glasgow and Scotland generally, and the industrial centres of England; if there are very strong bodies of the same at Slough motor depôt'. Edward Shortt replied: 'There are, or were, a few extremists employed at Slough, but they could not be described as constituting a Soviet'[23] While the actions at the plant may have disrupted work there, a mock funeral on the last day cannot be classified as revolutionary in the traditions of Lenin.

In May 1920, with the support of the Trades Union Congress (TUC), dockers and stevedores of London refused to load arms and ammunition onto a vessel, the *Jolly George*, bound for anti-Russian forces in Poland. This was an overtly political act by the unions but the action was not illegal, and those involved were sufficiently reputable that their representatives were invited to meet with the Prime Minister to argue their case. Moreover, many prominent Labour leaders continued to argue against political strikes.[24] Support for the Poles was not widespread. In response to anti-Semitic atrocities in Poland, including mass killings, rapes and theft, a national 'Day of Mourning' was observed on 26 June, and 100,000 were said to have attended a march to Hyde Park.[25] Many of the marchers were Jews from London's East End who had fled Poland before the war. Like most demonstrations at the time, it passed off peacefully.

The Aliens Restriction Act 1914 required non-British-born subjects to register and to obtain permits if they wished to travel more than 5 miles. They were prohibited from entering certain areas. Over 32,000 enemy aliens were held in internment camps or repatriated. In May 1915, there were anti-German riots in Liverpool, Manchester, Salford, Sheffield, Rotherham, Newcastle, South Wales, London and elsewhere. The number of Germans in Britain declined from 57,500 in 1914 to 22,254 in 1919. Immediately after the war, most Germans who had been resident in Britain before 1914, in some cases for decades, and had spent the war years in internment camps were deported to Germany. English-born wives and husbands had to decide whether to accompany their spouses.[26]

The very nature of the Save the Children Fund's activities, that is helping starving children across Europe, meant that there were occasional protests at meetings from members of the audience demanding that monies raised not be spent on the erstwhile enemy. And in November 1919, German delegates arriving for a meeting of the Fund were treated with great suspicion by the press. *The Times* reported they tried to avoid the limelight, and Dr Winkelsbach, a Dutch member of the Austrian delegation who had been a doctor in Vienna throughout the war, was at pains to stress his nationality: 'It was my duty, as all doctors will realise, to stay by their patients. I was absolutely neutral.'[27]

British soldiers entering Germany during the winter of 1918 found the locals surprisingly friendly despite the humiliation being meted out upon their country, and often rather easier to deal with than the grasping, difficult French and Belgian peasants they were used to. Guardsman Fen Noakes wrote home shortly after his battalion arrived in Düren, a small town between Aachen and Cologne:

> The inhabitants do not seem at all hostile – indeed I was greatly surprised at the pleasant manner in which we were received. They are not enthusiastic – one could not expect it – but they are very polite and seem anxious to please us. In the shops they serve us with many smiles and are strictly honest in changing French or English money.[28]

It was not only Germans who were perceived as responsible for the ills of the nation. In his maiden speech, Ernest Wild, the Tory MP for West Ham Upton, proclaimed 'we were going to support the Government in getting rid of aliens from this country'. He added that aliens were:

> at the bottom of one half, at least, of the vice of this Metropolis and of this country. The white slave traffic, unnatural vice, the exploitation of English girls whom they marry, and then live upon the proceeds of their prostitution, the brothel keepers who are too clever to be caught, because they keep in the background; the people with gambling hells who lead young men to destruction, and who bring in such horrible practices as doping and unnatural offences – that is the sort of atmosphere that has been introduced into this country by these people.[29]

There were also riots in ports and other areas against Chinese, Indian and black residents and their families. The reasons were as much economic as racist, but the black residents became the scapegoats for wider white working class frustrations. The merchant navy, upon whose ships the majority of these people worked, contracted rapidly as peacetime conditions returned. There were 5 people killed, dozens injured and at least 250 arrested. The causes were concerns over competition for the same jobs, particularly on ships, where black crewmen were paid less than their white colleagues, the same housing and often the same women. The demand led by the seamen's unions was made that local men who had returned from the war be given work.[30] It was not only workers who were resentful. The *Sheffield Mail* campaigned against Belgians who helped to construct the war memorial in Barnsley, while a letter to *The Times* justified further violence, arguing that 'intimate association between black or coloured men and white women is a thing of horror', the writer asking if it was appropriate to blame 'those white men who, seeing these conditions and loathing them, resort to violence?'.[31] In the Shetland Islands Norwegian whalers were blamed for the decline in the number of herring and special constables were drafted in to guard the stations after arson was attempted.[32]

However, there was no clear leadership or one agreed programme among the protesters. Repatriation committees were established in Hull, South Shields, Glasgow, Cardiff, Liverpool, Salford and other places which were home to a substantial number of black people. These bodies had no black representation. In 1919 the Home Office deported 3,000 Chinese seamen, recruited during the war, leaving only 711 in London by 1921. The 1919 Aliens Restrictions (Amendment) Act required foreign seafarers to register with the police on arrival in Britain. While this was new, the Act sought to support a return to a period when there had been fewer foreign seaman competing for jobs. The government deported some black men and offered £5 to anybody who agreed to be repatriated and resettled. Those who refused the offer lost their entitlement to poor relief.[33] Once the government acted, by providing help to the white unemployed and deporting people from the ethnic minorities, interest in attacking migrant labour diminished.

Veterans found that Britain had changed during the war, often, in their eyes, not for the better. And although the fallen were commemorated in memorials and ceremonies, many ex-servicemen felt that their sacrifices were not sufficiently recognized. Protests around the Peace Day celebrations in July 1919 were often about how ex-servicemen had not been invited to the festivities. Rather the money had been spent on feting local elites who had done well out of the war.

In Coventry, an historical pageant to mark Peace Day excluded munitions workers and war veterans, but included leading councillors. And while the older trades of silk weaving and watch-making were celebrated, newer industries which had contributed significantly to the war effort, such as bicycle and motor manufacture, were ignored. Ex-servicemen were not invited to join the parade until there were complaints and then they were only given minor roles, as historical extras. Discontent led to violence and over a 3-day period at least 7,000 people were involved in disturbances which included attacks on 35 shops deemed to be profiteers.

Ceremonies to mark the peace were not well-received elsewhere. There were also examples of crowds engaging in arson, looting and rioting in Doncaster and South Wales. In Wood Green, Middlesex there were attacks on the police. In Swindon up to 15,000 people were present when a ceremonial flagstaff was burnt and the Union Flag torn down. In Wolverhampton 2,000 people threw missiles at the police station after an arrest at the peace celebrations. This followed other incidents when crowds demanded the release of a prisoner. The police station in nearby Bilston was also besieged. Former munitions workers, the National Federation of Discharged and Demobilized Sailors and Soldiers and women's groups all complained about the high prices being charged for the peace banquet in Luton from which women were excluded.[34] Ex-servicemen complained that only 240 men, of the 4,000 in the town, had been invited to take part in the procession. They also noted the high rate of unemployment among former servicemen and the fact that some local men were still fighting in Russia.[35] A crowd of thousands stormed the town hall, burnt it down and damaged the surrounding shopping area. In nearby St Albans there was a certain smugness in the press report of a slap-up tea, dancing and a fireworks display: 'Instead of participating in setting the local Town Hall on fire (as at Luton) how much better it was to be seated with the St Albans ex-servicemen openly light-hearted and enjoying to the full the really first-class entertainment which had been provided.'[36]

In Ireland, there was the added complication of the ongoing campaign for independence. The 1919 victory parade in Dublin, which featured the display of union flags, nurses, soldiers and weaponry was boycotted by the Irish Nationalist veterans. Demobilized soldiers were cheered by the crowds but regular troops on the parade were greeted with silence. In the evening there was a scuffle, two soldiers were attacked and a police sergeant was shot.[37]

Protests by veterans were not just focused on Peace Day. A rally calling for jobs for ex-servicemen in Hyde Park in June 1919 led to fights with the police and women tram and bus drivers being attacked.[38] In Liverpool in April 1919, 5,000 marched for jobs, one of their complaints being, according to the *Walton Times*, that 'women are still occupying men's positions and that coloured men were being similarly retained'.[39] One of the organizations for ex-servicemen, the Comrades of the Great War, referred to: 'Those women you've dreamed of ethereal visions who cheered and inspired you to hang on when the whole world was slipping from under your feet – well they've got your job and they won't budge!'[40] In Liverpool the call was made for the replacement of bar maids while in Reading crowds visited employers to demand that women lose their jobs.[41] The British Legion demanded the expulsion of women and non-veterans from the civil service so that ex-servicemen could do their work. This aimed to spread jobs to unemployed former servicemen.[42] It was argued that women should not compete with men in the public sphere.[43]

In Luton 8,000 women had been employed on war work at George Kent Limited, but there were only 5,000 by January 1919. Many refused to return to domestic service as the pay was lower than the out of work donation and the job was equated with being, according to one woman reported in the *Luton News*, a 'slavey'.[44] Such attitudes were treated with contempt, with the *Daily Sketch* shrieking of the 'Scandal of the proposed retention of flappers [i.e. young women] while ex-soldiers cannot find jobs'.[45] Elsewhere, those who tried to avoid domestic service were in danger of losing their out-of-work donation payments, as a test case iron worker discovered.[46] Although the Manchester and Salford Women's Trades Council encouraged the formation of the Domestic Workers Union of Manchester and District, there was little support, it was in competition for members with other unions and it did not thrive.[47] Faced with unequal pay, a bar on married women from some work and little by way of union representation, women workers had to adjust to a world in which motherhood and domesticity were idealized and promoted. A wartime agreement that women should not compete for post-Armistice jobs was enforced. Women largely ceased to work on the buses and trams and the 1,080 in the Women's Police Service were reduced to a few hundred. By April 1919 there were 600,000 women registered as unemployed.[48] Many trades put their work forces on short-time and women who had worked in munitions or other industries were not permitted to register as unemployed as their 'normal' occupation was deemed to be housework.

However, there was continuing bitterness about the lack of work for veterans. One group of ex-servicemen who marched to Downing Street carried a banner with a slogan that was all too true:

REMEMBER
1914 YOUR COUNTRY NEEDS YOU
1918 WELL DONE
1920 FORGOTTEN![49]

Despite fine words, conditions for many veterans did not improve. The economic depression which arrived at the end of 1920 saw to this. Popular memories of their appalling and insensitive treatment was undoubtedly a contributory factor in the Labour Party's victory at the 1945 General Election.

A further area for disputes was the workplace. In Britain during the war the number of trade-union members doubled. More workers went on strike in 1919 than in any other year of the century except 1926 and 1962. There were more stoppages in 1920 than in any year until 1943, in mining, and until 1967, outside mining. Taking 1919 and 1920 together 2,959 stoppages were recorded, amounting to 61,537,000 days lost to industrial action.[50] These included strikes of the miners, transport workers, bakers and printers. In January 1919 there was, the Munitions Council reported, 'considerable trouble' among munitions workers in Manchester who faced redundancy.[51] There were 'labour troubles' at the National Factory in Richborough, Kent.[52] The government ordered the tanks onto the streets of

Glasgow to deal with a mass strike. Churchill called for the troops to be used to defeat a strike by electrical engineers in February 1919.[53] In August 1919 the police went on strike with over 50 per cent of the Liverpool and Birkenhead force on strike and 75 per cent of the police in Bootle.[54] At the same time in Lancashire there was also a bakers' strike, a tram drivers' strike and a call, by the local Labour Party, for a local general strike. In addition, over 450,000 cotton workers were out for 18 days.

The National Union of Railwaymen (NUR) used the media to gain public support presenting itself not as revolutionary, but as the supporter of working men. From February 1919, its leader, Jimmy Thomas, began to argue that the wartime bonus granted to railway workers should be retained. The government rejected this claim and in September negotiations collapsed. A strike was called. It was presented by the *Daily Express* as 'tyranny and oppression' with strikers being 'misled or frankly Bolshevist'.[55] On the first day of the strike demobilization was stopped and a ban placed on commercial display lighting.[56] Two days later the *Daily Chronicle* claimed that it was 'as if London were cut off by makeshift armies!'.[57] Virginia Woolf, living in deepest Sussex, felt equally cut off from London, although she supported the strike and sympathized with the railwaymen at her local station.

> We went down to the signalman [Tom Pargiter] with books and offers of help. His wife met us; he being at Newhaven. A fiery, impulsive, vigorous woman about to bear her fifth child. She was urging him to give in . . . With their strike pay they can't long keep off hunger. Then she couldn't see the rights of it. 'They're like children who've had their sweets and don't want to give up their penny,' she said, often enough to show that she'd used the argument often to him.[58]

News of a telegram sent by the Prime Minister to Caernarvon County Council regretting that he could not attend its meeting due to this 'anarchist conspiracy' provided the lead story in many newspapers.[59] The printers' union offered support to strikers. Some union chapels (branches) refused to set the type on some newspaper articles and the Labour Research Department placed several articles in the dailies in support of the strikers. The NUR ran targeted advertisements in the newspapers and a Will Dyson drawing of a dignified but poverty stricken worker with his four children, spouse, and mother captioned 'Is this man an anarchist?' was reissued as a poster. Leaflets were sent to clerics with a supportive message from the Bishop of Oxford. The Prime Minister compelled all cinemas to run a still-frame photo with his 2-second message of opposition to the strikers.[60] British Pathé made a 13-second film of J.R. Thomas and his message.[61] The *Daily Express* changed its view that the action was 'a challenge by a few conspirators to the liberties, the rights and the honour of Great Britain' and called for negotiations, arguing that the NUR 'have a case' and that the revolutionary forces in the country 'are negligible'.[62] The press began to characterize the strike as 'profoundly unrevolutionary'.[63] After nine days the government reopened negotiations guaranteeing no pay cuts. Thomas concluded an agreement viewed by the men as 'the best settlement ever made on their behalf'.[64] This was a demonstration that solidarity and constitutional action could be effective.[65] Moreover, the unions did not present themselves as a threat: they sought only limited changes.

While the trade disputes across the United Kingdom often had specific local causes, in Ireland nationalism was a unifying factor. In Ireland trade-union membership boomed and the Irish Trades Union Congress grew from 111,000 in 1914 to 300,000 in 1921. The number of days lost through strikes averaged 200,000 in the period 1914–16, 700,000 in 1917 and 1918 rising to 1.4 million in 1920. In Belfast alone 750,000 workdays were lost in 1919 through strike action. In April 1918, there was a widely supported one-day general strike against the prospect of the introduction of conscription in Ireland and almost every town in Ireland experienced its own general strike. In January 1919, in Bagenalstown, in County Carlow, a general strike led to the proclamation of a Provisional Soviet Government. In April 1919 Limerick Trades Council called a general strike which lasted a week. The organizers set prices and wages, issued money and established a police force. As many as 100,000 workers claimed to have taken part in marking May Day 1919. In June 1919, following a lock out of 2,700 labourers in Meath and Kildare, crops were destroyed, hiring fairs disrupted and there were bayonet and baton charges against the workers. When 400 soldiers ensured the transport of cattle to Belfast, union members refused to handle the animals, which had to be returned. In July 1919 2,500 trade unionists struck against 1,100 employers, sabotaging crops, livestock, auctions and hiring fairs. In November 300 labourers fought 120 Royal Irish Constabulary officers in the 'Battle of Fenor' in County Waterford.[66] There were 233 strikes in 1920, 4 times as many as during the war, including a 2-day national general strike in Ireland, demanding the release of prisoners detained by the British. A strike of Cork harbour workers shut down the harbour and Dublin dock workers refused to export food to Britain. Between May and December 1920 railway workers boycotted moving British troops and military supplies in Ireland.[67]

A fortnight after the Armistice Prime Minister Lloyd George rhetorically asked the people of Wolverhampton 'What is our task?' and answered 'To make Britain a fit country for heroes to live in'.[68] During the war the government had built housing for war workers near the factories where they worked and controlled rents. In England and Wales about three-quarters of households were in rented accommodation.[69] Much of it was very low standard and in the immediate post-war period there were vociferous campaigns for improvements. Across Woolwich the Tenants Association on the government built estates organized successful actions over rents and conditions. This body was chaired by a local Labour activist, Jack Mills. The vice-president was the local Labour MP Will Crooks. It did not advocate squatting, which was popular in the area, but action through Parliament. The approach was exemplified in the local Labour newspaper headline: 'Tenants – watch Parliament'.[70] In Coventry it was local shop stewards from Stoke Heath who formed the Tenants Defence League and organized a rent strike in 1919. This was in protest at prices, conditions and the corruption in the city council associated with the housing scheme. Over 6,000 people attended the League's open-air meetings and corrupt Liberal and Conservative councillors were forced to resign.[71]

A few people started to build for themselves. The land on farms in Laindon and Pitsea in Essex (now Basildon) which had long been bankrupt, for example, was sold off in small plots to people who built their own homes. The result was often the spread of poorly regulated, lightweight housing, frequently without mains sewerage and linked by primitive roads. While there were concerns about the sanitation in these shanty towns, they were evidence that people wanted a stake in society, not to destroy it and start again.[72]

Commercial developers also sought to meet the housing shortage. One of the most interesting of the new developments was Peacehaven. Originally conceived as a 'Garden City by the Sea', the village was the brainchild of businessman and entrepreneur Charles Neville. His aim was, on the surface, seemingly very simple: to create a town by the sea in Sussex. There, people would be able to purchase plots of land upon which they could build homes. First established in 1916 as New Anzac-on-Sea, the name of the town itself was chosen through a series of competitions run by Neville, who would choose the winning name and whomever had submitted it would receive £100 and a free plot of land. Interestingly, the runners up would also receive free plots but would have to pay a £50 conveyancing fee in order to claim them. There were also 12,500 runner up plots available meaning that people claiming them promised to be a significant money earner for Neville. The dubious merits of this competition led to Neville being sued by the *Daily Express*, the newspaper in which he had advertised the competition in the first place, over suggestions that it was little more than a fundraising scam. The *Express* would eventually win the lawsuit but by the time they did the publicity had already insured that Neville had achieved his goal. Building houses and the provision of services was more expensive and problematic than the purchasers had expected which meant that Peacehaven initially had no real logical layout.[73]

As the result of the protests, squatting and other forms of direct action over housing, rent controls were extended, and through the Housing Act of 1919 local authorities could bid for money to build council housing. The government was committed to social reform and 'the housing campaign provided a ready image for the whole programme of social reconstruction. To many, housing was the reconstruction programme.[74] However, the scheme was much less successful than anticipated. Between 1919 and 1924 only 176,914 houses were built by local authorities, with a further 221,543 built by private builders. Difficulties with supplies and labour meant that the promises of the Act were largely 'consigned to the waste paper basket'.[75] Nevertheless, the protests died away. People came to the conclusion that while housing was still needed, lobbying and voting might be more effective routes to achieving this than revolution.

The industrial confrontations of 1919 led the authorities to respond. As a result of the police strike (which led to 4 days of looting and rioting in Liverpool, a battleship and 2 destroyers being moored in the Mersey and tanks on the streets) over 2,000 striking police officers were dismissed. The Commissioner of the Metropolitan Police, Sir Nevil Macready, said that the force had been 'purged of these discontented elements'.[76] Lloyd George felt that the effect was to deflect the labour movement from Bolshevist and direct actionist courses back to legitimate trade unionism.[77] The war of independence in Ireland resulted in the internment of about 4,500 people in Ireland, the deaths of about 1,200 and numerous hunger strikes. Troops had been deployed on the streets of mainland Britain in 1919 in Glasgow in January and Luton in June. Royal Navy stokers were sent to pump out coal mines in Yorkshire during the summer of 1919 and plans were drawn up to use the Army to break strikes. Labour leader Arthur Henderson complained that the 'war machine' was being used to counter legitimate campaigns for change.[78] The political stability of the country appeared to be threatened by the links between rail and transport workers and the miners, the Triple Alliance.[79] The future Labour politician, Aneurin Bevan, recalled a conversation with the mineworkers union leader and president of the Triple Alliance, Robert Smillie:

Lloyd George sent for the Labour leaders, and they went, so Robert told me, 'truculently determined they would not be talked over by the seductive and eloquent Welshman.' At this, Bob's eyes twinkled in his grave, strong face. 'He was quite frank with us from the outset,' Bob went on. 'He said to us: "Gentlemen, you have fashioned, in the Triple Alliance of the unions represented by you, a most powerful instrument. I feel bound to tell you that in our opinion we are at your mercy. The Army is disaffected and cannot be relied upon. Trouble has occurred already in a number of camps . . . In these circumstances, if you carry out your threat and strike, then you will defeat us. But if you do so," went on Lloyd George, "have you weighed the consequences? The strike will be in defiance of the government of the country and by its very success will precipitate a constitutional crisis of the first importance. For, if a force arises in the state, which is stronger than the state itself, then it must be ready to take on the functions of the state, or withdraw and accept the authority of the state. Gentlemen," asked the Prime Minister quietly, "have you considered, and if you have, are you ready?" 'From that moment on,' said Robert Smillie, 'we were beaten and we knew we were'.[80]

As well as confrontation there was also preparation. Eric Geddes, a pre-war railway businessman who was the Conservative Minister of Transport between 1919 and 1921, saw it was the task of government not to order people to act or to send in the troops to impose order but to create the conditions whereby local businesses could maintain supplies. The Industrial Unrest Committee established under the Home Secretary became the Supply and Transport Committee under Eric Geddes. The country was divided into territories to be run by a 'District Commissioner', 70,000 volunteer 'citizen guards' were recruited and Food Controllers appointed. The government delegated responsibility. While the Home Office sometimes intervened, as in the case of a rail strike in Liverpool, chief constables were free to apply the law in different ways in different parts of the country.[81] The aim was to present anti-labour strategies as evidence of local communities' self-defence.

A further strategy, in the face of numerous threats, was for the government to make concessions. One minor example of this was a shortage in the supply of beer, largely because the barley used by brewers was diverted to making bread. A commission investigating strikes in 1917 found that 'The beer shortage is creating considerable unrest, and is interfering with the output of munitions and with the position of the country in this war. There is unrest, discontent, loss of work, and in some cases even strikes are threatened and indeed caused by the very fact there is a shortage of beer.'[82] Two years later there were riots in Manchester and other northern towns because of the continuing lack of beer. The shortage was even discussed by the Cabinet. In May 1919, the *Sheffield Evening Telegraph* reported that:

There are no open disorders, but in one instance, where landlord closed his house when the supply had not run out, customers protested, and followed this jumping the counter helping themselves to the beer. The Manchester Beer Consumers' Defence League are holding open air meetings with a view to securing better conditions and the compulsory opening houses. The Manchester police officials believe that unless there is a great improvement in the output of supplies very serious trouble will follow. District associations are being formed and parties are forcing themselves into licensed houses with a view to ascertaining whether there is any beer in the cellars. The low gravity is inducing people to drink far in excess of their usual quantities, and others are flying to methylated spirits. It is no uncommon thing to find houses in possession of supplies crowded almost to suffocation, and men helping themselves to the pumps, with the licensee looking on powerless. Beer queues are the order of the day. Some are 50 yards long, and people have been known walk miles to houses where beer is to be obtained. It is felt that the present hours are quite long enough, but when only one house in every hundred is open, it becomes a mad scramble.[83]

The government became very nervous about this in case these disturbances became something more serious. There were several discussions in Cabinet and eventually it was agreed to restore the production of beer to pre-war levels and at a higher strength than had previously been available.

In an attempt to stop strikes the government created a National Industrial Conference in February 1919 which was intended to foster co-operation between unions and employers and to bring about 'a British rather than a Russian revolution'.[84] The wartime involvement of unions and employers with the state in the mediation of economic interests was continued. Industrial interests became better represented in Whitehall and a Ministry of Labour was created. Numerous committees on specific trades reported to the Board of Trade and the Industrial Courts Act introduced State-financed arbitration. When it was recognized that the reduction in the hours worked could improve efficiency and reduce government expenditure on National Insurance, an Industrial Fatigue Research Board was created.[85] Committees with members representing employers and employees were formed for a number of industries and action taken in response to their reports led to improved health and greater output.[86] The Queen's Employment Advisory Committee on Women's Employment (a government-funded, voluntary body) provided a few grants for middle-class women to go to college and supported the training of young women in domestic tasks.[87] The historian Bill Schwarz dismissed such interventions as these were not part of an 'effort at popular mobilization but of administrative collectivism, an effort to tame the labour movement through a process of bureaucratic incorporation'.[88] The Ministry of Reconstruction saw its role as: 'to enable both employers and men to renew their pre-war activities . . . to pick up broken threads, to renew old habits and traditions, to go back as far as possible to the social and industrial situation as it existed at the outbreak of the war'.[89]

To resolve the miners' strike, the government established a Royal Commission on the mines led by Sir John Sankey, After only seventeen days it produced its first findings. It recommended that miners' pay be increased and hours decreased, but equivocated over demands that the mines be nationalized. Unemployment benefit was extended to almost all trades except domestic service. Within the civil service Whitley Council was an experiment in industrial democracy as it allowed management and workers to resolve issues without resorting to industrial action. Much of the reconstruction was summarized by historian R.H. Tawney as 'an experiment in improvisation'.[90]

Writing during the Second World War, the socialist George Orwell drew a conclusion which might be applied to much of the country in 1919. It was that 'the proletariat of Hammersmith will not rise and massacre the bourgeoisie of Kensington: they are not different enough'.[91] Towards the end of the year the *Sketch* concluded that: 'The year 1919 which began with such glowing anticipation has not been much fun at all'.[92] Given all the possible ways to describe 1919 this rather restrained one captures the mood of the sometimes sullen acceptance of limited changes coupled with sporadic expressions of resentment. People largely went on strike to improve their wages or conditions of labour and remained uninterested in making significant amendments to the political institutions. The police strike leader on Merseyside felt that that police force was 'the most important bulwark in society against the danger of Bolshevism'.[93] In Liverpool the reaction of the local labour movement to the police strike was 'ambivalent and sentiment was divided'.[94] In March 1919 the *Police Review* argued that: 'the police were never trade unionists by conviction; they joined out of necessity'.[95] Opposition to the post-war settlement was more likely to be intermittent grumbles rather than any coherent and consistent argument against it. Between the yearning for the past and the desire to disrupt lay the path of limited changes in social relations. It was this route that Britain took.

Chapter 3

Economic Reconstruction

In a poem which shared his concerns about the post-war period, 'Nineteen hundred and nineteen', the Irish poet William Butler Yeats wrote of the destructive and impermanence of the year. He then asked 'What matter that no cannon had been turned / Into a ploughshare?' The answer to this rhetorical question was that conversion of munitions was a matter of interest, but only for a brief period. This was because in 1919 the debate about the best direction for the economy was not won by those who wanted continuing government control over the economy. Rather it was won by those whose focus was on debt reduction and a system of currency regulation known as the gold standard. The advice of civil servants and the Governor of the Bank of England was to reduce the national debt and public expenditure, balance the budget, maintain deflationary policies and maintain relatively high levels of taxation.[1] The result was high unemployment and a lowering of wages.

The historian A.J.P. Taylor argued, with pardonable exaggeration, that 'until August 1914 a sensible, law-abiding Englishman could pass through life and hardly notice the existence of the state, beyond the post office and the policeman'.[2] By 1918 this was no longer the case. There had been conscription, direction of labour and State interventions in housing, education, scientific research and numerous other areas. Free trade was abandoned. There was State direction of businesses, control of imports and supplies, subsidization of food prices and regulation of rents.

Indirect control of the railways came almost immediately war broke out and soon repairs to the rolling stock were being deferred as munitions work and other forms of transport, including cart horses and cars, were commandeered. State control of the mines was promised by Lloyd George in 1915.[3] The Ministry of Munitions, established in 1915, controlled or built factories and, by 1918, was 'the biggest buying, importing, selling, manufacturing and distributing business in the world'.[4] Taxes rose and preference was given to products imported from the Empire. The Defence of the Realm Act enabled the government to take over factories and workshops, to impose curfews and censorship and to restrict movement to many areas of the country.

By the end of the war workers wanted more leisure time and improved living standards rather than a higher income. Before the war the standard working week was 54 hours. Unions in the shipbuilding and engineering trades had negotiated for a 47-hour week for men from 1919. The number of hours worked fell and this was not accompanied by a fall in money wages. The reduction in the working week drove wage and price inflation which were detrimental to industrial competitiveness.[5] For two years after the Armistice there was a short-lived boom in the economy based on pent-up demand and a rise in real wages. While there was a need for sharp cost-price reductions if markets at home and abroad were to be retained, the impact of the war and inflation made such adjustments difficult. There were wartime shortages, leading to extensive queues, and controls (notably following the introduction in 1917 of limited rationing for food). This resulted in a build-up of frustrated demands. People were unable to spend their incomes in the ways that they once had. Something in the order of £790 million was saved through the Post Office, the Trustees Saving Bank and in War Savings certificates.[6]

In 1919, the economist John Maynard Keynes looked back to what was seen as a past golden age:

> What an extraordinary episode in the economic progress of man that age was which came to an end in August, 1914! The greater part of the population, it is true, worked hard and lived at a low standard of comfort . . . [However a man of the middle and upper classes in London] could order by telephone, sipping his morning tea in bed, the various products of the whole earth, in such quantity as he might see fit, and reasonably expect their early delivery upon his doorstep; he could at the same moment and by the same means adventure his wealth in the natural resources and new enterprises of any quarter of the world, and share, without exertion or even trouble, in their prospective fruits and advantages; or he could decide to couple the security of his fortunes with the good faith of the townspeople of any substantial municipality in any continent that fancy or information might recommend. He could secure forthwith, if he wished it, cheap and comfortable means of transit to any country or climate without passport or other formality, could dispatch his servant to the neighbouring office of a bank for such supply of the precious metals as might seem convenient, and could then proceed abroad to foreign quarters, without knowledge of their religion, language, or customs, bearing coined wealth upon his person, and would consider himself greatly aggrieved and much surprised at the least interference. But, most important of all, he regarded this state of affairs as normal, certain, and permanent, except in the direction of further improvement, and any deviation from it as aberrant, scandalous, and avoidable.[7]

This yearning for a lost past disastrously permeated economic policymaking. The government sought a return to the Gold Standard. In 1914 Britain was one of fifty-nine countries on a gold standard. Each nation agreed to fix a gold value for its currency and to guarantee the inter-convertibility between its domestic currency and gold at a fixed official price. They also had to permit the relatively free international movement of gold and to ensure that its paper money was backed by gold. The belief was that this kept prices and exchange rates stable and that it automatically maintained a balance-of-payments equilibrium between countries. It protected the convertibility of sterling, imposed restraints on the discretionary powers of the monetary authorities, minimised the risk that the value of financial assets would be eroded by inflation and that there would be capital losses due to exchange rate fluctuations.[8] Leading contemporary economic opinion attributed British commercial supremacy and the City's financial ascendancy to international confidence in the gold convertibility of sterling.

The war was probably the most expensive conflict in British history. It was financed by spending 52 per cent of the GNP on defence, with additional help from inflation, US loans and the sale of overseas assets. Britain in effect came off the Gold Standard. Nevertheless, enthusiasm for this international system persisted. As Keynes noted in 1917: 'we have made a fetish of the Gold Standard. We have taken immense pride in it and constantly proclaimed to the world that it is the cornerstone of our policy'.[9]

This enthusiasm for gold was in part because the British Empire, which consisted of 12 million square miles and contained a quarter of the population of the world, expanded following the war. The outlook seemed good. Competition from Germany disappeared, Russia was involved in a civil war, the USA wanted to withdraw into itself and the French were allies. Productivity in Germany, France and the Soviet Union had declined in comparison with Britain. And British war damage was rather less than that of Germany, Russia, France, Austria-Hungary or Italy. While the United States was influential in the Caribbean, Japan was a regional power in east Asia, France and Italy sought influence in the Mediterranean and Britain remained a world power, indeed it was the only world power. Britain's greatness was, historian Russell Ally concluded, 'indissolubly identified with retaining London as the world's premier gold market'.[10]

However, international trading remained severely restricted. The revolutions and subsequent civil war in Russia meant that the world's largest wheat exporter in 1913 virtually ceased to trade. The new countries of Europe, which were created when the Austro-Hungarian Empire was broken up, swiftly erected trade barriers to protect their emerging economies. In 1913 Britain had an export surplus with India. In particular, British exports of cotton textiles to India were about 10 per cent of all British commodity trade. By the end of the war, India, having been cut off from British goods during the conflict, had begun its own textile production which it now sought to protect.

A decline of the pre-war export staple industries of coal, iron, steel, mechanical engineering, shipbuilding and textiles meant that Britain was unable to dominate the international economy. In order to assist peacetime economy, the government decided to postpone the removal of restrictions on imports from outside the Empire, to maintain public spending, to place an embargo on overseas lending and to relax controls over domestic investment. Faith was placed in the receipt of considerable sums of reparations imposed on Germany by the Treaty of Versailles.[11] In addition to the decline in trade there was an increase in debt. During the First World War the British national debt increased by more than a factor of ten in current prices, from £706 million at the end of March 1914 to £7,481 million at the end of March 1919. In January 1918, the government established a Committee on Currency and Foreign Exchanges. This was to 'consider the various problems which will arise in connection with currency and foreign exchanges during the period of reconstruction and report upon the steps required to bring about the restoration of normal conditions in due course'. The terms of reference were subsequently extended. Chaired by the Governor of the Bank of England, Lord Cuncliffe, the membership included Sir John Bradbury, the Joint Permanent Secretary to the Treasury and Arthur Cecil Pigou, Professor of Political Economy at Cambridge. It concluded that the most important problem to overcome was inflation. The priority was not to be the recovery of industry but the restoration of the Gold Standard. Economic historian Peter Cline felt that the Cunliffe Committee 'wrote the manifesto of the banking community, the ultimate aim of which was the return to the gold standard at pre-war parity'.[12] The enthusiasm for a system of multilateral trade and payments reflected the dominance of mercantile and financial activity over manufacturing industry. Cunliffe received twenty-one submissions of which only one, from the Federation of British Industries, represented a voice from industry. In August 1918 Cunliffe claimed that 'We are glad to find that there is no difference of opinion among the witnesses who appeared before us'.

The Committee stressed reliance upon a strong trade balance. The eventual aim was to restore pre-war British predominance in international trade. This was to be done by stabilizing the value of sterling in relation to the dollar at the pre-war exchange rate, equilibrium in the balance of payments and a reduction of the money in circulation. The intention was that a general deflation would follow after the war's conclusion in order to protect the foreign exchange rate. The State had to tighten commercial credit, cease government borrowing and eliminate the £300 million in 'paper money' issued during the war. Bank of England notes were backed by gold. This was not the case for the £335 million worth of government notes for 10s and £1. Cunliffe also demanded the reduction of the Floating Debt, the government's short-term credit. By the time of the Armistice the Floating Debt was over £1,400 million. The Committee wanted a reversion to the Bank's control over the money market, which had been lost during the first days of the war. It also noted the 'grave danger of a progressive credit expansion which will result in a foreign drain of gold menacing the convertibility of our note issue and so jeopardising the international trade position of the country'.[13] It offered no support for reconstruction or post-election political manoeuvring. In July 1919 Lloyd George accepted the recommendations of the final report of the Cunliffe Committee and called for an end to 'waste and extravagance'.[14]

Keynes noted the desire of 'the investing class' to return to the policy of buying and selling gold at a fixed price.[15] Before the war this had constrained governments and promoted economic stability. The expectation was that Britain would go back onto the Gold Standard, just as it had done after the Battle of Waterloo a century earlier. This took precedence over support for State investment in factory conversion or indeed almost all government funding. However, in March 1919 the country formally abandoned the Gold Standard which had been suspended in 1914.[16] The government had wanted to restore the Gold Standard at the pre-war parity, that is at the same rate of exchange with the dollar as had been the case in 1914. However, the British economy was now weaker than it had been in the past and the efforts to restore the Gold Standard had led to a reduction in imports, thus fuelling inflation, and higher unemployment.[17] Never above 8 per cent before the war, unemployment grew rapidly from later 1920 reaching 15 per cent in both 1921 and 1922, with a monthly peak of 21 per cent in June 1921.

Inflationary policies and balanced budgets, even at the expense of jobs, were seen as necessary if London was to return to its place at the financial centre of the world. The government also felt that disputes over taxation would be reduced and it would be able to raise more revenue if there was general consent to its policies. A reduction in the size and scope of the State would help ensure that taxation was seen to be balanced, fair, legitimate and effectively run by men of probity.[18]

These economic strategies did not go unchallenged. The war had interrupted the pre-war patterns of labour supply, investment and productivity and the period immediately after the Armistice was subject to dramatic economic fluctuations. The influential historian Richard Tawney felt that it was not until mid-1919, six months after the Armistice, that Lloyd George's coalition got its bearings and decided on its course. It was 'ready to be pushed. The pressure of business interests, the clamour of its supports, the noise made by the press, the advice of the Treasury, the economic situation, and – still more – the prevalent illusions about the economic situation, all pushed in one direction.'[19]

Others sought to drive the Prime Minister in another direction. In 1917 the economist J.A. Hobson asked: 'Is it not reasonable to suppose that the financial powers of the state, so successfully mobilized in the autumn of 1914 for the shattered fabric of private finance, can be made available for the purposes of assisting industrial and commercial recovery after the war?'[20]

There appeared to be a firm basis for future development. Plans were laid for the 'beating of swords into ploughshares' by sanctioning the drafting of a bill for the conversion of a demobilised Ministry of Munitions into a Ministry of Supply.[21] Churchill was among many others who supported a Ministry which would co-ordinate supplies to the services and reduce competition.[22]

During the war charities and trade unions had begun to run restaurants which offered subsidized food and in 1917 the government started to fund 50 per cent of the costs of these kitchens. Plans were laid for them to become permanent national institutions. Pubs in Carlisle and Enfield, taken over by the government during the war, remained in state control. There were specific proposals for the retention of State control of alcohol, milk and transport.[23]

The war revolutionized drinking in pubs as part of a move to ensure that productivity in factories was not affected by drunkenness. In 1914, pubs could open between 5.30am and late at night with some restrictions on Sundays. The average strength of beer was 7 per cent alcohol by volume (ABV).[24] The cause of the changes lay in fears over drunkenness among the working classes that might affect production of war goods. In the words of Lloyd George, then Minister for Munitions, who told the Shipbuilding Employers Federation in March 1915 that Britain was: 'Fighting Germany, Austria and Drink, and as far as I can see the greatest of these three deadly foes is Drink.'[25] Strict controls were imposed on brewers cutting the strength of their beer and restricting the opening hours of public houses and, even, trying the control the behaviour of the men and women who visited them. For example, it became illegal to 'treat', that is to buy a round. Breweries and pubs in Carlisle were nationalized in 1916. It was an experiment to reduce drunkenness among local munition workers, through providing better pubs and weaker beer. Despite the protests of the temperance movement, which wanted the pubs closed, the experiment worked. Alcohol related crimes fell considerably. The government wanted to extend the experiment nationwide but the proposal was successfully opposed by the brewers.

After the Armistice, most of the wartime restrictions remained. Pub opening hours were just 5½ hours a day between noon and 2.30pm and 5.30pm and 9pm, with further restrictions on Sundays. Despite complaints, it took until 1921 for a slight relaxation in opening hours by an hour a day. The *Bystander*, in 1929, grumbled, accurately, that these restrictions, not just for the Society set, but for pub-goers in general, were 'humiliating discomforts as a permanent result of having won the War'.[26] It was not until 2004 that pub hours were finally liberalized.

The beer served in pubs remained rather weaker than had been the custom before the war. At roughly 3.5 per cent ABV it was less than half the strength it had been in 1914, although it was stronger than had been available during 1917 and 1918, when shortages of grain were at their greatest. It was also considerably more expensive, even allowing for wartime inflation, as taxes had risen by 430 per cent during the war. It was no surprise that beer consumption fell from 30 million barrels a year in 1914 to 13 million barrels in 1919.[27]

Convictions for drunkenness fell by 200,000 in 1914 to less than 30,000 in 1919. The moderate wing of the temperance movement had achieved many of its aims. Lord D'Abernon, chairman of the Central Control Board (which regulated the sale of liquor), said: 'I am pleased that the main cause for the reduction of alcohol consumption is to be found in a) high taxation b) wise limitation and spacing of opening hours permitted for the sale of drink. . . . We can congratulate ourselves on a reform accomplished without social perturbation.'[28]

In February 1918 the Minister of Reconstruction, Christopher Addison, warned that 'a discontented population and an ill-repaired machine offer, as it seems to me, an improvident means of debt reduction'.[29] On the left Beatrice and Sydney Webb felt that the State should be used to ensure orderly change:

> We must face the practical certainty that if the transition from capitalism to socialism is not intelligently anticipated, planned and guided by the rulers of the people, the people, when the breaking strain is reached, will resort to sabotage to force whatever government is left to tackle the job of reconstruction; and the danger is that the sabotage may go so far as to make the job impossible . . . our obsolescent institutions have been allowed to strain human endurance to breaking point instead of being modified.[30]

On the right, the historian Martin Pugh has suggested that some Conservatives, such as Stanley Baldwin, thought of the State as 'a benign and positive vehicle for promoting the interests of the community'.[31] Eric Geddes, the Conservative Minister of Transport, argued that 'you must be prepared to spend money on after-the-war problems as you did during the during-the-war problems. That must be found, and added to our war debt if necessary'.[32]

Against them stood the Treasury which sought to reverse the wartime position by reducing public expenditure and wages. The Treasury's policy was to balance expenditure at the lowest reasonable figure. During the war Treasury responsibilities included exchange-rate policy, external borrowing and managing war debt. Its influence was reduced when inflationary deficit financing was introduced and the national debt was increased. The proportion of national expenditure by the government rose from 8 per cent in 1914 to 50 per cent in 1918.[33] After the war the Treasury insisted on balanced budgets and monetary stabilization through the management of the bank rate and the rejection of public investment. It took responsibility for supervising and controlling all the operations of central government in so far as these affected the financial position, as well as for carrying out financial policy.[34]

In August 1919, the Cabinet agreed not to discuss proposals from departments involving expenditure until the Treasury had had the chance to study them. If the Treasury opposed a proposal, the spending department concerned had to notify the Treasury that an appeal to the Cabinet was pending. Its demands for austerity, budget cuts, monetary deflation and the removal of most import controls, were implemented. In the face of rapidly rising interest on the internal debt (it rose to 22.4 per cent of receipts by 1920) the Prime Minister argued that 'ruthless cutting of expenditure was imperative' and a cut in government spending of 75 per cent was introduced towards the end of 1919.[35] There was a brief inflationary boom, followed by the fastest economic collapse in British history. The Cabinet accepted the notion that Ministers should prioritize expenditure within balanced budgets. On Treasury advice Austin Chamberlain, the Chancellor of the Exchequer between 1919 and 1921, raised interest rates and removed the barrier to foreign lending.[36] In May 1919 Austin Chamberlain reduced planned expenditure by 36 per cent from £2,579 million in 1918–19 to £1,660 million in 1919–20. The annual deficit was reduced from £1,690 million to £326 million. This was one of the most deflationary budgets on record. However, it was still a plan for 60 per cent more central government expenditure than in 1914. In this context the deficit of £326 million was condemned as inflationary by those in the grip of the idea that government could best be classified as waste.[37]

The strong bias towards commercial and financial interests within Westminster and Whitehall buttressed the influence of the Treasury. Few of the civil servants who advised Ministers had an interest in industry and many were dismissive of trade as an activity. The bankers favoured free trade and the Foreign Office argued that the prestige of having a currency based on the Gold Standard and a city which provided overseas loans helped to maintain British influence abroad. Treasury officials took the view that the market system was the best way to allocate resources, that the discipline of the Gold Standard was of value and there should be close ties to the Bank of England.[38] The role of the City was strengthened when five large banks emerged following a number of amalgamations during 1918 and 1919. The pace of the movement led to an investigation by a Committee on Bank Amalgamations, which recommended that future amalgamations be subject to the approval of the Treasury and the Board of Trade.[39]

The Treasury was not alone in its views. Andrew McDonald concluded that the campaign to restore the Gold Standard and a balanced budget by the *Daily*

Mirror, *Daily Mail* and *The Times* was 'the most vigorously prosecuted and most sustained of its kind since the inception of the mass popular press of the 1890s'. The campaign traded in sensational stories of public waste, railing against the excesses of a so-called 'spendocrat' bureaucracy. The different titles tailored their approach to suit their target readership, but essentially, they spoke to certain basic middle-class and lower middle-class values: an intolerance of extravagance, a pride in the value of thrift and a faith in prudent housekeeping. Reduced public spending would, quite simply, bring lower taxes and a fall in the cost of living. The *Daily Mail* spoke about the 'new poor', that is the middle-class victims of inflation. Any more deleterious effects of deflation were ignored.[40] Moreover, the 'relentless press attention elevated public economy until it became the common language of all politicians'.[41] The National Union of Manufacturers and the Federation of British Industries, both formed in 1916, and the National Confederation of Employers' Organizations, created in 1919, also had concerns about control from Whitehall and urged the government to abolish wartime restrictions.

Despite Treasury influence, the State did maintain its influence in a number of ways particularly before the savage cuts in public spending took hold. The Defence of the Realm Act 1914 (DORA) provided the government with a range of controls over people's lives, conscription and a system of strict controls over those workers who were not conscripted were introduced and some powers, notably strike-breaking powers, were not relinquished after the war.[42] Between 1916 and 1920, a number of new ministries were created included Shipping, Food, Health, Labour, Transport and Pensions. There was also a number of government agencies established, including the Forestry Commission and the Department of Scientific and Industrial Research. Duties introduced in 1915 to protect industry were retained in 1919 and increased in 1921. The Wages (Temporary Regulation) Act in 1918 and an Out-of-work Donation initially assisted ex-servicemen before they found work and was extended to all workers in November 1918, and the Unemployment Insurance Act 1920 extended coverage to a further 8 million people. Welfare provision was extended under the Old Age Pensions Act 1919 and the National Health Insurance Act 1920. The Education Act 1918 increased schooling provision. Local education authorities could enforce school attendance, and restrict the employment of children of school age. They also became responsible for education and training and they could offer scholarships and maintenance allowances. Houses were built under the Housing and Town Planning Act 1919. The Land Settlement (Facilities) Act 1919 allowed counties to provide ex-service personnel with smallholdings.

The wartime ministries were soon scrapped, the new Ministry of Health, which administered public health and the Poor Law, had a limited role, and the Air Ministry (responsible for the RAF) only just survived being abolished. The role of the State was also diminished when expenditure on health insurance and housing was emphatically cut. By and large, the Treasury won the argument over the size and scope of the State. Although an expectation that the State could intervene into any area of life had been created, postwar stability was achieved through remarkably little advance in the responsibilities of the State. During the war, a woman who was suspected of having venereal disease could be forced to submit to a gynaecological examination. Anyone with a sexually transmitted disease could be prosecuted for having sexual intercourse with a serviceman, even if she was married to him. A pioneer of studies of social policy, Richard Titmuss, concluded that the war led to only one permanent reform, the free treatment of venereal disease.[43]

The debates in Whitehall and Westminster had echoes and repercussions at the local level. Although there were campaigns against the withdrawal of government services, as we have seen most people were happy to just have a job and a quiet life. More specifically campaigns for the State to retain its assets and convert factories from wartime production to the making of goods for peacetime ran aground. Those State factories which remained in government hands could only sell to the State sector, and only then if there were no private sources available. National Factories could not be sold to the Labour or Co-operative movement or local authorities. There was less need for the State to manufacture goods once the railways and the mines were returned to private hands.

There were calls for the conversion from munitions production of numerous wartime factories run by the government. In January 1919 shop stewards in Waddon in South London produced 'a scheme for the better utilisation, of National Aircraft Factories, particularly the factory at Waddon'. They wanted it converted to peacetime production. This campaign connected them to shop stewards at the National Aero Engine Factory, Hayes and the National Aircraft Factory, Aintree.[44] There were similar campaigns at the Waltham Abbey Gunpowder Factory and the Enfield Royal Small Arms Factory. In December 1919 workers at the Belsize Motor Works, in the Clayton district of Manchester, organized a series of meetings to demand that decontrol be halted.[45] In Coventry and Newcastle there were campaigns for conversion and trade unions, trades councils and the Scottish TUC took up the issue.[46] A deputation of civic chiefs of industrial centres affected by the withdrawal of orders for battleships asked the Prime Minister to provide alternative work. The Scottish TUC and several Labour MPs and trade councils supported diversification from the production of armaments. The Hills Committee of the Ministry of Reconstruction suggested that national factories be used for training women.[47] There was support for women to retain the work they had started during the war when almost 2 million women took on jobs previously reserved for men.

During the war, the government opened 218 new or adapted factories, producing every type of munition of war. After the war many of these 'national factories' were converted from armaments production after the war. There are examples of one changing production in order to make artificial silk, another making cars and a third becoming the factory where Crosse & Blackwell made Branston pickle. Cadbury's converted an ammunition factory to chocolate production and there were also a dyeing and cleaning works and a paper mill.[48] Bamford and Co. of Stockport shifted from making 18lb shells to building marine propellers for the Admiralty and the Trafford Park Tractor Assembly modified its military tractors for civilian use. The Munitions Council commended Thomas Fildes of Ancoats. The firm added legs to their canister fuses and sold the resulting items as ornaments.[49] In Cricklewood, S. Smith & Sons opened a factory in 1915 to manufacture fuses, instruments and accessories. It shifted to making electrical motors, aircraft accessories and electric clocks. The Government Cartridge Factory, Edmonton was purchased by Rego Tailoring. The National Balloon Factory, based in the former Bohemia Picture Palace, Finchley, was sold to the Kiwi boot polish company. A purpose-built government cartridge factory, the Birmingham Metal and Munitions Co., was sold as an electrical works. A National Gauge Factory in Walthamstow was sold to a dyeing and cleaning company. Parts of factories were sold, with a hut from the National Filling Factory, Banbury, re-erected as a coffin store by a local undertaker.

Conversion from wartime production was not always straightforward. Prices and markets were uncertain and there were difficulties with obtaining raw supplies.[50] The aircraft builders A.V. Roe failed to make the transition from metal working to making furniture. Armstrong, Whitworth & Co., Openshaw, found that the machinery for making armour plate and gun mountings was 'in the main too heavy for private orders'.[51] In Dudley the National Projectile Factory, built by A. Harper, Sons and Bean in 1915, produced shells, repaired guns and worked on aero engines. Immediately after the war the company used it to produce cars. The company went into receivership in 1920.

Galloway Engineering, which had built aero engines components and then, following the war, tractor and truck motors, designed and built Galloway cars. Led by Dorothée Pullinger, sixty women engineers designed the first cars aimed at women drivers and the only such cars to go into general production. Recognizing that on average women were shorter than men, the Galloway had a raised seat to improve sight-lines, a lowered dashboard and a smaller steering wheel. Instead of the gear lever and the brake lever being on the outside of the car, across the driver's door where they could obstruct skirts, the handbrake was situated near the driver's seat and the gears were placed in the middle. The rear view mirror was also a first. It had a more reliable engine and more storage space than comparable vehicles. Priced at £550, the car 'made by ladies for others of their sex' was designed to be economical and easy to maintain.[52] Unfortunately, they were not a commercial success. Around 4,000 Galloways were produced, maybe 200 cars at the Tongland factory which closed in 1923. Production then moved to Heathall, about 20 miles away, where a larger Galloway was made until 1928.[53]

One of the most significant campaigns for conversion in the State sector was organized in Woolwich. For decades before the war only one industry – armaments – dominated the town. The Arsenal grew in size fifteen-fold during the period 1914–18 and the Armistice brought with it the fear of job losses. Between the summer of 1918 and the early 1920s there was a concerted 'Peace Arsenal' campaign for the conversion of the site to the production of materials required in peacetime. This post-war campaign had echoes of a similar pre-war campaign. The people of the town had prospered during the Boer War of 1899–1902 and then suffered unemployment when its conclusion led to thousands of dismissals. There were campaigns for jobs run by local churches, friendly societies, the Chamber of Commerce and civic figures. The local council encouraged migration. There were protest marches and both mass meetings and meetings with the Secretary of State for War and the Prime Minister. A petition was sent to the King and there were government inquiries. A committee chaired by the Labour Party leader, Arthur Henderson, considered the possibility of State production of non-munitions work.

As a result of foreign competition, standardization, new production methods and the concentration of industry, the status of engineers had been considerably reduced.[54] Engineering shop stewards argued that diversification into locomotive production could efficiently ease economic recovery, by providing both an item that would meet an urgent need for engines as the result of wartime destruction, and provide employment in a one-industry town facing mass redundancies. It would also reduce the probability of resultant widespread evictions and social unrest. Also implicit was the availability of skilled men being given the opportunity to make prestigious locomotives.[55] There was experience, as the Arsenal had its own internal railway system of 120 miles of standard gauge track and also narrow-gauge track.[56] Locomotives were so expensive that they were frequently repaired rather than scrapped and there was also expertise in this work at the Arsenal. Repair of locomotives was deemed to be munitions work.[57] Moreover, the certainties of the pre-war years were embodied in the skilled, male task of locomotive construction. When the engineers' union depicted 'Industry' on its insignia, it symbolized this with an image of a locomotive When Lloyd George sought to disparage the Russian Revolution he noted that the Russians could not repair locomotives with the doctrines of Karl Marx. When the chair of the Arsenal Joint Shop Stewards Committee, Jack Mills, addressed the issue of productivity in a speech to the TUC he focused on 'the derelict engines at Derby, waiting to be repaired, cargoes waiting for locomotives, food rotting for lack of transport'.[58] Although some working practices had changed during the war, effectively reducing the status of engineers, this was not the case with the construction of locomotives where the principles of the craft traditions remained untouched. The Labour politician Ramsay MacDonald made this point when he told a crowd in Woolwich that 'when swords will be beaten into pruning hooks, I want the machines of the Arsenal to be making the pruning-hooks . . . I want the machines to be turned by the same skilled hands to make things that the nation and men will use'.[59]

There were protest marches, meetings with ministers and Lloyd George and a Committee of Inquiry under the Liberal MP Thomas McKinnon Wood, which examined the case for alternative work. There was support from within the Ministry of Munitions and both the Labour and Conservative MPs for Woolwich supported the case for what one of them, Sir Kingsley Wood, called a 'a great peace arsenal'.[60] The two Labour MPs who sat on the Committee felt that the site should be used to produce and repair rail rolling stock and items for municipalities.[61] The Committee concluded that repair work was better undertaken under government control and called for improvements to the management structure. However, few of its recommendations were implemented.[62] A standing advisory committee was established to implement some of the recommendations and this also promoted the idea of the Arsenal being used to fulfil government contracts. Other committees examined safety and explored the possibility of private companies using the site. The workers' representatives argued that there was an experienced workforce on hand, with otherwise idle government machinery and equipment which could be used to rebuild.

Requests to Woolwich Arsenal from the Phosphor Bronze Co., for drop stamping work, from R. Hoe & Co., for printing machinery, and for heavy machinery from Smith Brothers & Co. were rejected. Orders from the Royal Mint were accepted to make over 6 million campaign medals that were issued to the discharged servicemen for service overseas during the First World War.[63] Churchill promised orders for Local Government Board equipment and also orders for 1,000 locomotives and up to 40,000 wagons.[64] The Arsenal also produced items for the Post Office, the Indian Postal Service, Admiralty, Anatolian Railways, the Board of Trade and the Ministry of Food. It made tractors, dairy appliances, house-building materials, notably doors, and a range of other items.

The Prime Minister, Lloyd George, promised that 500 locomotives would be made at Woolwich. A master at oratory, he made a visit to Woolwich when alternative work was at its zenith with 8,000 people making wagons, medals, penny blanks and locomotives. Another 5,000 were working on motor vehicle and wagon repairs and producing items for the Admiralty and Post Office.[65] The *Evening Standard* reported that the Arsenal would be a 'great railway centre' and other newspapers echoed this account.[66] However, the *Woolwich Labour Pioneer* correctly concluded that he had promised little. It then reported that his 'pledges appear to have gone by the board' and that he had been 'captured' by the 'flinty faced men who look as if they have done well out of the war'.[67] Furthermore, making the locomotives took far longer than was planned. Only thirteen had been completed by the end of 1921. By May 1922 there were forty-five locomotives. A debate in the Commons revealed that each cost £15,600, at a time when a commercially produced locomotive of the same type cost £9,000.[68] The Arsenal was not designed to make such engines nor did the workforce have the right specialist skills. A further five locomotives were completed and the rest of the order cancelled.[69] Sales were made to Southern Rail, Metropolitan Railway and in Ireland.[70] As a former mayor of Woolwich acknowledged, they became a 'deadly weapon against the policy of alternative work'.[71]

The government increased some taxes. There was consideration of a turnover tax, a type of sales tax and also interest in indirect taxation. In 1919, the indirect taxation on beer, spirits and death duties was raised. However, beer consumption had fallen during the war, from 89 million gallons in 1914 to 37 million in 1918, and the additional beer duties brought in much less than expected.

There was also support from the Labour Party and Andrew Bonar Law (the Lord Privy Seal and leader of the Conservative Party) and among orthodox economists, notably A.C. Pigou and some Treasury officials, for a capital levy. This was a scheme to transfer savings from the private to the public sector through a one-off graduated tax on personal capital personal property, including land and accumulated wealth. Some saw this as a device for extending government ownership, arguing that the government could accept payment in land or shares.[72] However, the Treasury while prepared to budget for a deficit, were disinclined to make any fundamental change to the tax system. Although a new corporation profits tax was introduced, the rate of this, the single innovation in postwar fiscal policy, was reduced in 1923 and it was abolished in 1924. A Profiteering Act was passed in 1919 to meet widespread concerns that there had been considerable profiteering by industries, trades and shops during the war. Tribunals determined whether prices were fair. A study by historian Margaret Morris suggested that the Act was 'more a political propaganda exercise and less part of a serious economic policy'.[73]

Some of the taxation imposed during the war, notably the Excess Profits Duty, was retained. By the end of the war, when it was at 80 per cent, it was responsible for 36 per cent of government revenue.[74] The Duty was cut to 40 per cent but then in June 1920 raised to 60 per cent before being abolished in 1921. Income tax was reduced from its wartime peak of 6s in the pound and the tax-free allowance for children was raised and extended to wives. Income tax was still four times higher than it had been in 1914, when those on incomes of £10,000 paid only 8 per cent. The proportion of revenue derived from income tax and super tax rose from 29 per cent in 1913 to 36 per cent in 1919. Death duties had risen from 15 per cent in 1914 to 40 per cent in 1919. In 1920 the Finance Act placed an income tax exemption limit of £135 which did not entirely roll back the wartime expansion of the tax base. Married men with children received more generous allowances so as to encourage population growth.[75] Taxation continued to rise until it reached 32 per cent of national income in 1921 compared with 8 per cent in 1913 and around 20 per cent in the period 1924–30.

The cuts to spending and the high interest rates reduced demand. There was also high unemployment in some areas. Across many industries prices fell and growth rates were slow. The Bank of England raised its discount rate from 5 to 6 per cent in November 1919 and then to 7 per cent in April 1920. This was in place for a year and exemplified the commitment to a deflationist policy. Stanley Baldwin, the Financial Secretary to the Treasury, conflated the notions of sound finance and small government and employed a phrase later adapted by John F. Kennedy: 'Until the time comes when the ordinary man, instead of asking himself, "What can I get out of the state?" will ask himself, "What can I do for the state?", we shall never be able to put that drag on Governments which is absolutely essential in the interests of sound finance.'[76]

The inflationary and deflationary strategies, the trade problems, the focus on a return to gold and the cuts in government spending by 54 per cent over two years meant that a deficit of £1.6 billion became a surplus of £231 million. However, this was designated to pay off the debt rather than to invest in converting plant.[77]

It would be wrong to say that financially and economically Britain returned to a pre-war economy. Too much had happened to prevent this. There were permanent changes to the economic landscape in the relationship between the State and the private sectors, permanently higher taxes and the creation of new government offices such as the Ministry of Health. However, at the point that the threat to profits was judged to be greater than the threat of social instability, the plans for State support for economic diversification, for expenditure on reconstruction and for an interventionist economy were cast aside. Whitehall's centralized planning, economic organization and modernization were dismissed as wartime aberrations. Rather, the focus remained on reducing government spending in order to service the debt and on the international Gold Standard as the pillar of Western civilization. Associated with peace and prosperity before the war, for it to fall was seen as catastrophic, even though it came to mean deflation and an over-valuation of sterling which lost export markets and jobs. Ironically, expenditure of unemployment benefits led public expenditure to remain high. Across much of Europe political legitimacy had been lost and so too had economic stability. However, more peaceable Britain abandoned much State intervention, relied on a patch-up of its laissez-faire economic system and enjoyed relative political stability.

Chapter 4

Political Reconstruction

In the months immediately following the Armistice the parliamentary system was challenged as never before. In place of the pre-war struggles between Unionists and Liberals there were Labour and the Conservatives. Constitutional changes, the impact of coalition politics and the reforming of the two main parties within Westminster and at local level are key components in understanding this situation. What emerged was a stronger political system with Parliament at its heart.

On 14 November, a few days after the Armistice, the Prime Minister of the Coalition Government, the Liberal Lloyd George, called a General Election for 14 December. Since the previous General Election, eight years before, registration had been simplified, constituency boundaries had been altered to make for greater equalization of voter numbers and there were now 707 constituencies, an increase of 37 since 1910. More significant was that there were far more first-time voters than in the past partly because the election had been delayed due to the war and because the parliamentary franchise had been considerably extended to women over 30 who were householders, the wives of householders, occupiers of property of £5 or more annual value or university graduates voting in a university constituency. It was probably the minimum the government could offer to satisfy campaigners for the extension of the franchise to women. Crucially in the eyes of MPs, the female elector was likely to be 'a mature wife and mother primarily concerned with the preservation of her home life' and 'unlikely to be interested in a career or radical feminist issues'. The Tories assumed, probably correctly, that the new electors as a result were more likely to vote Conservative.[1]

In early 1918, a bill was rushed through Parliament that enabled women to stand for election to the House of Commons on equal terms with men, with no age barrier. However, only one woman – Constance de Markevicz – was elected at the 1918 General Election, and as a member of Sinn Fein she refused to take her seat. The first woman to enter the chamber of the House of Commons was an unusual choice, the American millionairess Nancy Astor, who fought the seat of Plymouth Sutton at a by-election in November 1919 when her husband was elevated to the Lords. She was hampered in the popular campaign as a result of her published and at times vocal teetotalism and her ignorance of current political issues. Her tendency to say odd or outlandish things sometimes made her appear unstable. On one occasion, while canvassing in Plymouth, she was greeted at a door by a girl whose mother was away. As Mrs Astor was unfamiliar with the area, she had been given a naval officer as an escort. The girl said: 'but she [my mother] said if a lady comes with a sailor they're to use the upstairs room and leave ten bob'. Mrs Astor remained an MP until 1945.[2]

Although the franchise had been extended several times during the nineteenth century it was still the case that 40–5 per cent of the male population, 5 million men, mostly industrial workers, was not permitted to vote and there were relatively few electors in London, northern towns and industrial areas with poorer inhabitants. Householders were favoured over tenants, young unmarried men living at home and the very poorest people.[3] Now 5.6 million more men, almost all of those aged 21 years of age or over, were included in the electorate and service personnel posted overseas were enfranchised if they were 19 or over, irrespective of gender. It was widely held that all those who fought in the war should have the right to vote. So, while only 3,372 women qualified in this way it established that citizenship was based on eligibility, not sex. This idea was reinforced by the decision to exclude male conscientious objectors for five years. In total, the electorate had expanded nearly three times from 7,710,000 to 21,393,000 voters. The changes towards near universal suffrage led to the party system being reinvigorated at national and local levels. Bill Schwarz summarized the overall effect of the changes: 'However radical these reforms may seem by the numbers enfranchised, they were the most conservative that the government imagined it could squeeze through. Even then, the effects were mitigated by the 1918 Redistribution Act which handed to the Conservatives at least seventy safe seats.'[4]

W.S. Gilbert's jocular lyric that 'every boy and every gal. That's born into the world alive. Is either a little Liberal Or else a little Conservative!' might have been true in 1882 but was not by 1918. There were challenges to the idea of a two-party system. The election saw 'upwards of fifteen hundred candidates under more than a dozen different banners, cranks and faddists adding an extra bit to the prevailing confusion'.[5] They included four candidates for the Highland Land League, three Independent Progressives and a Christian Socialist. The Conservatives faced the breakaway Nationalist Party from August 1917. Four Labour MPs formed a National Democratic Party, there was the possibility of the formation of the Trade Union Labour Party and the Independent Labour Party discussed affiliation to the Comintern, an international communist body. The Women's Party, launched in 1917, called for equality for women and support for the war. It attacked the labour movement but its progressive feminist and industrial programmes also diverged from Conservative thinking.[6] The National Association of Discharged Sailors and Soldiers, formed in 1916, stood candidates, as did the Silver Badge Party, which was formed in 1918, and the National Federation of Discharged and Demobilized Sailors and Soldiers, formed in 1917, put up twenty-nine candidates.[7] Of the candidates standing on this single issue, only one was returned.[8]

The General Election did not mark the end of the new alliances. At the Co-operative Movement Congress in 1919, the nascent Co-operative Party proposed to open negotiations for what it termed a 'United Democratic or People's Party' with Labour, although a formal agreement was only made in 1927. In 1920 the British Socialist Party joined with other bodies to form the Communist Party and the non-party Women's Election Committee was created to promote women candidates. In 1921, the newspaper proprietor Lord Rothermere created his Anti-Waste League to campaign for smaller government and the Scots National League was formed in London.[9]

These new parties received little support in 1918 or subsequently. The new female electorate was more middle class than the population as a whole and a high percentage of them turned out to vote. By contrast, the early polling date, lack of permission to vote and of reliable information kept many soldiers from voting at the General Election in December 1918.[10] Just under 11 million people went to the polls. Even so, this was more than double the number who had voted in 1910. During the 1918 election campaign the Liberal and Unionist leaders formed a coalition with 362 Conservatives (333 of whom were elected), 145 Liberals (136 of whom were elected), 18 National Democratic Party and 6 Independents. Each of these candidates had a letter of endorsement from the Coalition leadership known as the 'coupon'.[11] The coupon marginalized many Liberals who were associated with the former Liberal leader, Herbert Asquith and fought the election in nationwide opposition to Labour. By contrast, 'every Conservative candidate is *ex officio* a Coalition candidate'.[12] Liberals who had the coupon (and thus no Conservative opponents) were returned but so too were some Conservatives who did not have a coupon (some of whom had Liberal opponents). Asquith, for example, was defeated by a Conservative who had been refused the coupon. In the Liberal stronghold of Manchester, the Conservatives won every seat they contested, even though their candidates only had coupons in five of their eight seats, while the Liberals won no seats. Fewer than twenty Liberals defeated a Coalition candidate and fewer still won a three-cornered contest.[13] It was not the coupon but the decision of the Conservatives whether or not to run candidates that decided the outcome. The Liberals were not even united in opposition. Thirty-six non-coalition Liberals were elected but nine then accepted the Coalition whip. Other Liberals were general supporters of the Coalition. *The Times* estimated that only about fourteen Liberals could be relied upon to consistently oppose the government. The Liberal Party received 350,000 more votes than Labour but declined in popularity over the course of subsequent by-elections. Independent Liberals won three seats in by-elections in March and April 1919 but then came last in three more by-elections and only won two more before the next General Election, both in Liberal strongholds. Taking the twenty-four by-elections between 1918 and

1922 contested by the three main parties, the Coalition received 40.1 per cent of the votes, Labour 35.1 per cent and the Independent Liberals 24.8 per cent.[14] The National Liberals formed their own party in 1920 while Coalition Liberals faded from view as a distinct grouping.

Before the 1918 election the House of Commons comprised 281 Unionist (Conservative) MPs, including 5 who styled themselves the National Party, 260 Liberals, 77 Irish Nationalists, 6 Sinn Fein and one Independent. Seats previously held by five Unionists and one Irish Nationalist were vacant. At the previous General Election the Liberals had won the most seats and formed the government, so they did very badly in 1918. In part, this was because the party was split down the middle. But there had been other less obvious changes in society to which the Liberals had not adapted. Before the war the vast majority of middle-class Anglicans were Conservative. Nonconformists often voted Liberal and this reflected the issues the party had traditionally campaigned upon.[15] But by 1918 the Liberals' links to nonconformity had been broken and the war and redistributive policies dominated the manifestoes.[16] Christian belief was less important, not helped by the seeming irrelevance of the responses of the churches to the calamities of the First World War. More and more people had common experiences of schooling, factory life and leisure pursuits such as watching professional football. Over 10 million electors, more than half the electorate, did not vote and half of those who did vote selected a Coalition candidate. The new Commons saw 382 Unionists of all shades, about 60 per cent of the House. While Labour had won 2.5 million votes to the Unionists' 3.5, these proportions were not reflected in the Commons where, in practice, government members outnumbered the combined opposition by more than three to one. The Coalition's domination was helped by the refusal of the 73 MPs from Sinn Fein to take their seats in Westminster.

The creation of a coalition meant that the old loyalties, chapel or church, were not reflected on the ballot paper. The pre-war conflicts, notably the wave of strikes, women's suffrage, Britain's declining role in the world, Ireland and the House of Lords, were largely marginalized during the election campaign. More dominant was a tale of patriotic subjects who had done their duty for King and country. Politics had moved away from the values associated with the Liberals and towards notions of country and community. The Labour Party failed to make much headway during the campaign, but secured its position as the representative of the working class. A new version of two-party politics was being constructed which was reflected in the press.[17] The Conservatives received support in many newspapers and Labour's Arthur Henderson met with Lord Northcliffe and arranged for Labour to be given space in the *Daily Mail* and the London-focused *Evening Standard*. George Lansbury advertised in the

Daily Express during the 1918 election campaign, despite the disclaimer that the paper ran.[18] Such large-scale campaigns focused attention on the election as a two-sided event.

'Many Matters Caused Anxiety to the Peace Parliament in its First Session' – The View of a Lobby Correspondent

A strange House of Commons assembled on February 4, 1919. It was unfamiliar in composition and character . . . Coalitionists overflowed three-quarters of the chamber, occupying not only the Ministerial side, but also the benches below the Opposition gangway . . . Largely composed of rich men, well advanced in years and new to its life, the House early revealed considerable power of expert criticism in business affairs, but was naturally amenable to the influence of the Government. It was not as a rule, a well-attended House. An unusually small proportion of the new men, unskilled and unpractised, were desirous of Parliamentary distinction or interested in the everyday work. Attendance was affected by the development of the system of Grand Committees. Members who spent the early part of the day in the rooms upstairs had little desire to sit on the benches and listen to speeches in the evening. Many matters caused anxiety to the Peace Parliament in its first session. There were demobilisation troubles, Irish defiances of British rule, rent difficulties, profiteering complaints, the miners' demands, the cry of nationalisation, the general industrial unrest, the threat of direct action by Labour for political objects and the national railway strike, behind which the Prime Minister found an anarchist conspiracy and in consequence of which with stringent rationing, the prohibition of pastries, reduced lighting in the entertainment area, Hyde Park a milk depôt, and enrolment of special constables and transport drivers, London resumed some of the aspects and conditions of war time. There were problems of health and housing which formed the subject of legislation. Our intervention in North Russia and the continuance of military service till peace was assured encountered opposition . . .

Alexander Macintosh, *From Gladstone to Lloyd George; Parliament in Peace and War* (Hodder & Stroughton, 1919), pp. 305–7.

While the results, summarized as 'essentially a victory of the Right' by historian Chris Cook, the Labour Party also made gains.[19] The party was better prepared for the 1918 election than it had been for previous ones. In 1914 Labour was a federation of affiliated trade unions and socialist societies with individual members in only a few places and no set programme. By November 1918 it had become a party with constituency organizations with individual members as well as affiliates and a commitment to the 'common ownership of the means of production'. The party was relatively stable in financial terms as in 1911 MPs' salaries began to be paid by Parliament. In 1913 trade unions were permitted to ballot to collect money for the party and the trade-union membership rose from 4 million in 1914 to 8 million by 1919.[20] It won 57 seats (from 361 candidates) compared with 42 seats (from 56 candidates) in 1910. It gained 22.7 per cent of the votes, compared with 7.2 per cent in 1910.[21] The number of votes gained was seven times higher than in 1910. Moreover, it won hundreds of local council seats in the next few years as it consolidated its rise in the political sphere.[22]

Labour appealed to the younger voters. According to Michael Childs: 'the coming of age of workers born in the late Victorian and Edwardian period explains in part the coming of age of Labour'.[23] It benefitted from the idea that the wartime State control of industries and the State fixing of rents and profits had been efficient. This wartime collectivism, it argued, could provide the basis for a peacetime alternative to laissez-faire capitalism. It became associated with campaigns to convert State wartime production to the State production of items needed in peacetime. This involved negotiation, rather than revolution. The rise of Labour is also linked to the longer term change of people identifying with their social class and voting accordingly.[24] However, Labour also attracted people from across the electorate, not only from the working class. Arthur Strauss, a partner in a metal brokers, was elected as a Conservative MP in 1910, stood as an independent Labour candidate in 1918 and later joined the Labour Party. William Royce, a former President of the local Conservative Association, won Holland–with–Boston for Labour in 1918.

Labour's manifesto in 1918, *Labour and the New Social Order,* began by addressing the issue of peace, not by focusing on economic disasters and industrial confrontations. It demanded the immediate withdrawal of Allied forces from Russia, self-government for Ireland and India, the repeal of the Defence of the Realm Act, an end to conscription and the release of political prisoners (that is conscientious objectors). It also declared 'there must be no sex party: the Labour Party is the Women's Party'. It stressed that its programme was 'comprehensive, constructive' and to be achieved by 'constitutional means'. It outlined how a democratically elected Labour government would legislate for nationalization and wealth redistribution.

Some within the labour and trade-union movement, including Herbert Morrison and Ernest Bevin, supported direct action to prevent British involvement in the war against the newly created USSR. The 'high point of Labour's dalliance with direct action at national level' was the creation of councils of action in 1920. These were to co-ordinate workers' actions, including demonstrations.[25] This was followed by a move towards making an appeal as the party associated with moderation and efficiency and 'an effort to attract middle-class professional members and voters'.[26] In general, the focus on effecting change through Parliament, rather than by other means, was the reason for the existence of Labour.[27] Ralph Milliband concluded that: 'Of political parties claiming socialism to be their aim, the Labour Party has always been one of the most dogmatic – not about socialism, but about the parliamentary system. Empirical and flexible about all else, its leaders have always made devotion to that system their fixed point of reference and the conditioning factor of their political behaviour.'[28] He went on to argue that the party promoted 'piecemeal collectivism within a predominantly capitalist society'.[29] Labour leaders may have assumed that the political and social system could not be overturned.[30] Labour leader J.R. Clynes expressed the concern that direct action would encourage others beyond the Labour movement to employ such tactics. It was his recognition of the centrality of Parliament, rather than as an example of direct action, which meant that when in 1921 two Labour MPs were ordered to withdraw (following their comments made about the government's unemployment policy) Clynes led the other Labour MPs from the Chamber.[31] Taking a similar line, Henderson said that direct action alienated voters.[32] He sought to guide the 'mass movement along the path of constitutional change'.[33]

Constitutional Labour

'[A] Constitution which enables an engine-cleaner of yesterday to be a Secretary of State today is a great Constitution', J.H. Thomas.[34] James Henry Thomas, 1874–1949, was illegitimate, left school aged 12 and rose to become General Secretary of the National Union of Railwaymen, 1916–31. He served as a local councillor and then as a Labour, later National Labour, MP and Minister, 1910–36.[35] While never on the left of the party, nevertheless, in 1920 Thomas felt that: 'I do not think there is anyone today who fails to realise that the old order of things can never be re-established'. He went on, in *When Labour Rules*, to describe 'The England of To-morrow':

No man will have occasion to protest against the conditions under which he is expected to live; no man will be able to state that some one is living on his sweated labour; and no man will be able to proclaim that he lacks the opportunity to improve his lot if he wishes to do so.

There will be no profiteers, no unemployment, no slums, no hungry children. No man will be expected to work an excessive number of hours, and no man who is fit for work will be permitted to shirk it; the right to live upon the accumulated wealth of another will no longer exist; the right to the best and highest education the country can afford will no longer be the exclusive privilege of a favoured class, but will be open to all whose talents show that they will benefit by receiving it; the only qualifications for the higher civil service will be character and ability.

[. . .] Another feature of the England of to-morrow will be the National ownership of Railways, Mines, Canals, Harbours, and Roads. Also, there is no reason against, but plenty of reasons in favour of the public ownership of the great lines of steamers.

[. . .] a great army of University Extension lecturers will be employed to give popular instruction, which will be available to all during the winter months, and there will be a National Theatre and a National Opera.[36]

Many Labour MPs in 1918 were former union officials. The party helped to embed trade unions into the new political system and give them a stake in parliamentary democracy. The Parliamentary Labour Party and the Party Conference was dominated by forty-nine MPs sponsored by trade unions and former union officials, and all too often deemed to be of little value to the union. Many had supported the war, were on the right of the party and largely focused on trade-union matters.[37] The inaugural meeting of the Durham Divisional Labour Party was held in 1918 in a hall belonging to the Durham Miners' Association and led by union officials, one of whom, Jack Lawson, became the MP in 1919.[38]

Labour's leadership believed that they had 'a role in the state, hence they opposed direct action'.[39] Labour's commitment to free trade, Home Rule, social welfare and Gladstonian foreign policy made it appealing to some Liberals. It was attractive to some Conservatives because it made an appeal to patriotic pleasure-seeking, elements of working class culture. It was a Labour MP, Will Crooks, who started the singing of the National Anthem in the Commons when the war was declared and it was Jack Jones MP whose love of football, cricket and drinking endeared him to many voters during a period when royal visits, racing and football were far more popular than Bolshevism.

The political structures of the modern British State proved to be robust when threatened by the actions of a few revolutionaries. Labour saw change in terms of an evolutionary process, a series of historical stages, leading to socialism. Once the benefits of social ownership were understood, more would be demanded and socialist consciousness would develop.[40] On the other side of the House of Commons the Prime Minister, Lloyd George, argued that it was important 'to give the impression we are not a "class" Government. The strength of this Government must be that it holds the balance evenly between classes'.[41]

In the Conservative Party too there were changes. MPs represented a wider range of interests than had been the case in the past. As many of those who might have expected to go into Parliament had died during the war or were still on active service, the social base of Conservative MPs changed. There were more businessmen, merchants and manufacturers from provincial towns and fewer young men from titled or landowning families or the sons of MPs. In contrast to the past, 168 of the 382 Unionist MPs in 1918 had no experience of politics. It was also an unusually elderly parliamentary party with only 23 per cent of the new members aged under 40. These were men too old for the services with experience of business not politics. Moreover, far fewer had attended either a public school or the universities of Oxford or Cambridge. In 1918 one Unionist son of a distinguished family Lord Henry Bentinck noted his party was becoming 'thoroughly commercialised and vulgarized. . . . Plutocracy be ennobled, decorated, knighted, and enriched. That way lies disruption and damnation.'[42]

> No longer was the tone of the party to be set by men from what can best be described as the old ruling class – the aristocracy and county families, imbued with the spirit of 'noblesse oblige' and serenely confident in their role, who long had sent their sons into parliament early in life after seeing them educated at the proper schools and colleges.[43]

Into the old bottle of the Conservative and Unionist Party had been poured the new wine of industrialists. Men whom Stanley Baldwin famously described as: 'A lot of hard-faced men who look as if they had done very well out of the war.'

The emergence of a stable, two-party system was also helped when, for the first time, constituency boundaries were largely the same as local government boundaries. There was an effort to make the number of voters in each seat roughly equal. Many smaller seats were abolished while some larger ones were divided. Industrial towns received more representation. In 1915 the largest constituency, Romford, numbered 60,878 electors while the smallest, Kilkenny, had only 1,702.[44]

The redistribution to London, Birmingham, Glasgow and Liverpool from rural areas benefitted the Conservatives at the expense of the Liberals. There were also complaints that the boundaries had broken up communities. The leader of the Labour Party, Ramsay MacDonald, who lost his seat in 1918 and lost again at a by-election in 1921, argued that the outcome of the changes was the creation of 'artificial' constituencies in which 'the electorate had been dissolved into separate individuals'.[45] And *Liberal Agent* concluded that redistribution had led to 'a neurotic and butterfly type of elector'.[46] These views about the apparent break-up of society were widely held not just by politicians.

Politicians on all sides conceptualized the electorate as easily swayed and often ignorant. They worried that their opponents were effective propagandists. The dockers' leader, Ernest Bevin, felt that the lack of support for Labour was due to the 'mental poverty' of the electorate.[47] He and others felt that, put simply, the Labour Party's role was to educate people so that society could progress towards the Socialist Commonwealth. It had to overcome what Labour leader Ramsay MacDonald called 'the marshalled opposition of mass habit'.[48] People needed to be helped to develop the appropriate wisdom, knowledge and understanding. This was a lengthy and difficult process for 'the masses retain the love of primitive man for gaudy ornament and sparkling plaything', and 'slowly, very slowly, do intelligence and reflection permeate the mass'.[49] As Edinburgh's *Labour Standard* complained, the working class conceptualized education to be of less importance than 'a street corner brawl'.[50] Ramsay MacDonald blamed his failure to be elected in 1918 on the female voters, 'the sad flotsam and jetsam of wild emotion', and went on to argue that he felt many of the electorate, who 'take no rational or abiding interest in politics or in their national affairs', were 'non-rational and irresponsible' and could be influenced by propaganda as 'the minds of masses of men' were so limited that it could be 'sheer folly and perversity to allow this mass to pass important political judgements'. A single Conservative candidate could turn voters 'into a mere mob', whereas socialism was rational and conservative.[51] Labour, he felt, 'strives to transform through education, through raising the standards of mental and moral qualities, through the acceptance of programmes by reason of their justice, rationality and wisdom'.[52]

The Tories largely had the press behind them. They also set up various lobbying groups. One such was the shadowy National Propaganda. It was formed in December 1919 and chaired by Reginald 'Blinker' Hall MP, and wartime Director of the Naval Intelligence Division at the Admiralty. It aimed to promote free enterprise and it kept files on left-wing activists.[53]

Before the war politics was forthright and robust with pleas for fair play and free speech being seen as 'advertisements of weakness'.[54] Until 1918 'volatile meetings and political disruption remained widely accepted as an inevitable, even legitimate, feature of a healthy polity'.[55] Meetings, however, were not really a feature of the 1918 election. Although schools were used for meetings, many of the large public buildings in London and elsewhere had been commandeered by the government and so were unavailable.[56] In Sunderland the prevalence of influenza led to the candidates' decision to avoid 'house-to-house canvassing during the election campaign and not to convey electors in carriages on the polling day'.[57]

After the war, there were concerns that men returning from the fighting would have become less deferential, more brutal and susceptible to calls for the overthrow of the social order. The *Manchester Guardian* argued that during the campaign Lloyd George did nothing to restrain 'the cheap violence of his followers; rather, it must be said, he has played up to it'.[58] It also noted the defiance of the police by rioters in Wolverhampton. It concluded that men's 'readiness to fly to violence and defy authority' was a result of the war.[59] The Conservatives, in turn, vilified disturbances and associated rowdyism with Bolshevism and Labour.[60] The reactionary rabble-rouser Horatio Bottomley, elected as an Independent MP in 1918, argued that those constituencies where the electorate failed to behave 'decently' should be disenfranchised.[61]

By way of response Labour leaders promoted education over disorderly entertainment. The *Labour Organiser*, in April 1921, noted the importance of encouraging 'the quiet, ordinary citizen' to recognize 'the power of Labour to govern'. The message was reiterated at local level. Greenwich Labour Party organized the distribution of leaflets outside Conservative meetings, declaring that 'Good Labour men are good sportsmen and give their opponents a fair hearing'.[62] Labour claimed that the electorate wanted 'reasoned argument . . . devoid of the band, banner and shouting'.[63]

Local politics and local government remained of great importance, which was reflected by the decision of Whitehall during the war to devolve many matters to councils such as food rationing. At the municipal level Labour sought to present a similar message, that it wished to govern for the locality, rather than being focused on class action. Labour identified particularly with working class communities and saw that councils could be one of the main agencies for the enactment of its policies. It was determined to be a constitutional party that promoted education and worked hard to build communities. The development of local rationing schemes and the appointment of labour representatives on pensions and conscription appeal tribunals had provided administrative roles for Labour activists. They became the bulwarks of the idea that the State apparatus was the most appropriate means of securing social justice. In many areas Labour was effectively organized. By 1920 there was a divisional Labour Party in every constituency in Manchester and inner city Ardwick soon boasted 4,000 members.[64] For Labour, 'the most centralized and disciplined of the three parties', the 'importance of local peculiarities' remained.[65]

There were non-union members, often women and middle class, who helped to foster neighbourliness and ensured that the character of Labour politics 'changed from a party based on certain trade unions to one based on neighbourhood organisations'.[66] In east London the Labour Party made a formal pact with the United Irish League, had close ties to the Irish Self-Determination League and offered opportunities for integration into the body politic to Catholics, who had traditionally been marginalized in local affairs. There were twelve Catholics among the forty-three victorious Labour Party Stepney councillors elected in 1919.[67] Labour also involved women 'as canvassers and fund-raisers' far more than the Conservatives, partly because it had fewer financial resources.[68] It was through their associational life that people participated, trusted one another, gained skills, spread ideas and, by building networks outside the State, constructed a strong political system.

In turn, the Tories also sought to appeal to the new female electorate. It formed the Women's Unionist Organization, which built on the Primrose League that had been established by the Conservatives for their female supporters back in the 1880s. It was followed by Unionist Women's Institutes, a 'proliferation of localized anti-socialist discourses', and published the *Conservative Woman*.

That 'the local dimension remained vital to British politics' helped to ensure that opportunities for decision-making and engagement were spread across the country.[69] In 1918 most local Conservative associations in London engaged in 'practically no canvassing'. This had generally been the case at elections before the war, when the electorate was much smaller. They did not have the systems in place to reach the new voters. However, by the time of the General Election in 1923 the majority of associations had contacted over half their electorates.[70] Within the Coalition it was the local associations which voiced their opposition to the development of a single new party merging the Conservatives and Coalition Liberals and played a significant role in preventing it.[71]

Although the count was delayed due to the need to transport ballot papers, it was the first General Election to be held on a single day as in the past polling took place on different days in different constituencies. This change 'is likely to have shifted the focus of elections to the national stage and weakened the hold of local customs'.[72] This concentrated attention on Lloyd George, who assumed the mantle of national saviour. Although the creation and maintenance of the wartime Coalition had ensured changes within the Commons as 'backbenchers had discovered that they had power and that they were more than mere voting fodder', the decline in the role of MPs continued.[73] They were 'increasingly spectators in the drama of politics'.[74] There was also personal hostility to Lloyd George and in by-elections several candidates stood as anti-Coalition Conservatives. By 1922 this reaffirmation of Conservatism split the Unionist Party and had led to a coup against the Coalition.

The development of local branches of political parties and of the voluntary sector spread stability across the reconstituted political spectrum. The settlement was implemented by national leaders but cemented at local level. Local political bodies were encouraged. Voluntary organizations, unions, co-operative societies and pressure groups had long mobilized citizens, bound them to one another and involved them in public affairs. Although political parties were suspicious of rival bodies, the engagement of voluntary non-party associations helped to steady, not to challenge, the political structures.[75]

Such bodies were particularly important during the war, raising millions of pounds for the Red Cross and other hospitals, sending parcels to prisoners of war and socks to men at the front, collecting sphagnum moss used to heal wounds. Of the work of the Young Men's Christian Association (YMCA), which ran canteens for the forces, Will Crooks said: 'Why, they could no more do without the YMCA than they could do without munitions at the front.'[76] They continued to play these roles after the war, although the relationship between the State and charity changed. The State was now recognized as being the senior partner in the provision of welfare to the needy. The National Federation of Women's Institutes was initially a state-funded wartime body which aimed to improve food production. It became independent after the war and played a significant role in anchoring British politics against extremism. The League of Nations Union, founded in 1918, 'comprises persons of all classes and many schools of thought: it would be fatal to our unity if our propaganda were to be made a vehicle for the views of any particular group'.[77] It provided a space for members to engage in associational culture and discuss issues, run campaigns and become educated citizens. The Save the Children Fund, founded in 1919, was the first of a new generation of charities. It was as much a pressure group as a charity. As a result, it was much less deferential, but also very much more successful than its competitors. By the end of 1919 missions of nurses, doctors and relief workers had been sent to many places across Central and Eastern Europe where they were most needed. And in a great coup they had persuaded the government to give £1 towards famine relief for every pound the Fund raised.[78]

Across Europe new political formations were being put in place with Lenin promoting communism and in 1922 Mussolini declaring himself *Duce*, leader of a fascist movement in Italy. In the face of unrest and unemployment, the British solution to the postwar problems was to rebuild a two-party system. The Conservatives became dominated by industrialists. Labour, opened up to individual members working within their own communities as well as trade unions, succeeded the Liberals as the alternative. Both parties developed a view of the electorate as liable to be swayed by propaganda and in need of education. Both became committed to constitutional, Parliamentary politics, rather than violence and direct action. Both recognized the other party as an integrated, integral, constitutional bulwark of the revised structure. Between the two parties there was considerable agreement about democracy, the need for some State intervention and for what was known as 'sound finance'. Postwar stability rested on the continuation, and the development, of support for parliamentary constitutionalism, the importance of politics locally and of a vibrant voluntary sector. In practice, apart from two short periods, politics between the wars was dominated by the Conservatives, either governing alone or in coalition. However, it was the events of 1919–20 which secured the notion of two big parties taking turns to govern and being committed to promotion through the media and to winning voters by persuasion at local level.

There were widely differing views about the defeated enemy. They were subtle and varied by class. Robert Graves and Alan Hodge thought that in the immediate postwar period Germany was officially regarded as a 'moral outcast' and that: 'Nothing of German origin could be sold in shops and the wartime ban on German classical music remained in force for some time.' The press remained virulently 'anti-Hun', as the phrase went. On the whole newspapers, particularly the *Daily Mail*, argued that Germany should be severely punished for its actions. *Punch* published a cartoon in February 1919 referring to the continuing British naval blockade of Germany showing a German criminal saying to the Allied policeman, 'Stop you are hurting me', and then aside, 'If only I whine enough I may be able to wriggle out of this yet.'[79] Most of the few remaining Germans living in Britain were expelled during 1919. After the scuttling of the German High Seas Fleet at Scapa Flow in June 1919, its commander Admiral von Reuter was sent to an internment camp at Oswestry where he was attacked by an angry crowd and struck in the face by a rotten egg.[80]

Much concern was expressed at the harshness of the Peace Treaty, although public opinion was broadly in favour of it. *The Times* called it: 'a great historic memorial . . . of the war we have fought and the victory we have won'. But warned that 'A settlement so wide, so intricate and so technical teems, of necessity, with opportunities for evasion and bad faith.'[81] The *Yorkshire Telegraph and Star* said that 'Germany is to be severely punished, but the time will come when she has paid the penalty, and it is not in our nature to be vindictive.' Only the voice piece of the labour movement, the *Daily Herald*, opposed the treaty.[82]

In May 1919, the Asquith Liberal MP Commander Joseph Kenworthy told a meeting at the Royal Albert Hall that: 'This abortion of a peace treaty, this bastard child of the "Little Welsh Wizard" and the old, worn out man-eating tiger, Clemenceau, had passed beyond the boundaries of tragedy and entered the field of comedy. [It] would have to be modified because it was found to be absolutely impossible.'[83] Kenworthy had just become MP for Hull Central beating the Coalition candidate in a by-election where he advocated 'a good, an early and non-revengeful peace.[84] The economist John Maynard Keynes' angry attack on the Treaty, *The Economic Consequences of the Peace*, outsold best-selling novels on both sides of the Atlantic. And over time it helped turn public opinion against the Peace Treaty. Keynes accurately declared that even the modest Treasury estimate of the amount of reparations of £2 billion was probably beyond Germany's ability to pay. In fact, Germany paid less than £1.1 billion of reparations in total between 1918 and 1932.[85]

A few people, ex-soldiers for the most part like Charles Carrington, felt that so far as being too harsh on Germany, the terms of the Treaty of Versailles had been too mild. In particular, they felt Germany's war leaders should have been prosecuted and publicly humiliated. The Allies did not make the same mistake in 1945, when they established the war crimes tribunal at Nuremberg and later rebuilt the German state anew in democratic colours.[86]

Chapter 5

Adjusting to Peace

It is important to consider how two key segments of society adjusted to peace. Older women gained the vote, which was seen as a reward for war service. And many now worked in jobs that before the war would have been seen as inconceivable as women's work. But in other ways women's roles in society had hardly changed. Older women were permitted to vote but, perhaps because they were often wives and mothers focused on homes, many voted Conservative.[1] Conversely, the disabled ex-serviceman was a new participant within society, one whose needs had to be met, as had been promised by the wartime rhetoric of the war hero, but at the lowest possible cost.

As well as the vote and the right to stand for Parliament (see Chapter 4) during the following year at least seven important measures leading to large improvements in the status of women passed into law. These included the Sex Disqualification Removal Act 1919, which, among other things, enabled women to enter certain professions and to take up public roles from which they had previously been debarred. However, female civil servants were still expected to resign their position on marriage. They were permitted to become barristers, solicitors and magistrates and to sit on juries. In 1918 there was a doubling, to 10s per week, of the sum fathers could be obliged to pay toward the maintenance of an illegitimate child. The Nurses Registration Act 1919 improved the professional status of women as well as the quality of care available to them. The Maternity and Child Welfare Act 1918 improved health and welfare facilities for mothers and children, and improvements in the inheritance rights of women under Scottish law and the Industrial Courts Act 1919 appointed women to the newly established courts of arbitration on pay and working conditions.

In truth, the real gains made as a result of the war were small. Those women who benefitted were overwhelmingly middle class. No action, for example, was taken on equal pay.[2] The trade-union leader Mary McArthur was despondent: 'Reconstruction has been for some time our favourite shibboleth. Shall I be accused of faintheartedness if I say that, at this moment, the new world looks uncommonly like the old one, rolling along as stupidly and blindly as ever and that all it has got from the war is an extra bitterness or two.'[3]

During the war tens of thousands of women entered the factories and offices to fill the gaps left by men joining up or to boost the war economy. Between July 1914 and July 1918, the number of women employed in Britain rose by nearly 1.5 million, with virtually all of them engaged in new occupations or hired as substitutes for men. In engineering, where large numbers of women were employed, the figures rose from about 170,000 women in the industry before 1914 to 594,000 in 1918. As the academic Norbert Soldon noted, women during the war:

> Planed, moulded, mortised and dovetailed in sawmills, drove trucks in flour and oil and cake mills; made upholstery and tyre tubes; bottled beer and manufactured furniture; worked in cement factories and foundries and tanneries, in jute mills and wool mills; broke limestone and loaded bricks in steel works and worked as riveters in shipbuilding yards. They could be found in car factories, in quarrying and surface mining and brickmaking. They worked as porters and carriage cleaners on the railways; in power station and gas works and on sewage farms; as policewomen and park attendants and street and chimney sweeps. Only underground mining, stevedoring and steel and iron smelting were still all male.[4]

A hundred thousand or so young women also served in the forces, driving vehicles, waiting tables and working in offices.

With the Armistice, the munitions factories rapidly began to close. Gerry Rabin notes this led to: 'a quite spectacular and virtually unresisted migration (or ejection) of female munitions workers from their wartime jobs'. By June 1919, the Ministry of Munitions had let 90 per cent of its women employees, the so-called munitionettes, go from its factories. Many women, especially married women, were impatient to go anyway, they told the Ministry that they wanted to leave the war factories if family members were on leave or had been demobilized.[5] The National Shell Filling Factory at Barnbow, West Yorkshire employed 16,000 workers. As soon as the Armistice was declared, operations ceased. Many workers left the factory immediately 'and swelled the crowds that made festivity in the streets of Leeds; others returned to assist in partial operations after two days stoppage; and in very short order all employment on munitions was at an end'.[6]

Some muntionettes took matters into their own hands. On 19 November 1918, about 6,000 munitions workers, mainly from Woolwich, marched on Parliament demanding 'immediate guarantees for the future'. They marched in 'good order wearing their munitions badges' and carried banners that read 'Shall Peace Mean Starvation' and 'Rise Like Lions Out Of Slumber. In Unconquerable Number.' Their protest came to nothing.[7]

A few girls did not wait to be let go – they walked out. On Armistice Day itself, Jennie Johnson, from Newcastle who had hated the factory where she was working, when the announcement of peace was made:

So I put my hat and coat on. I went into the cloakroom and the foreman said, 'Where are you going?' I said, 'Home'. He said, 'You can't'. He came up to see my father and he said how silly I was. I'd lose all my money. Anyhow I got the money. But I was delighted just to go. It was the best day of my life to be walking out and I never went back again . . . It was the first time in my life, I'd ever done what I'd wanted.[8]

Jennie soon found a job at a local cinema, which she really enjoyed. Jennie was lucky: the women who left the factories in the weeks after the Armistice had little difficulty finding work. However, if they were discharged during 1919 matters were different because the jobs were no longer there. For many former munition workers, the alternative was the dole. Fortunately, the Out of Work Donation, which was meant to tide servicemen over until they found work, was extended to civilian workers just after the Armistice. By April 1919, just under ½ million women and 31,000 girls under 18 were drawing the Donation. The scheme was meant to be temporary but it was extended several times well into 1921.[9]

The women who enlisted in the services were also rapidly demobilized and many entered the job market. Ruby Ord had served in the Women's Auxiliary Corps (WAAC):

Once we were back in England, everyone was occupied trying to get a job. It was very difficult if you had been a WAAC, because you weren't favourably looked on by people at home. We had done something that was outrageous for women to do. We had gone to France and left our homes – so we had quite a job getting fixed up with work when we got back. I got a job by accident, purely because my sister got married, and her husband gave me work.[10]

Many women were happy to return to domestic life to look after their menfolk and children. Only about 10 per cent of women continued to work after their marriage. This was more or less the same proportion as before the war.

But those women, whether single or married, who sought work faced considerable difficulties. Trade unions had traditionally fought to stop women taking work which had been done by men. In part, this was because they wanted to maintain current employment practices that benefitted skilled workers. They were also suspicious of the ability of women to do the work. Women, however, were attractive to employers because they were paid less. There was also considerable pressure on employers to take on returning servicemen. Indeed, the Restoration of Pre-War Practices Act 1919 made it a legal obligation. Most women accepted that this ought to be the case. The trade unionist Barbara Drake, writing in 1920, argued:

Male trade unionists were determined to reimpose their restrictions on female labour. Nor was the decision opposed by industrial women, who were quick to acknowledge the common justice of the men's claim that pledges given by government and the employers must be redeemed in full. The necessity seemed, indeed, so plain to men and women trade unionists that the only matter for surprise was that they should have had to insist upon it.[11]

What alternatives were there for working class women? The obvious choice was to become domestic servants, for which there was a huge demand. The personal columns of *The Times* and other papers were full of adverts for domestics: 'Single-handed cook and house-parlour maid for family of two; some help given; must be good-tempered; good wages, according to capabilities. Required immediately good cook and kitchen maid. Quiet place in Kent: £48 and £20; good references required.'[12] It was hard, dreary and badly paid work, from which perhaps as many as 100,000 munitionettes and factory workers had fled during the war.[13] And few willingly returned, the numbers of female servants enumerated in the census fell from 1.4 million in 1911 to just over a million a decade later, although domestic service still remained the biggest employer of women. A government committee was set up in 1919 to investigate why fewer girls wanted to enter service, but came to no real conclusion.[14]

Resentment about women workers remained even after they had lost their jobs, as this extract from the *Tottenham and Edmonton Weekly Herald* for 17 January 1919 makes clear with its references to fur coats: 'A queue of over 1,000 women and girls was to be seen outside the Tottenham Employment Exchange on Friday morning. They were waiting to receive their 25s out-of-work bonus. It was a well-dressed queue; the musquash and seal coat, eloquent of the former munition worker, was not absent, while most of the queue-ists appeared to be under 21.' The same edition of the newspaper featured 187 advertisements for domestic servants, and about 100 more for female assistants for businesses and laundries.

By the Armistice the dynamic between mistress and maid had changed for good. The *Manchester Guardian* pointed out: 'Very few girls will go into domestic service after experiencing the freedom of limited hours and their own home.'[15] And in the *Daily Mail* the journalist Ward Muir wrote about 'Mary' his 'Aunt Matilda's' (Mrs Egerton-Browne) general servant. Mary had spent the war years working in a factory:

For one thing Mary has lost, for ever and ever, the 'respectfulness' which, – well, made her imagine that to wait on Mrs Egerton-Browne, who had been too stupid ever to earn a penny in her life, was the natural and proper fate for a clever girl in Mary's 'position' – that is without the means to be as idle as her mistress . . . I have seen Mary's bedroom furnished with a 'servant's set'. I have seen the bare little kitchen in which Mary wasn't allowed to receive admirers . . . but in which she was supposed to sit very contentedly for six evenings of the week. And I don't think that Mary will come rushing back.[16]

Increasingly, there were alternative employment for 'clever young women' like Mary. Office and clerical work was one alternative. The number of female office workers rose from 178,000 in 1911 to 560,000 in 1921, despite considerable opposition from their male counterparts, although they were still paid less than men.[17]

Call of the Home Unheeded by Many Girls – Bristol Scheme to Solve Problem

A meeting of employers and mistresses, arranged by the Local Advisory Committee was held yesterday in the lesser Colston Hall in regard to the question of domestic service in Bristol.[18] Miss B M Sparks explained in opening the meeting that it was imperative that some scheme be evolved by which girls should be brought back to work in the homes, and to do this the conditions of domestic service must be brought into line with those of other industries, both in regarding details of conditions and wages.[19] A draft scheme has been drawn up by the Women's Sub-Committee of the Local Advisory Committee and it would be explained by Mr Broad and suggestions regarding the scheme were invited.[20]

Miss Baron pointed out that the subject was the most pressing among those affecting women's work. Women coming out of munitions industries who were in domestic service before the war showed no inclination to go back into service.[21] This was not only the case in Bristol but all over the country and Local Advisory Committees set up in connection with Employment Exchanges to deal with employment questions were finding everywhere that this question was most pressing.[22] The girls' point of view must be regarded as well as the employers'. The girls had an opportunity of doing another kind of work during the war. They have more freedom, definite hours of work and more companionship in their work. They had also felt that every bit of their work was tremendously worthwhile doing and helped in the war. They did not want to give up their freedom and companionship, or the better status they had enjoyed. To give an idea of what was happening in Bristol; there were something like 1,900 unemployed claiming donations at present, a large number of whom were probably in domestic service before the war. The Exchange had been inundated with vacancies since the meeting of domestic workers about a fortnight ago. There were 400 vacancies at present for domestics to live in, and 150 for daily workers. To show how few girls were going back to domestic service, during the four weeks ended 7 February, nineteen women were placed to live in and 53 daily workers. It seemed as if something must be done to change the conditions and make domestic service more attractive. Long hours and lack of freedom were the chief objections. Various schemes had been drawn up by various bodies, one of which provided for the girls to live together in a hostel and wear a special uniform and be under a certain amount of discipline.

Mr L Broad [outlined] the scheme which as suggested for Bristol . . . [A] 'Whitley' council representing employers and employed was to be constituted and from it a rota to vet prospective domestics and mistresses.[23]

Wages and hours. The following minimum wages would apply for resident domestics; Cooks 21 years and upwards £30; house parlour-maids, parlourmaids and housemaids 18 years, £22, 19 years, £24, 20 years, £26, 21 years and upwards, £28. General: 18 years £20, 19 years, £22, 20 years, £24, 21 years and upwards, £26. Between maids; 18 years, £15, 19 years, £20. These wages were in addition to full board and washing. The women would be given two hours daily, irrespective of meal times, a half-day holiday every week, a half-day on Sundays and two weeks holiday a year on full wages. For meal times they would have half-hour for breakfast, one hour for dinner and half-hour for tea. Employers would be asked to sign an agreement on these conditions and give an assurance that the situation was a good and comfortable one and the sleeping accommodation was satisfactory. There would be a month's notice on either side. Any complaint as to conditions of service should be referred to the weekly rota. With regard to daily and part-time workers, general work without meals should be 4d an hour (exclusive of meal times) and 6d without meals.

Criticism of the scheme was invited, and there was some discussion of details. Replying to a question as to the scheme having the effect of raising wages of girls at present employed at lower rates, Mr Broad said the scheme might have that effect. . . . One lady thought such conditions would make the girl more the mistress than the employer herself . . .

Bristol Evening News, 19 February 1919

The war had changed women, particularly those under about 30, for good. If working class girls had found freedom in the factories and the middle classes in the armed services, it was harder for those from the upper classes. Barbara Cartland, who was a teenager during the war and grew up in an impoverished gentry family, remembered that: 'We lived in manless homes. We were brought up by women and Edwardian women at that. We were fenced around with narrow restrictive social customs, nurtured on snobbery . . .'[24] It was hard to break free from bourgeois conventions to work in factories or offices. Many upper class women contributed to the war effort by running voluntary organizations, and their daughters were expected to play their part as well.

Observers mused about how the aftermath of the war would affect women. After a trip on the London Underground Edward Heron-Allen noted in his diary in July 1918:

I continue to be vastly interested in the crowds one meets in the tubes in the mornings and evenings – 90 per cent being composed of girls and women. What on earth is to become of them after the War? As many of them have said to me, it will be quite impossible for them to settle down again to the normal, ornamental esurient life of the pre-war girl, hedged around by the rules laid down by their Victorian parents.[25]

Robert Graves and Alan Hodge plainly stated that 'The Great War . . . freed the Englishwoman'. More nuanced, Viscount D'Abernon, the chairman of the Liquor Control Board, thought that the war had increased women's self-confidence, which was the result of 'occupation, steady wages and an independent self-supporting career', which was 'beneficial to the community'.[26] This new confidence was shown in the way women began to dress and styled themselves with short hair and short skirts. The historian Noreen Branson noted that: 'Black stockings went out and "flesh-coloured" ones came in, in a delicate hint that legs might be looked at instead of hidden away.'[27] All were wartime measures that had been enthusiastically adopted by fashionable young women – 'flappers' as they were referred to by the press.

The tubular look of women in the 1920 fashion plates were complemented by the new sack-like blouses and woollen jumpers. The *Sunday Express* protested that the cut of many of these was so startlingly low that 'surely they would not be welcomed in ordinary business offices'.[28] One change that observers often remarked upon was that women now smoked. According to the *Spectator*:

> Now, though the habit is far from universal so far as individuals are concerned, it is in a fair way, to conquer every class. The lady smokes in the drawing-room and her parlour-maid smokes in the pantry. The Factory Girl smokes, the College Girl smokes, the Bachelor Woman and the Young Married Woman all smoke, some of course to excess.[29]

The Duke of Portland, who found it hard to adjust to the nineteenth century let alone the twentieth, grumbled in his memoirs, that: 'It is neither becoming or attractive for an otherwise pretty and charming young woman to appear with a half-smoked cigarette hanging from her vividly painted lips and with henna-stained nails at the end of nicotine-stained fingers.'[30]

There was a backlash. The press mercilessly mocked the flapper and her free and easy ways. The same accusations against flappers as had been made against munitionettes resurfaced, that they had too much money, too few morals and were disrespectful towards their elders and betters. The Bishop of London harrumphed that the 'disgraceful conduct of young women and girls and that of officers and men, who in association with them had disgraced their uniform must cease, and there must be an entire change of the rotten state of public opinion on morals'.[31] When Eric Geddes became minister of the new Ministry of Transport he insisted that no flappers be employed: 'He objects to low necked blouses, "flashy" dresses, gossip in corridors and organised tea parties.' The personnel officer only found two suitable girls: 'Although they are only 17 . . . they are not a bit "flapperish". They are staid young things, good hard workers, and not over-fond of tea and jumpers, and they are never found gossiping.'[32] There were also additional concerns about post-war women. During the war Noel Pemberton Billing MP claimed that the Germans had made a list of 47,000 English people who were 'sexual perverts'. In February 1918 an editorial in his newspaper, the *Vigilante*, which was headed 'The cult of the clitoris', implied that one of these 'perverts' was Maud Allan, a

Canadian dancer. She sued Noel Pemberton Billing MP for criminal libel and after a widely reported courtroom battle, she lost the case. In 1920 Arabella Kennealy's *Feminism and Sex Extinction* saw the chief feature of the women's movement as 'masculinism'. Lesbians, it seemed, were 'incapable of parenthood' and were thus a threat to evolution. It was against this background that an attempt was made to bring lesbians within the scope of the criminal law. Frederick Macquisten MP sought to extend the 1885 legislation, which prohibited acts of gross indecency between men, so that such acts between women were outlawed. This clause was passed in the Commons but rejected by the Lords.[33]

The war made a difference to women's lives. Many had new experiences in factories or in the forces. The change was particularly true for girls and young women – flappers – who did not have the responsibilities that their mothers had. In some cases the change was very small. Beatrice Browne, who served as a typist with the Women's Royal Naval Service, felt that this was an important time for women: 'Because up until then, we were brought up in a very, very strict Victorian stilted youth. It gradually got that you were free, and when the war was over, that first war, you got more freedom. I know I had, I was allowed out later at home when I got back.'[34] The war didn't lead to equality and opportunities. There were small but important changes that over time transformed women's place in society.

One of the biggest problems facing society in the immediate post-war period was how to cope with disabled veterans. Official statistics show that about a quarter of all returning soldiers – 1.6 million men in total – had been wounded in some way.[35] The most common injury was a gunshot wound, which was generally a small flesh wound. Even when veterans had had no physical wounds they were likely to have been affected by their experiences at the front, very likely developing symptoms of neurasthenia (also referred to as shell-shock) or what we know as Post-Traumatic Stress Disorder (PTSD).

Before the First World War the care and rehabilitation of veterans had been minimal. Such men were normally helped either by their family or incited the sympathy of passers-by through begging. A very few were assisted by charities. The Soldiers and Sailors Help Society and Lord Roberts' Workshops, which aimed to train disabled veterans, both of which were founded in the 1890s, were the main bodies working in the field, with the Soldiers and Sailors Families Association (SSFA). The SSFA was established by Sir James Gildea in 1885 to help the families of men fighting overseas. It was founded following a letter in *The Times*, in which Gildea wrote: 'A further responsibility and duty now devolves on the country to see that the wives and children of those ordered on active service are not altogether forgotten, and that the cry of poverty or want be not added to those of suspense and anxiety.'[36] However, although the Admiralty had run an asylum for insane former officers and ratings in Hoxton during the Napoleonic Wars, there was little understanding of the mental stress of service in the forces.[37]

Within weeks of the declaration of war in August 1914 the first disabled men returned home. By the following February, 360 men a month were being discharged back into civilian life.[38] Little provision had been made for them. The assumption was that, as happened in previous wars, their needs would be met by charity. And to a degree this was the case. During the war, the British Red Cross Society opened 3,244 convalescent hospitals in grand homes, large and small, across Britain and Ireland. In its final report the Society said that 'the whole movement formed a splendid spectacle of patriotism which has far surpassed sanguine expectations'.[39] In addition, hundreds of thousands of pounds of donations were raised for a range of new institutions to care for permanently disabled veterans, such as St Dunstan's Home for the Blind, which was founded in 1915, and the most important of them, the Star and Garter Home. The Home began as the result of concerns that severely paralysed and disabled men would have nowhere to go to once they had been discharged from hospital. It was set up in 1916 as a result of an appeal made by Queen Mary in an old hotel on the top of Richmond Hill. The Home encapsulated the problem faced by all these institutions. Initially, it provided beds for just sixty men, even though they could have been filled ten times over.

Almost 95 per cent of the injured were from the other ranks. Many of those who joined up saw the Army as an escape from poverty. On 2 January 1917, the *Islington Gazette* reported that 'Campbell Road is as patriotic a Road as any in Islington, 300 of its men have joined HM Forces and over 30 have made the great sacrifice. Campbell Road decided to have a War Shrine and on Friday this was unveiled by the Mayoress of Islington.' And there was a lavish street party to celebrate the peace in 1919. However, those who returned to Campbell Road after demobilization were ill-served. Henry Grant had had a gun shot wound but could find no work for eleven years, James Leary also had a gun shot wound and became a beggar. George Thomas had an injured hand and was reduced to peddling without a licence, a crime for which he was convicted in 1919. Reginald Inskipp, blinded by a bayonet, was grinding an organ for a living by 1921. Jim Dunn's family lived seven in a room on the road. His father suffered from 'neurasthenia', the popular term at the time.[40] Many disabled veterans moved to Campbell Road because it was one of the few places they could afford. This had its own problems as living there made getting a job difficult. 'I have written for hundreds of jobs', complained 'A British Legionite' in a letter to the local newspaper, 'and when I mention Campbell Road it is all up, simply because the street has a bad name'.[41]

As it became clear that the voluntary sector could not cope, nor could be expected to cope, the State stepped in, workhouse infirmaries and existing hospitals were taken over and turned into military hospitals. And by 1917, purpose-built hospitals were appearing across the country. One of the most important was Queen Mary's Hospital in Sidcup, which opened in August 1917 to help rebuild the faces of unfortunate servicemen who had been horribly disfigured by fire or had been shot in the face. At least 60,000 men were recorded as having been wounded in this way, among them Private Joseph Pickard, who had his nose shot off by a sniper. At Sidcup he was offered 'a Wellington nose or a Roman nose? I said I didn't care what, so long as I got one'.[42]

As the war came to an end, it was clear that hundreds of thousands of ex-servicemen would need continuing treatment. By Christmas 1918, over 500,000 men had already been discharged from the forces during the war as being disabled.[43] For many it was enough that they received a pension to compensate for the loss of a finger during battle or the inability to work as the result of breathing in mustard gas during a gas attack. Others would need permanent care. This could place a huge burden on the tax payer, from which the government flinched, despite promises made during the war to induce men to enlist. There was also, as Peter Leese suggests, the 'requirement to sustain the existing distribution of wealth – to preserve the social system, as it functioned before the Great War'.[44]

The original intention was to set up a body to be called the King's Fund for the Disabled to administer the system, which would be financed in part by voluntary donations. This was a failure, because the potential donors overwhelmingly believed that support for veterans should be provided by the State. In January 1919, the Minister of Pensions, Sir Laming Worthington Evans, wrote to Sir Douglas Haig that:

> A great deal of opposition has been raised in the country to the King's Fund on the grounds that the pensioners require their rights not charity, and also on the ground that the administration of a voluntary fund by the Minister of Pensions, or through the Pensions Offices enables the state to shirk its duty and places it obligations upon the voluntary fund.[45]

The Fund was formally disbanded in November 1919, and the £1.5 million that had been raised was handed over to the SSFA. Although some charities continued to provide some specialist care for the most severely disabled men, responsibility for this largely passed to the Ministry of Pensions, which undertook to administer both the payment of pensions and run various training schemes to provide training in order to get men back into employment.

The government also established the King's National Roll, whereby companies undertook to employ a certain number of disabled veterans. It was launched in September 1919 with a Royal Proclamation read from town halls and pulpits alike. It passionately implored the public that 'it is a dear obligation upon all who, not least through the endeavours of these men under the mercy of Almighty God, enjoy the blessing of victorious peace, to make acknowledgements of that they have suffered on our behalf'. It was a voluntary scheme in which companies pledged to employ a certain number of disabled ex-servicemen. The civil service increased the number of such men it employed and reserved certain work for contractors who were members of the scheme. Within a week 1,452 firms had registered, but the enlistment was patchy. In Lancashire, for example, 2,736 men were registered, yet 3,500 had yet to sign on, and in Plymouth the Mayor had to ring major employers imploring them to take on men. Even so 89,000 disabled men were employed by the end of 1920, which rose to 259,00 by the end of 1921. Within a few years 90 per cent of eligible veterans had joined, most of whom were found places. Meaghan Kowalski, the historian of the Scheme, concludes that it 'made a considerable difference to the standard of living of each and every one of the men it successfully employed'.[46]

Claimants for a disability pension had to appear before a medical board, where they were assessed as to the extent of the wounds and awarded pay as the percentage of the whole. A full pension was given in cases of 100 per cent incapacity. But very few received this. The severest bodily wounds, the loss of a right arm from the shoulder down, was worth 14s a week. The award was 14s if the arm was missing from below the shoulder, but above the elbow, and then the rate dropped to 11s and 6d for limbs missing below the elbow. Unless the applicant was left-handed, to lose a left arm or parts thereof was worth 1s.[47]

The process left many men feeling humiliated and bitter, particularly after the cuts in government expenditure imposed after the 'Geddes Axe' in 1922 reduced the amount paid in pension and made it harder to qualify. Private Ernie Rhodes dislocated his shoulder and lost part of his leg while in the trenches. He put in for a pension:

> I told them exactly what happened and my former corporal sent them a report. He wrote down exactly what injuries I had received during the war, and eventually I got awarded a thirty per cent disability pension. Then within a week or so, I'd just got home from work, and my mum says 'there is a letter from the pension's people,' and these are the words – and let us not forget, I went to France twice and I was only a boy when I was conscripted – 'We have over-ruled a decision arrived at in Manchester. We have found your injuries are neither caused nor brought on by your army service.' God strike me dead if that is a lie! That made me very bitter.[48]

Private B.W. Downes wrote scathingly in his memoirs of his encounters with the Medical Board. They were, he believed, in the hands of retired doctors whose ideas were narrow-minded and out of date, medics 'who assess what pensions, if any, would grudgingly be given to a man crippled in service to his country'. He described the encounter with a medical board:

> Mackenzie and his friend, the MP for Brighton, pressed for a medical board for me and I duly appeared before one. The Chairman of the Board said they had assessed my hip and leg wounds at 20 per cent disability but they were got giving men anything for the chest wound as in their opinion it was due to shell shock or 'war neurasthenia' – 'as we call it,' he observed pretentiously and would disappear after a while in civvy street [. . .] when I communicated the diagnosis to the Worthing specialist I was given another medical board and even after more than fifty years I would recognise it with its same workhouse green painted walls and the same short shrift accorded malefactors, with a meagre ten per cent added to my wounds disability based originally on the 1914 cost of living when whisky was 3s 6d a bottle.[49]

Downes was clearly an educated, well-connected man, able to argue his case well and unafraid of bureaucracy. Most veterans were not in his position. Frank Richards, of the Royal Welch Fusiliers, suffered from haemorrhoids, which foolishly he hadn't told the medical officer about on his demobilization. Despite having been in the front line for almost all of the four years of the War he was rated A1. As the pain increased he tried to self-medicate. 'In two years and a half I drunk enough medicine to float the British Navy and swallowed enough of pills which if they had been made into cannon balls would have knocked down all the concrete pillboxes on the Western Front.'[50] For most ex-servicemen, particularly those who were not well off, the greatest humiliation was trying to get or improve a disability pension. The petty rules and regulations seemed to be out to trap the applicant and penalize the unwary. In the eyes of many applicants, the undeserving always seem to have been well-rewarded. Frank Richards grumbled that:

> In the village where I was living the majority of men receiving disability pensions in that year 1923, were men who had served at bases or had never left the British Isles and had never seen the sky over the firing line. Some of them in this year of 1932 are now drawing life pensions and larger ones than the men who were wounded or disabled in action.[51]

Eventually he was forced to apply to Ministry of Pensions medical board for a disability pension. He was awarded 8*s* a week for sixty-five weeks. And a more serious problem of rheumatism was disallowed because he had not been admitted to hospital with it, while in the Army.

Help in dealing with the Ministry came from the various veterans' organizations. In Belfast, for example, between July 1918 and March 1919, the Comrades of the Great War had lobbied on 12,000 grievances and was in the process of tackling 500 more.[52] It was possible to appeal against any decision. In 1919 applicants had about a 1 in 2 chance of success.[53] But any successful application could be reviewed by the Ministry's Special Medical Board. It's first chairman was Sir John Collie, a doctor who was deeply suspicious of all claims of illness. In a speech just after his appointment, Sir John said, 'Personally I have always believed that hard work and continuous work is the only way to be continuously happy, and that in one form or another it is the salvation of those who are suffering from functional nervous disease [that is shell shock].' He rejected any treatment that offended his own 'common sense approach' and dismissed psychoanalysis as mere quackery.[54] Initially, a lot of the pensions work was done by volunteers, made up for the most part of local do-gooders whom it was assumed would know local applicants and their circumstances. Applicants resented having to approach such people who might well judge them not only on their merits but also whether they drank or cohabited with a woman. Matters improved slightly when representatives from veterans' organizations were appointed at the end of 1919. However, at least five departments were concerned with pensions – the War Office, the Admiralty, the Air Ministry, the Ministry of Labour and the Ministry of Pensions, and men often fell into the gaps between these bodies. Monthly reports to the Ministry of Pensions noted that in Portsmouth 'Men are often disqualified through technical difficulties', while in Leicester there was 'a tendency to "get rid" of applicants rather than examine the case and offer all that the Government could do'.[55] Sir Douglas Haig gave evidence to a Commons Committee in the case of a second lieutenant, who was in a tuberculosis sanatorium, for which 4s 6d a day was deducted from his pension of £175. His wife and family had to eke out an existence on £93, without any children's allowance. 'However, his little boy has just died', added Sir Douglas Haig, 'probably from starvation, so this would save the Government £24 a year.'[56]

Along with trench foot and gas poisoning, shell shock is regarded as being one of the great disorders of the First World War and it has long fascinated academics and novelists. According to a lecture given by the American academic George Mosse in 1998: 'For the cultural historian, shell shock provides an excellent example of the fusion of medical diagnosis and social prejudice.'[57] It was something which, unlike say a broken limb, could not easily be identified. In its mildest form men might be startled by sudden loud noise, but at its most extreme men suffered from violent shaking and a loss of the power of speech. Put simply it was caused by a soldier's inability to endure for a prolonged period the horrors of the battlefield. In class-obsessed Britain, in some ways, the worst aspect was that it affected men from all social classes, whether they be square-jawed Anglo-Saxon he-men or the stunted products from the slums. However, as late as 1917, one psychologist could maintain that products of public schools were less prone to shell-shock, for they had had the benefit of that 'atmosphere . . . in which character and manliness are developed side by side with learning', and which 'seems to prevent neurasthenia'.[58]

One battalion medical officer – a brave and gallant soldier and by no means a shirker – told the War Office inquiry into shell shock about his experiences. During the horrors of Passchendaele in 1917, he had seen his battalion wiped out four times in three months. The medical officer recounted how, after a series of shocks had warned him that he was near breaking-point, it was the sight of a line of horses belonging to dead comrades which had led him to crack; he hid himself and cried for a week.

> Well, I think that was 'shell shock' I had. I lost control when I went into the dugout and concealed myself, and also for that week in which I could not control my tears; but after that, beyond some nightmares and dreams when I went down the line, after the six months down the line I went up the line again, and I had no difficulty whatever in controlling myself – not the slightest.[59]

Before the First World War shell shock had not been recognized as a medical condition, although with hindsight it is clear that many Victorian ex-servicemen, particularly those who were unable to settle down and took to the roads as tramps, exhibited it.[60] During the war, its diagnosis and cure remained controversial. Army commanders were inclined to dismiss shell shock as being mere malingering, to be cured by stiff discipline. To modern psychiatrists it is clear that many of those 'Shot at Dawn' for cowardice had some form of Post-Traumatic Stress Disorder (PTSD).[61]

Neurasthenia was first described in scientific terms in 1915 by Dr Aldren Turner, who had been despatched by the War Office to investigate 'this new disorder' that was affecting officers and men alike. He said that it was:

> a form of temporary 'nervous breakdown' scarcely justifying the name of neurasthenia, which would seem to be characteristic of the present war . . . ascribed to a sudden or alarming psychical cause such as witnessing a ghastly sight or a harassing experience . . . the patient becomes 'nervy', unduly emotional and shaky, and most typical of all his sleep is disturbed by bad dreams . . . of experiences through which he has passed. Even the waking hours may be distressful from acute recollections of these events. Recovery is satisfactory, especially if the patient is sent home for complete rest.[62]

As the war progressed the problem got worse, and 40 per cent of men wounded in the Battle of the Somme had some form of shell shock. The Army high command was not sympathetic, viewing the disorder as being a contagious psychological response of the 'weak' to protracted fighting and worried that it might spread like flu among the troops. They ignored the pitiful breakdown of loyal and brave soldiers. However, during 1917 rest camps were set up behind the lines to treat sufferers which greatly reduced the numbers affected to less than 1 per cent of the casualties of the Battle of Passchendaele. By 1918 there were six specialist neurological hospitals for officers – of which Craiglockhart near Edinburgh (known as 'Dottyville' by Graves and Siegfried Sassoon) is the best known – as well as thirteen for other ranks.[63] In his novel *England, their England*, A.G. MacDonnell provided a picture of a thinly disguised Craiglockhart. The military commander did not accept that shell shock was a legitimate concern. His remedy 'consisted of finding out the main likes and dislikes of each patient and then ordering them to abstain from the former and apply themselves diligently to the latter [Those] who disliked noise were allotted rooms on the main road.'

The effects of shell shock to a greater or larger degree were widespread among ex-servicemen, although in 1921 only 65,000 veterans claimed a disability pension for neurasthenia. But, as late as 1939, 120,000 ex-servicemen were receiving pensions or had received final awards for war-related 'primary psychiatric disability': 15 per cent of all war pensions still being paid.[64] Anecdotally, Robert Graves and Alan Hodge thought that all veterans who had served in the trenches or been 'under two or three rolling artillery barrages' suffered shell shock to a 'greater or lesser degree'.[65]

Many sufferers were shamed by their condition, particularly as, unlike many war wounds, it could not be seen by the public. Sergeant William Esplin was greeted by a 'welcoming' crowd at Netley Hospital in Southampton:

> Alas, it so happened not many of our number wore bandages: we bore few signs, outward and visible, that we had been wounded. We were not the battle-stained heroes who had been expected. There was a silence which could be felt. We hung our heads in inexplicable shame. 'Let's get off home', a buxomy, loud-voiced dame counselled. 'Them's only some of the barmy ones.'[66]

In *Goodbye to All That*, Robert Graves describes how he was affected. At home in Harlech: 'Shells used to come bursting on my bed at midnight, even though Nancy [his wife] shared it with me; strangers in daytime would assume the faces of friends who had been killed.' He would climb the local hills and plan imaginary attacks and plot defensive points. Later, when he returned to his studies in Oxford:

> In the middle of a lecture I would have a sudden very clear experience of men on the march up the Bethune–La Bassée road; the men would be singing, while French children ran along us, calling out 'Tommee, Tommee give me bullee beef', and I could smell the stench of the knacker's yard just outside the town.[67]

Graves' experience was not uncommon. Many never fully recovered. Thomas Olive explained how his wartime experiences manifested themselves after his return to civilian life:

> I used to have little breakdowns now and then and my wife used to be very frightened. It more or less used to happen at night, when I was in bed. I used to spring up off the bed, you know; it used to frighten her. My daughter, incidentally, is terribly nervous, she's terribly nervous. My wife says it's all my fault. Well, I had shell shock, you see. I got blown up, you see, and it affected my whole system. I got a pension for about oh, what was it, about nine shillings a week.[68]

Some of those who suffered from shell shock were able to cope with it after the war, and even found that it lessened over time. But others – such as Bertram Steward's friend – were never able to readjust.

> The strain of continual bombardment – continual, not just one bomb and then a quarter of an hour and another one but continual bombardment all the time pounding and pounding away. Now I think that's what people didn't understand, they heard of people having shell shock but what happened was everybody had shell shock who went through that sort of thing. It manifested itself in different ways. One of my friends who went out there, when he came back after the war he was accustomed to shut himself up in his home or in his garden and he wouldn't come out at all and nobody could get him to. He finished up – he was a great athlete, a good boy at school – he finished up in a lunatic asylum and died only within a year or two of the finish of the war.[69]

Indeed, to become used again to civilian life could set off attacks, in the words of two contemporary doctors, by: 'surrendering of the privileges of the soldier's life for the humdrum commonplaceness of civilian life, the question of pension, of adequate recognition for past suffering, the feeling of injustice engendered by the present distribution of wealth in society'.[70]

Most victims were looked after as best they could be by their families. Wives, as we have seen, must have found it very hard and it was very rare to receive any advice, let alone training, in dealing with their spouses' difficulties. The worst cases, however, ended up in the county lunatic asylums, where conditions were rarely pleasant. In 1921, some 9,000 veterans were being treated in this way. Sir Frederick Milner, President of the Ex-Services Welfare Society, was appalled: 'Have you ever tried to imagine the thoughts of some pathetic victim of "shell shock" when in a lucid moment, he realises that he is a prisoner in a pauper madhouse.'[71]

In a few cases shell shock was the cause of a man's criminal behaviour. In January 1919 Lieutenant Colonel Norman Rutherford of the Royal Army Medical Corps shot Major Miles Seton, apparently under the delusion that the major had an evil influence over his, Rutherford's, wife and children. At his trial *The Times* suspected that 'the long strain of the war, more than one actual experience of shell-shock in action . . . proved together too much for his intellect'. The jury found him guilty but insane citing neurasthenia as a cause.[72] However, it was hard for counsel to persuade the courts that their client's activities were due to shell shock. The courts were deeply sceptical of such defence arguments. The medical officer for Birmingham's prisons thought that: 'Doubtless this is in some cases quite genuine . . . but in other cases it is simply used as a catch word, and has taken the place of the "drink" excuse . . .'.[73]

To many observers it appeared that thousands of soldiers had entered a no man's land. Crying and shaking (often signs of shell shock), they had become 'feminised'. By 1918 there were over twenty Army hospitals for shell shock casualties in the United Kingdom. This did not fit with the image of the solid and untroubled and uncomplaining military hero, as presented in numerous stories for boys by authors such as G.H. Henty. Meanwhile, women who had literally and figuratively 'worn the trousers' on the home front had become more like men. With their bobbed hair and shorter skirts they had seized new economic and political opportunities and were thought to be undermining traditional values. The cultural values of civilization appeared under threat. As Barbara Cartland's gardener grumbled: 'Oi reckons if women start a-looking like men, we'll soon have 'em thinking like men. And they'll be a-bossing us like men.'[74] However, social values were adapted not overthrown. While after women were accommodated as politicians and lawyers, many more became domestic servants. Moreover, despite the lingering male mental casualties, soldiers returned and many resumed their position as head of the family.

Chapter 6

Commemoration

The years 1919 and 1920 saw several nationwide commemorations of the sacrifice made by the nation during the war, together with many others locally. They reflected a national feeling of grief in the loss of over 700,000 young men on the battlefield, but also there was a strong feeling that their sacrifice as well as the efforts made by their comrades should not be forgotten, and a grim satisfaction that Germany had been defeated.[1] These events were largely centred on the day that the conflict came to an end – Armistice Day, 11 November 1918.

During October and early November 1918, newspapers had been publishing a constant stream of reports that the Germans were near to collapse and discussing the terms that might be inflicted on the defeated nation. A German delegation crossed the front line on 8 November to be presented with a series of demands that they had no choice but to accept. There was almost no negotiation: the French were determined to prevent any suggestion of talks, and the Germans too weak to insist on it. In the early morning of Monday, 11 November, having heard that the Kaiser had abdicated and revolution was threatening to break out at home, the German delegation signed the agreement. It was to come into effect at 11am that day.

Telegrams were sent to all units on the Western Front. The message read: 'Hostilities will cease at 1100hrs. Troops will stand fast at the line reached at that time, which will be reported by wire to GHQ. Offensive precautions will be maintained. There will be no intercourse of any description with the enemy until instructions are received from GHQ. Further instructions will follow.'[2]

Here it took time for the news to sink in, as Robert Graves and Alan Hodge wrote: 'It was as if the kitchen clock had stopped . . . and the household were uncertain as to when the potatoes should be put on to boil if at all'. The adjutant who compiled the unit war diary for the 18th Kings Royal Rifle Corps noted that: 'News of cessation of hostilities received very quietly and without any demonstration whatever. It was evident that the minds of all had become accustomed to a condition of war as natural and permanent, that the mere announcement of a different state of affairs conveyed little or nothing to them.'[3] The few celebrations at the front were muted because initially, at least, nobody knew how long the Armistice would last.[4]

Things were very different at home. An official announcement was made at 10.20am and telegraphed across the country. In London, Edward Heron-Allen was working at the War Office:

At 11am a signal maroon was fired from the roof of every police and fire station in London. One was fired from Adastral House immediately overhead and shook me almost out of my chair! Many people – for we had no warning that the news would be announced thus – thought that a daylight air-raid was being signalled, and began to fly for shelter. But within five minutes everyone realised the truth, and then London went mad.[5]

Lady Mary Cameron was one of the clerks at Adastral House, then the headquarters of the Air Ministry:

A notice was posted in the main office saying that as the Armistice had been signed everyone was given permission to pay off work at three PM instead of the usual six o'clock. I learned on authority that about two per cent of the employees actually remained at work until three o'clock but I cannot guarantee that, as directly the first maroon banged in the air, I left my office and seated on the back of an Air Force mechanic's motor cycle I set off to see what was happening in London.[6]

The rector of Great Leighs near Chelmsford noted that the news reached the town just after 11am:

The works there immediately went on holiday. 'Jim' Carpenter who works at the Marconi Works . . . when he came back said the workers were so excited that it would have been no use carrying on . . . The news was passed on to Great Leighs Post Office and the cottagers were very excited . . . There was a considerable display of flags along the Great Road [in Great Leighs]. Jesse S. Wright had an enormous Union Jack at his gate, near Deers Bridge, Mrs Jennings at 'the Victoria' (coffee house), Mr A.G. Port, shopkeeper, Mrs Humpfreys, bicycle shop, Mrs H. Hicks, Supply Stores – all had flags out. St Anne's (public house) contented itself with a written notice in one of its windows 'Armistice signed. Hostilities cease today.'[7]

London was full of drunken celebrators, although how anybody could get drunk on weak wartime beer remains a mystery. Virginia Woolf found: '[Londoners] celebrated peace in their sordid way, staggering up the muddy pavements in the rain, decked with flags themselves & voluble at sight of other people's flags . . . Taxicabs were crowded with whole families, grandmothers & babies, showing off & yet there was no centre, no form for all this wandering emotion to take.'[8]

Lady Mary Cameron remembered that:

> The whole city was in uproar. Nothing has ever been seen like it before and probably never will be seen again . . . Every car and taxi was full, with occupants on the roof, radiator, mud guards and any other place that would hold a human body. Everybody was drunk with excitement and liquor . . . Stranger embraced stranger in the street, private cars were overcrowded with bosom friends who had not known of each other's existence until an hour before . . . Noise: taxi horns, trumpets, shouts, laughter; tears.[9]

In the Lancashire mill town of Bury, things were quieter: 'By the middle of the day the main streets were full of people dressed in their best clothes. Wartime songs could be heard here and there, but citizens were noticeably restrained . . . [their mood] was somewhere between elation and blankness, as if they were not quite sure what to feel.'[10]

Outside London in St Albans the local paper reported that on the receipt of the news at the town hall, where the county council was in session, 'the chairman the Rt Hon T.F. Halsey at once stopped the meeting, and with the rest of the council stepped on the balcony, and proclaimed that the armistice had been signed'. Later that day, Biddy Hodges, then a small child, remembered being held up to see over the fence at Belmont Hill. 'The Torch Bearers marched down Holywell Hill and massed on the Belmont playing fields.' In the evening another huge crowd gathered in Market Place, the city band played, the street lights were lit again and there was singing, dancing and flag waving.[11]

For many families, Armistice Day brought only sad memories of sons, brothers and lovers who would never return. Vera Brittain, who lost her dearly loved brother, fiancé and many friends, was repelled by the scenes of drunkenness:

> I detached myself from the others and walked slowly up Whitehall with my heart sinking in a sudden cold dismay . . . For the first time I realised with all that full realisation meant, how completely everything that had hitherto made up my life had vanished with Edward and Roland, with Victor and Geoffrey. The War was over; a new age was beginning; the dead were dead and would never return again.[12]

Three weeks after the signing of the Peace Treaty with Germany Britain celebrated Peace Day with processions, fetes and fireworks. The reasons behind the celebrations were not altogether clear. The date selected, Saturday, 19 July, had no special significance.[13] It seems to have been chosen largely because General Pershing and 3,000 American doughboys were passing though London on their return home. The authorities wanted a properly organized event, instead of the riotous mayhem which erupted following the Armistice, which saw the loss of hundreds of thousands of pounds war production as workers took to the street to celebrate peace.[14]

There was the fear that such celebrations, unless orchestrated by the State, could turn into something more ominous. After observing the Armistice celebrations in London Beatrice Webb noted that: 'The peoples are everywhere rejoicing. Thrones are everywhere crashing and the men of property are everywhere secretly trembling . . . How soon will the tide of revolution catch up with the tide of victory? That is a question which is exercising Whitehall and Buckingham Palace and which is causing anxiety even among the more thoughtful democrats.'[15]

The signing of the Peace Treaty at the end of June caused similar, although rather smaller, unofficial celebrations. *The Times* reported that there were 'few or none of the signs of people rejoicing unrestrainedly in the removal of a heavy burden, which marked the November celebration. [In Trafalgar Square] the crowd were, in general calm and smiling . . . Suburbia [later] was hilariously noisy with fireworks and mock bombs.'[16]

However, at Great Leighs in Essex, the Revd Andrew Clark recorded:

Major Caldwell says the RAF men at 'Brooklands' went crazy last night. At midnight they had out a big portable searchlight and ran it along the road, flashing towards Chelmsford, frightening all the horses in the place. They disturbed the people by their shouting. They kept on to 2am, when they went to the Colonel's house and cheered until he came out and sent them off to quarters.[17]

The authorities hoped that the day would mark both national thanksgiving for the nearly five years of sacrifices, but also point the way forward to a better postwar future. This was picked up by commentators. In the *Illustrated London News*, E.B. Osborn warned: 'this Pageant of Peace so hardly won . . . lays on us as a sacred duty, the remembrance of the undying dead in all our works and days. They gave their lives that we might enter safely into a more spacious and better age . . .'.[18] *The Times* preferred to remind its readers that:

No thoughtful man could look on the military spectacle without seeing, too, a procession of memories often too poignant and too full for dry eyes . . . Today a new epoch begins in which like Caesar, we count nothing done so long as aught remains to be done. We carry forward the memories of the past to inspire us, but our eyes need to be set on the path before us, where if only we are worthy, still greater achievement lies.[19]

This, too, was stressed by Lloyd George in an impromptu speech made to cheering crowds in Downing Street:

It is now for us to set our own house in order at home and if we set about it with the courage, the spirit, the resolution and the unity of purpose with which we have achieved this great victory then we shall make this country not merely one which has wiped out all ravages of war, but a country which shall be a model to the world, not only for the valour of its sons, but as a well-ordered, as a prosperous, as a happy and contented community.[20]

The centrepiece of the celebrations was a procession of troops from the victorious nations along the Mall marching past the King at the Victoria Memorial outside Buckingham Palace. Only Canada and Newfoundland did not take part, because all of their forces had already returned home. Three officers from Japan and a single Thai soldier emphasized that the Allied victory had truly been a global one. For the first time, 1,500 personnel and volunteers from the women's auxiliary services and voluntary organizations took part in such a procession.

Space was reserved for disabled ex-servicemen in their blue uniforms along the Mall. E.B. Osborn described 'the broken, yet persistent curve of dusky blue made by the uniforms of convalescent fighting, which was continued on the south side with quiet pleasure by the occasional scarlet capes of nurses sitting in the curving stand . . .'.[21]

Hundreds of thousands of people flocked to London to glimpse the procession, see the fireworks and take part in events laid on for their children in Hyde Park. The numbers were greater than had witnessed the Diamond Jubilee in 1897 or the Coronation of George V in 1911. *The Times* described the desperate search for accommodation: 'Many people who had come two days before the celebrations in the hope of finding sleeping room, after a long day's search gave up in despair and returned home. While others slept overnight in Trafalgar Square or along the route itself.'[22]

The crowds lining the route were on the whole well behaved enjoying the spectacle. Near Albert Gate, where the crowd was thickest, young women ran into the roadway to throw roses in the path of Marshal Foch and Sir Douglas Haig. And so many thousands of fainting cases were reported that the ambulance authorities gave up count.[23]

For many the highlight of the procession was the Cenotaph memorial in Whitehall. Servicemen and women turned their eyes towards it and saluted as they passed as a mark of respect to the deceased. It was erected at the last moment, over the objections of the Prime Minister, who feared it would reek too much of Catholic symbolism for the tastes of the staunchly Protestant British people. The monument was designed by Sir Edward Lutyens, seemingly almost on the back of an envelope, although in fact he had already been working on a similar design. The temporary construction immediately became popular with the public, clearly meeting an unexpressed need for a national place for remembrance. The architectural historian Allen Greenberg suggests empathetically that the simplicity of Cenotaph embodied the 'acceptance of death and a sense of the fragility and uniqueness of each individual. [It was] perhaps the one part of the peace celebration that spoke of nothing but death, of duty well done, and remembrance'.[24]

Within an hour of its unveiling on the morning of the 19th the *Illustrated London News* reported: 'A little group of bereaved relatives of ones in the war gathered . . . and laid at its base their tribute to "The Glorious Dead". So their wreaths remained their while the great pageant passed by, silent witnesses to the private grief that all underlies all public rejoicings over Victory.'[25]

In the days after the celebrations there grew up a feeling that the Cenotaph should be kept. As early as the Monday after the parade, a letter appeared in *The Times* calling for the monument 'to be retained either in its present form or rendered in granite or stone . . .'.[26] However, the design was sometimes attacked because of its lack of religious symbols. The *Catholic Herald* called it 'nothing more or less than a pagan monument, insulting to Christianity, Atheist, Mohammedan, Buddhist, Jew, men of any religion or none'.[27] Yet, this was its strength. It appealed to all regardless of class or creed.

Almost every town and village joined in the Peace Day festivities. In Sheffield, *The Times* reported 'enthusiastic scenes . . . In the afternoon, there were teas for the widows and children of those who have fallen in the war and at night bands and dancing in the parks.' Across the Pennines at Grasmere after a church service 'a procession of village councillors, children with flags in hand, inhabitants and visitors [went] through the gaily decorated sports field where there were flat races, wrestling, a fell race and other events'.[28]

A few towns refused to take part. In Exeter, the city council decided that 'it being felt the middle and lower classes did not wish any public celebrations'. In other places, such as Chertsey, ex-servicemen's organizations refused to participate protesting at unsettled pension claims and the lack of employment for their members.[29] And in a few places, notably Luton and Coventry, there were riots by veterans who felt excluded by the celebrations.

There seems to have been a general sense of unease about the whole event, perhaps not helped by pouring rain. It seemed somehow artificial. Philip Gibbs later wrote:

> It was a magnificent pageant of the fighting men and merchant seamen and women from the services. One forgot for a little while the failure to make homes for heroes or to redeem any of the promises held out to the nation. This was our Victory Day and a tribute by vast crowds to those who had saved us in time of war. That night London went mad, but the most part of it was a decent joyous madness without any vice in it. I was caught up in the surging crowds who linked arms and were cheering and singing.[30]

Virginia Woolf thought: 'There's something calculated & politic & insincere about these peace rejoicings. Moreover, they are carried out with no beauty & not much spontaneity.'[31] For many people it was a rare opportunity to let their hair down. Virginia Woolf described the scenes in Richmond: 'A woman of the upper classes was supported dead drunk between two men partially drunk', and the fireworks seen from the top of Richmond Hill, 'these rockets were beautiful; the light on the faces of the crowd was strange; yet of course there was grey mist muffling everything & taking the blaze of the fire'.[32]

As a mark of national sentiment, the first anniversary of the Armistice was probably a better guide, for it was almost entirely spontaneous and not arranged by the authorities. This is how the people really wanted to commemorate the losses of the Great War, not through victory parades or organised entertainments.

After the success of the Peace Day in July the government expected that little attempt would be made to celebrate the first anniversary of the Armistice. As late as 4 November, the Cabinet discussed 'the Anniversary of the signing of the Armistice', when it agreed to propose a nationwide period of silence. The idea came from Sir Percy Fitzpatrick, who had been the British High Commissioner in South Africa during the war where they had observed a 'three-minute pause' every noon, allowing all South Africans to reflect upon the sacrifices being made on their behalf: 'Only those who have felt it can understand the overmastering effect in action and reaction of a multitude moved suddenly to one thought and one purpose.'[33]

The Cabinet cautiously supported the proposal: 'That the advantage of the realisation by the nation of the magnitude of its deliverance from the great perils of the War, outweighed the main objection that a precedent would be established which, in remote years, after the passing of the present generation, might conceivably prove inconvenient.'[34] Members felt that 3 minutes would be too long, so instead proposed a minute's silence to the King, who in turn suggested

2 minutes. On 7 November, all the national newspapers carried a request from the monarch for a 2-minute silence at 11am, that: 'there may be for the brief space of two minutes a complete suspension of all our normal activities'.[35] The King was confident that: 'No elaborate organisation appears to be required. At a given signal, which can easily be arranged to suit the circumstances of each locality, I believe that we shall all gladly interrupt our business and pleasure, whatever it may be, and unite in this simple service of Silence and Remembrance.'

On the day itself the newspapers carried further reminders and editorials extolling the Silence. And, indeed, it was universally observed. In Plymouth, for example: 'As the hour struck a great silence swept over the town. People halted in their walks, chatter ceased as if by magic, traffic stopped and the rumbling noise of industry stayed.'[36] In London the Stock Exchange ceased trading and a murder trial at the Old Bailey was interrupted. The entire railway network ground to a halt and in factories machinery was switched off or left unattended.

In the noisy cities the silence was particularly noticeable: 'Nobody can notice what a silent London – still for two minutes – is like. No traffic, no business, no talking – nothing for a brief but sacred space of time.' In the 'awful silence' *The Times* thought there was 'a glimpse into the soul of the Nation'. At Piccadilly Circus, as busy with traffic then as now, the traffic was still thundering through as the first maroon sounded. By the time the second maroon was heard, there was absolute quiet. The man late for work no longer raced for his bus, a window cleaner stayed his ladder, the violet seller fell silent. The only sound was the splash of the fountain near Eros.[37]

On Whitehall crowds gathered around the Cenotaph, now looking rather tatty, the King and Queen laid a wreath, as did the Prime Minister. *The Times* reported that at the first stroke of Big Ben announcing the hour of 11: 'Here and there an old soldier could be detected slipping unconsciously into the posture of attention.' There was a sudden sharp sound of a woman's sob, and *The Times* reporter saw 'streaming eyes of all too many man' which attested to the 'genuineness of the moment'.[38]

And almost as suddenly as everything had stopped, the nation resumed its everyday activities.

Armistice Day, 1920 was centred on a funeral. On that day, the British 'Unknown Warrior of the Great War' was laid to rest at the end of the West Nave in Westminster Abbey. At the same time the rebuilt Cenotaph was rededicated by the King.

The idea of such a burial seems first to have come to a chaplain at the front, the Revd David Railton, when he noticed in 1916 in a back garden at Armentières a grave with a rough cross on which were pencilled the words 'An Unknown British Soldier'. In August 1920, he wrote to the Dean of Westminster, Herbert Ryle, through whose energies Railton's proposal was carried into effect. Each step of the selection of the body, its removal to London and then the final ceremony was marked by particular symbolism.

The body was chosen from unknown British servicemen exhumed from four areas on the Western Front where the fighting had been particularly severe: the Aisne, the Somme, Arras and Ypres. The remains were brought to the chapel at St Pol on the night of 7 November. The General Officer in charge of troops in France and Flanders, Brigadier General L.J. Wyatt, with Colonel Gell, went into the chapel alone, where the bodies on stretchers were covered by Union Flags. They had no idea from which area the bodies had come. General Wyatt selected one and the two officers placed it in a plain coffin and sealed it. The other three bodies were reburied.

Next day the body was escorted to Boulogne to rest overnight and then the coffin was placed inside another which had been sent over specially from England made of 2 in-thick oak from a tree which had grown at Hampton Court Palace, lined with zinc. Within the wrought iron bands of this coffin had been placed a sixteenth-century crusader's sword from the Tower of London collection. The coffin arrived at Platform 8 at Victoria station late on 10 November, where it laid in state overnight guarded by a platoon of Grenadier Guards.

Next morning, the coffin was placed on a gun carriage drawn by six black horses and began its journey through the crowd-lined streets, making its first stop in Whitehall where the Cenotaph, newly rebuilt in Portland stone, was unveiled by King George V. Here the King placed his wreath of red roses and bay leaves on the coffin. His card read: 'In proud memory of those Warriors who died unknown in the Great War. Unknown, and yet well-known; as dying, and behold they live.' One observer saw that among the watching masses hats, removed as the silent crowds 'uncovered' at the approach, were not returned to heads, even 20 minutes after the procession had passed into Westminster Abbey. It was as if the extended emotion and the indelible memory of the coffin had brought a near total paralysis.[39]

Then the carriage made its way to the north door of Westminster Abbey, a few hundred yards away. The coffin was carried into the church on the shoulders of pall bearers made up of generals and admirals followed by the King, members of the Royal Family and Ministers of State,

The coffin was borne to the west end of the Nave through a guard of honour of 100 holders of the Victoria Cross, under the command of Colonel Freyburg VC. During the burial service, the King stepped forward and dropped a handful of French earth onto the coffin as it was lowered into the grave.

Servicemen kept watch while thousands of mourners filed past. Many of the mourners were widows or mothers who had lost sons. Special permission had been given to make a recording of the service but only the two hymns were of good enough quality to be included in what was the first electrical recording of a church service ever to be sold to the public.[40]

Herbert Thompson, who was an inmate at St Dunstan's Home for Blind Ex-Servicemen, wrote in the *Daily Express* of his experience:

> The ceremony in the Abbey left an indelible impression on my mind – a feeling of ineffable sadness and melancholy, yet there was a message of inspiration and hope. I felt as if the spirit of the Unknown Warrior had whispered in my ear, 'Courage, brother, hope on.' . . . I came to the Abbey glad that I had been chosen from among so many. I went away sorrowing but with a message of hope locked in my heart.[41]

Both the Tomb and the Cenotaph touched the hearts of millions. In the 3 days that followed its rededication the Cenotaph was visited by 400,000 people.[42] But for many the Tomb of the Unknown Warrior allowed grieving families to have some contact 'with what at least could be imagined to be the real body of the lost son or husband was a terrible necessity for so many of these who knew nothing of the fate of those they had lost'. Yet ex-servicemen themselves seem to have been little moved by the Tomb, perhaps they were too aware of the numbers of unmarked corpses remaining on the battlefields.[43]

Any history of Britain in the immediate aftermath of the First World War must reflect the grief of families who had lost sons and husbands and the feeling of the sacrifice that their deaths meant to the men who had returned and to the local communities where they had once lived. It is difficult for people a century later to understand how prevalent this feeling was.

In particular, the nation's grief was centred on Sir Edward Lutyen's simple stone Cenotaph. It was an accidental memorial which people took immediately to heart. In thanking the architect for his work, the Prime Minister wrote a few days after the redication that: 'The Cenotaph by its very simplicity fittingly expresses the memory in which the people hold all those who so bravely fought and died for their country. How well it represents the feeling of the nation has been manifested by the stream of pilgrims who have passed the Cenotaph during the past week.'[44]

Opposition to these commemorations was muted. Some families at least did not want to have their losses grieved in this public way. Many ex-servicemen grumbled about how badly treated they had been on their discharge from the forces and how the money spent on the celebrations would have been better spent on providing work for them, but only in a few places did they take matters into their own hands. A few papers were less than happy about the way in which the events were organized. The left-leaning *Daily Herald*, for example, initially opposed to the internment of the Unknown Warrior describing it as being: 'the emotional doping of the people', was later persuaded by the strength of the popular reaction: 'As we stood there in silence, while the muffled drums began to whisper, as it were a million miles away and grew into the sound of a rushing wind, the stone atrocities faded, the vulgarity and bad taste were forgotten, the pomp and circumstance forgiven.'[45]

There were examples of ex-servicemen using remembrance occasions to reminisce or disrupt. At the Cenotaph in 1921 the unemployed sang 'Bubbles' (a song popular with Millwall football fans at the time) and carried placards stating 'The Dead are remembered, but we are forgotten'.[46] In 1922 thousands of former service personnel marched past the Cenotaph, their medals replaced with pawn tickets.[47] However, in general, remembrance became 'an annual event in which social and political unity was reaffirmed. Other views and criticisms of the Great War were regarded as doing dishonour to the dead'.[48] *The Times* insisted that bereaved women dress and act in a manner which demonstrated their patriotism.[49] Indicating that the losses were felt by all they could be used to transmit 'the pain to those who had been lucky enough to suffer no immediate loss'.[50] This notion of an 'adoptive kinship' of solidarity was echoed by the person who proposed the 2-minute Silence, Sir Percy Fitzpatrick. He felt that its role could be to aid social integration, 'to remind us of the greater things we hold in common'.[51]

The vast majority of the fallen lay where they fell on the battlefields of France and Flanders. The years 1919 and 1920 saw the beginning of recovery in what became known as the Devastated Areas, that is the land through which the Western Front had wriggled from the North Sea to the Swiss border. Writing to his mother just before the Armistice, the Revd 'Tubby' Clayton described:

Every time one goes across the devastated area, it is more impressive, although already the shellholes are clothed with green, and the industrious Flemish folk are dwelling in pill-boxes and have even bought some cows with them . . . On each side there is a crescendo of desolation. Trees first scarred, then blasted, then stumps, then non-existent. Houses first roofless, then barely recognisable, then pieces of wall with dugouts against or under them, then brick-heaps; the vanished utterly. If you dug you might find bricks, even floors and cellars; but it is wiser not to. For the rest, wire all rusted and tangled, rotting sandbags, broken wheels, piles of unused shells, boxes of ammunition, timber for the roads, duckboard tracks, grotesque direction posts in two languages, dead mules flung into inadequate shell holes go on in one vast nightmare across the rise and fall of the ground . . .[52]

But by 1920 nature, and the hard work of the returning inhabitants, was already beginning to improve matters. According to one guide book:

> Nature is hard at work on the battlefields, nursing them back to health. She has it all her own way now. Already many of the scars of war have softened down: soon they will be gone altogether, and the old familiar landmarks will be gone. It will be no easy matter to pick up the trench lines and to recognise the positions held by ourselves and the enemy. It will be harder still to picture those days of mud and strife and dreariness, and to see with the mind's eye life as it used to be on the Western Front.[53]

Clifford Lane, who served on the Western Front, recalled the dangers of returning there in 1920:

> I took my wife soon after we were married to Belgium and we stayed for about a week. And we wanted to find the grave of her brother, which we did. But, in doing so, we found that it was still dangerous, very dangerous, to travel across fields and things like that because there were still shells, bombs, anything lying about. Every now and then there'd be an explosion where, I suppose, the Belgian Army were destroying live shells, you see. Every now and again people would shout to us, 'Stop! Don't come any further.' So, I thought, 'To hell with this, I'm not going to risk my wife's life and my own life again!' So, we stopped exploring after that. We kept to the main roads, the Menin Road. And we never had any more trouble, but it was really highly dangerous for some years after that.[54]

A priority for all of the former combatants was to recover and rebury the mangled bodies, who had been posted as being missing during the war. For the British, Labour Companies and Graves Concentration Units were set up under the control of the military authorities. These units searched for the graves and remains of the war dead and conducting the battlefield exhumation and reburials where necessary. The cemeteries were established and maintained by the Imperial War Graves Commission.[55]

Despite the difficulty and unpleasantness of the work, the exhumation squads were methodical and meticulous in their searches. Most had seen active service themselves and were painstaking in their search for anything that would help identify a fallen comrade. Nevertheless, battlefield conditions meant that many of these vital indicators were lost and a high proportion of the bodies found remained unknown. It was the job of the officer in charge of these search parties to record details about each body recovered, including the location where the remains were discovered, whether a cross was found on the grave and any regimental particulars or other means of identification found at the time. In 1920, the first three war cemeteries opened at Le Treport, Forceville and Louvencourt. They were of an experimental nature. The most successful was judged to be the one at Forceville. This comprised a walled cemetery with uniform headstones in a garden setting which became the model for all future British war cemeteries around the world.[56]

Even so, well into the early 1920s individual grave markers and small cemeteries could be found all along the old front line. In his guide Lieutenant Colonel Lowe wrote that: 'The little crosses in the hillside mark the rest billets of our rest comrades of the trenches.' He offered succour to his readers, many of whom were searching for family members who had fallen in France and Flanders, that 'They really haven't left us: they are only on ahead, like scouts finding the way.'[57]

Within months of the Armistice a new tourist industry had sprung up along the Western Front. It catered for the families who sought the last resting place of their beloved, sightseers who wanted to see the places they had read so much about and a surprising number of ex-servicemen wishing to revisit the places where they had fought.

Huts were built to shelter and feed the tourists. In France, a charity established St Barnabas Hostels in Calais, Boulogne and Hazebrouck (near Lille), which provided 'a sympathetic home atmosphere for those visiting graves and are entirely free from the Tourist Agent element'.[58]

The centre of this tourism was Ypres, which had seen some of the fiercest fighting of the war. The battlefields themselves lay just a few miles away.[59] The town had all but been destroyed by the fighting. In 1919, Winston Churchill proposed that the ruins of Ypres be left in perpetuity as a memorial to the British lives lost in the salient.[60] However, this was not really practical, so by July 1920 the British had agreed with the Belgian authorities that just the Cathedral and the Cloth Hall be left in ruins as a memorial. In fact both the Cathedral and the Cloth Hall were eventually rebuilt. Local people did not want to be reminded any more than they had to be of what they had endured during the war. The Hall now houses the superb In Flanders Fields Museum.[61]

For years visitors were accommodated in large huts. Their bodily needs were met by makeshift restaurants and estaminets (bars). Lieutenant Colonel Beckles Willson, who ran the Ypres League in the town, complained to the Belgian Foreign Minister in July 1919 that:

> It is of course inevitable that in view of the incoming of tens of thousands
> of tourists, many former residents of the town, not of the better class, will
> wish to return and rebuild their shops and estaminets; what is earnestly
> hoped by us and in fact . . . by the whole world is that the noble Grand

Place and adjoining ruins shall not be vulgarised and desecrated by the erection of cheap and gaudily painted barraquements . . .

Even as I write six new huts are in the process of erection – all estaminets. One which is painted sky blue boldly calls itself The British Tavern which exposes us daily to the rebuke of Belgian and French visitors who imagine we are responsible for this eyesore . . . At present these thoughtless entrepreneurs are defeating their own interests by utterly spoiling a glorious site, far more interesting than the Forum or Pompeii, besides arousing the indignation of every right-thinking visitor.[62]

Although there were grumbles about this 'desecration' it met a real need.

Then as now visitors often toured the battlefields in organized parties, which had the advantage that everything as well as a guide was included. In 1919 Thomas Cook offered a deluxe tour for 35 guineas and a popular one for £9 9s. Alternatively, you could hire a car and a driver to take you out to the places you particularly wanted to visit. The Wipers Auto Service offered 'Private Touring Cars for Hire' and urged readers of its advertisements: 'Don't waste your cash – come to us.'[63]

Many of the visitors were women grieving the loss of loved ones. One ex-soldier, who took tours out to the cemeteries, told the journalist H.V. Morton that: 'It hurts to see the women who come here hoping to find graves, walking about reading other people's crosses and crying a bit.'[64]

It is hard to work out how many tourists visited the Western Front in the years immediately after the end of the war. Despite all the difficulties of travelling through the Devastated Areas they must have been in the tens of thousands. The Church Army alone conducted 5,000 relatives of the dead across the Channel between November 1919 and June 1920. Thomas Cook, too, reported a high demand for its tours, suggesting that the reasons were due to inflated wages at home and the desire of people to see the battlefields.[65]

Chapter 7

Local Memorials

By the time of the Armistice, memorials were already being constructed, often in the form of unofficial street shrines. During 1916 the first street shrines appeared in working class areas of the East End and elsewhere to mark the service of local men. The first was set up in south Hackney in August 1916 and soon spread across the country. Those for St Albans are now on display in the city's Abbey. Prior to the war memorials generally had been to victorious leaders, Nelson's Column in Trafalgar Square, for example, or to regimental officers. But after the war the emphasis shifted so that all combatants on local war memorials were to be commemorated equally. Of course, there was nothing to stop families from erecting their own memorial, although these are rare in public places outside churches.

There were many different perspectives as to who should be commemorated, what values should be illuminated, what form the memorials should take and where they should be placed. Memorials echoed one another and taken together presented the idea of a shared grief across a united nation. This function has been emphasized by the historian George Mosse. He has argued that memorials offered displacement from the unpleasant brutalities of war, made 'an inherently unpalatable past acceptable' and that this was 'important not just for the purpose of consolation but above all for the justification of the nation in whose name the war had been fought'.[1]

Rather than the symbol of the nation being in London alone, memorials were found everywhere. Before the war men might have doffed their caps to the squire. After the war men would habitually raise their hats or otherwise acknowledge the Cenotaph when passing it.[2] Such rituals were echoed in almost every village, where the commemoration of the war dead became 'the backdrop against which post-war lives were lived'.[3] This helped to connect strangers and to cement communities.

Across the country memorials presented the dead, regardless of their war work, as being heroic. The Order of Service for the Memorial Service in Bermondsey stressed: 'On land and sea all have been heroes. Each one we lose is a lost hero! Everyone who steps into the breach to fill the gap becomes a hero too!' The memorials offered reasons for the deaths and helped to transform chaos and loss into order, solemnity and meaningful destiny.

They were an expression of the gratitude of those left behind and becoming symbols of resolution. Local memorials have been categorized as 'official acts of closure [. . .] that bring war to a grand and affirming conclusion'.[4] As seen in the previous chapter, the War Office had ruled in 1915 that bodies could not be repatriated. Many bodies had been blown to pieces, buried in mud, not discovered by burial parties or not identified. A network of cemeteries was built in the war areas by the Imperial War Graves Commission for those men whose bodies were found and grand memorials built to commemorate those who had no known grave. But for many families, particularly the vast majority who were unable to travel to visit the plots where their loved ones lay, there arose 'a universal preoccupation. The need to bring the dead home, to put the dead to rest, symbolically or physically, was pervasive'.[5] Memorials in Britain became a symbolic means of bringing soldiers home.

Most of the 50,000 war memorials, large and small, public and private, were dedicated in some way to 'the glorious dead'. They reminded people to remember the sacrifices made by local men rather than to raise questions about duty and patriotism.[6] Some memorials included civilians, women and, in several cases, animals, but most just commemorated the men who had died. Many described the war as being a crusade, and despite the sacrifice a triumph. Others were non-denominational and spoke of peace or justice. In theory, at least, the memorials were for the expression of private grief and to comfort the bereaved, although in practice they reflected the collective mourning of the community as a whole. The memorials also became the symbols of the pervasive atmosphere of quiet patriotism and 'collective bereavement'.[7]

The memorials provided rationales for the war, reminding people of shared values and, in some cases, provided community amenities. They reflect the, often parochial, concerns of the residents of villages and towns. The memorials 'commemorate not only past events but the moments of their own creation'.[8] Built in the shadow of contemporary debates about the war, collectively the memorials speak of a nation's solidarity and unity around mourning.[9] The memorials represented and encouraged social cohesion, and also a steadfast localism. According to the historian Kate Tiller: 'Local war memorials speak of both the dead and the living. . . . They are the embodiment of grass roots responses to one of the most formative and distinctive experiences of the twentieth-century life, involvement in mass modern war.'[10]

We are all familiar with war memorials in the high street and memorial plaques in churches and schools. There are some 55,000 such memorials across the United Kingdom. A very large proportion date from the immediate postwar period, being commissioned in 1919 and dedicated in 1920 or 1921.

Commemorating the war dead in this way is not a modern phenomenon. Many parish churches have plaques remembering the sons of the local gentry who gave their lives for 'King and Country' in the Napoleonic and Boer wars as well as in other now almost forgotten colonial conflicts. What is unique is how widespread and all-encompassing those from the First World War are.

It was decided early on in the war that all service personnel would be buried in cemeteries near where they fell. The Imperial War Graves Commission, which was responsible for administering the cemeteries, thought: 'One could never explain why Lord and Lady This was able to have a body . . . while plain Mrs Smith, a labourer's wife or widow could not'.[11] Apart from a lucky few who could afford to travel to the battle areas to visit their dear one's grave, families could only grieve at a remove. Communities wanted to commemorate the sacrifice of those who had not returned. But, as Professor Jay Winter reminds us, two motifs, 'war as both noble and uplifting and tragic and unendurably sad', are present to varying degrees in every memorial.[12] Villages and towns consciously or unconsciously wanted to mark Allied victory as well as to mourn the dead. Indeed, there is some evidence that, except in a very general way, these memorials provided little consolation to bereaved families. For many widows and mothers, however, as we have seen, solace seemed more readily available through the Cenotaph and the national services which took place around it.[13]

Each community chose to commemorate the war dead in its own way depending on local inclination and the money available. There was no central direction or funding and none was offered. Jay Winter argues that this form of remembrance was born out of the shared experience of people at local level which was 'a palpable, messy activity which produces collective remembrance'.[14] This is true up to a point, but in most places it was the local elites who decided the form of commemoration and raised the money for the local civic memorial.

As well as the village, town and city memorials plaques are also found in churches, schools and workplaces. Not every community chose to build statues and crosses: there are also memorial hospitals and playing fields. When consulted, which wasn't all that common, bereaved families and the returning veterans usually nominated something practical rather than a memorial. In Cambridge, ex-servicemen suggested cottages for disabled former soldiers. In Newport on the Isle of Wight, where a public meeting heard from both widows and veterans:

Mr. Cousins, for the Discharged and Demobilised Soldiers' and Sailors Society said those he represented preferred a cottage hospital. Mrs Spencer, who said she had lost three brothers in the war, and her husband had been wounded six times, expressed the view that those who had given their lives would prefer that a memorial should take the form of helping those who could not help themselves. Mr McKinley, for the Comrades of the Great War, said the great majority of preferred a cottage hospital, and failing that something in the way of public baths.[15]

On the surface the histories of most village and town memorials, that is the ones generally to be found on the High Street, in front of the town hall or in near the parish church, are not dissimilar. Initially, a public meeting was held to decide that there should be a memorial and what form it should take. A committee would be elected, almost always made up of the great and good, to raise money, acquire any land required and organize the design and construction. Few places could afford the top architects of the day, like Lutyens or Sir Reginald Blomfield, but there were many lesser sculptors and architects, such as the sculptor Albert Tofts, who did a more than workmanlike job. The quality of their designs is such that most war memorials have hardly dated.

The organizing committee also decided whether the names of the fallen would appear on the memorial or in a separate roll of honour. It is usual for names to appear on village and district memorials, sometimes including everybody from the locality who served even if they returned safely. Appeals for names might be published in newspapers and, in most places, canvassers went from door to door to find individuals who should be so commemorated, as well as to solicit funds to pay for the memorial. Not every grieving family wanted their sons and husbands included, while others helpfully nominated friends and relatives who seem to have no obvious connection to the place where they are commemorated.

Initially, there would be great plans, but these almost always had to be scaled back because less money was raised than had been hoped. Despite extensive canvassing, it was rare for working class families of the fallen to have made any contribution, which may suggest that the proposed memorials had little appeal. In Newport, the secretary of the memorial committee noted that the public response had been 'poor', although he later crossed it out and substituted 'inadequate'. One exception was Cambridge where a well-organized campaign during 'Tribute Week' raised contributions from nearly one in two of the borough's families. Even so the town did not reach its target.[16]

Eventually there would be a grand unveiling of the civic memorial. Some recently retired senior officer or the local squire would be invited to do the honours. At Northrop in North Wales, which was perhaps typical of local ceremonies, the local paper reported:

> In the calm of the sunset hour, the memorial . . . was unveiled in the old parish church . . . before a large congregation and many relatives of the forty sons who had fallen.
>
> Lord Justice Bankes [the local squire] unveiled the memorial and expressed everyone's thoughts. Rev T H Vaughan spoke consolation and Rev J H Davies [a Congregationalist minister] read an appropriate lesson,

the choir sung, bells rang out a muffled appeal and Northop Band played in the village street 'Eternal Rest'. It was intended that this should be 'The Last Post' but through some mishap in the arrangements this did not occur.[17]

But these civic memorials only tell half the story. There are tens of thousands of unofficial ones in churches, workplaces and schools. Jon Mein has identified forty in St Albans alone from street shrines to scholarships for bright children at local schools.[18]

At St Luke's Church in Kew, for example, there is a splendid faux terracotta tablet, designed by Sir Robert Lorimer – a prominent church architect of the day – commemorating the hundred or so men from the parish who did not return. Also in the church are plaques to Major Henry Johnston VC who won his Victoria Cross during the Battle of the Aisne in the early days of the war and a screen erected by Ernest and Annie Clarke as a 'thank offering' for their four sons 'preserved during the Great War'.

The Cenotaph in Whitehall did not celebrate individual heroism or leadership. Initially, it was to be a temporary structure but it soon came to be seen as a tomb to no one person, but all people and as permanent and important.[19] Several places, such as Bristol, followed the pattern set by the Cenotaph.[20] The cenotaph in Letchworth was described in the local newspaper as constructed because of a 'craving that has arisen among our citizens. Some definite time was needed, some definite place [for] public expression'. A mausoleum, a tomb, was built 'empty, and yet to us so full of meaning'.[21] In St Anne's-on-the-Sea the cenotaph includes a relief of wounded soldiers. In Chadderton, Greater Manchester, there is an additional figure. It is of a mourning soldier, at ease and helmeted.

Local memorials were expressions of community pride and a justification for the sacrifices made. The memorial in Evesham was a 'perfect personification of our victorious men who fought for England [in] the most righteous war this country has ever waged'.[22] In Sleaford, the committee established to propose a memorial sought to ensure that the memorial should be 'worthy of the town'. In Bradford the city council committee on a war memorial was instructed 'to find the basis of an agreed proposal for making the object of a War memorial worthy of the City'.[23] One memorial in the city specifically praised the strength of the local fighters and quoted Jeremiah, 'And Lo, a mighty army came out of the north'.[24] A memorial at the Beckton Gas Light and Coke Company included an eternal flame, connecting the dead with the company's product.[25] In Keld, North Yorkshire the memorial stone was from a local quarry and dressed by local masons. Part of a dry stone wall, it is situated where the four dead men used to meet, near the pub and with a view of the river. The poem on it was written by a local teacher.[26] In Newcastle a wooden board with decorative frame and a wreath carved in relief has the words

'In grateful memory of those members of the staff of Bainbridge & Co who gave their lives for their country'.[27]

National unity was also strengthened by the creation of memorials for others besides combatants. By recognizing the contribution made by women in particular the memorials present an image of the postwar nation in which all citizens could feel included.

In Wigton, Cumberland the urban district council funded a recreation ground to commemorate all who had served.[28] The Lyness Royal Navy Cemetery has a memorial to four people, one female, who served on a hospital ship and who, in August 1918, during their free time, went sailing and hit a mine.[29] Bradford has a memorial of a stone uniformed fireman with hose in hand and on a plinth. This is in commemoration of the 'devotion to duty' of those firefighters killed in a munitions works' explosion in 1916.[30] Often memorials which feature female forms show women as heroic mothers who were supportive of the sacrifices made by their martyred sons.[31] In Stromness on the Orkneys, there is a single representational mourning female figure on top of a plinth.[32] In St Anne's-on-the-Sea there is a seated mother and child. In St Cuthbert's Church, Fir Vale, Sheffield, there are five-light stained glass windows. On these figures depict the Resurrection and Ascension and widows left behind after their husbands were killed in the war.[33] A memorial, paid for by Sir George Renwick, in Newcastle shows soldiers taking leave of their families and the figure of winged victory.[34] In Townley Park, Burnley three sculpted men, representing the three services, rise from a Portland Stone block which looks a little like the Cenotaph. Bronze women are alongside the block, looking up. At the unveiling ceremony, according to the *Burnley Express*, it was made clear that one of these women was a mother with a wreath 'and as she stoops, the cenotaph shapes itself in her heart into the features of her son'.[35] There is a memorial window to women killed in explosions at the National Filling Factory at Barnbow near Leeds.[36] In Hammersmith Cemetery there is memorial to those eleven women and two men 'who died for their country in the explosion at Blake's munition factory'.[37] When a member of the Women's Army Auxiliary Corps, a clerk in Aldershot, died of tuberculosis she was buried in the Military Cemetery with a salvo over her open grave. A fellow WAAC recalled that there were 'Full Military Honours, gun-carriage team of black horses, coffin with Union Jack, a full military band and some hundreds of us, taken from the whole area to parade and line the streets'.[38] In St Mary's Church, Cardigan, there is a window inscribed in 'grateful memory of the men and women of this parish who gave their lives'.[39] There is a stone of remembrance 'in memory of the men and women of Taff Wells and Nantgarw who sacrificed their lives so that we may live'.[40]

Women when represented on memorials were often portrayed as nurses. After all, they often cared for men during their last hours. One of the four bronze figures on Exeter's War Memorial is a nurse, along with a soldier, a sailor and a prisoner of war. In St Cadfan's Church, Tywyn, Meirionnydd, the memorial porch honours the 251 men and 20 women who served and the '30 soldiers and a nursing sister' who gave their lives 'for the honour of the Empire and the liberties of the world'.[41] In addition to a list of 'Emberton's fallen heroes' in All Saints, Emberton, there is a plaque with a St John's Ambulance Brigade badge and the words 'To the glory of God and in honoured memory of Nurse Nellie Decoma Brown of this parish who died July 2nd 1921 after three years of suffering following four years of active service in the Great War 1914–1918'.[42]

The most famous nurse of the war was Edith Cavell. She was a nurse from Norfolk who spent many years living in Belgium. Nurse Cavell was tried and shot by the Germans for helping sick and wounded British soldiers in Brussels. Famously, her dying words were supposedly that 'patriotism is not enough. I must have no hate in my heart.' In Norwich there is a bust depicting Edith Cavell wearing her nurse's uniform. The plinth includes a life-size carving of a soldier. The inscription reads 'Edith Cavell, nurse, patriot and martyr'. There is also a memorial to Cavell opposite the National Portrait Gallery in London. Cavell is shown in her uniform and among the inscriptions are 'Humanity', 'Devotion', 'Fortitude', 'Sacrifice' and 'Faithful until death'. The woman and child depicted at the top of the cross symbolize the protection of Belgium by the British. Edith Cavell was not a member of the armed forces of any Commonwealth country nor was she working for a Commonwealth division of the Red Cross.

As the prayer read when the Findon War Memorial was opened indicates, memorials became places where symbolically bodies came to rest:

Whose bodies are buried in divers lands
Or engulfed in deep waters
Gather them, we beseech Thee, from the East and the West
From the North and the South,
And bring them to the Heavenly City.[43]

A memorial leaflet produced by the Brixton Independent Church read 'To us they return no more, but in the motherland of England they lie, gathered and secure for ever'.[44] Claiming the dead for the nation reiterated a popular explanation for the war. Symbolically transferring the bodies promoted a sense of how homes had been part of the struggle and how generations and families were reconciled.

In the absence of bodies there were some memorials which provided physical representations of the dead. Rochdale, Manchester and Southampton each commissioned a sculpted, draped corpse. In Bradford there are figures of soldiers with bayonets fixed, and in Burnley sculpted service personnel. Others show a soldier mourning his fallen comrades. The sculptor Albert Toft's soldier figure, bare-headed, in prayer and with rifle reversed, can be found in several locations – Streatham, Stone, Leamington Spa, Thornton Cleveleys and on the site of the metal manufacturing company Guest, Keen and Nettlefords.

Some representations were derived from neoclassical ideas about the perfect form. They were used to symbolize men who had been familiar faces around the town, who may well have suffered from malnutrition before the war and disfigurement prior to death during it. In a few places there were attempts to convey the conditions in the trenches, rendering this as the central experience of the war. In Hale the bronze, 7ft-tall soldier has leggings tied around his lower limbs to prevent mud adhering to his trousers, which was a common addition to British Army uniforms.[45] The inscription on the memorial in Alloa includes the carving of three soldiers emerging from, or perhaps half-buried in, a muddy mound around which barbed wire and debris can be seen.[46] The most graphic representation of the war is probably found in Charles Jagger and Lionel Pearson's memorial to the Royal Artillery at Hyde Park Corner which includes a sculpture of a 9.2in Mk 1 howitzer surrounded by scenes of the war.

Individuals and groups of comrades were also commemorated. Many churches have windows commemorating individual parishioners. In Abbey Dore, Hertfordshire, the church has a stained glass window commemorating 'squire Captain R C B Partridge' and his name also appears on the wooded village memorial.[47] Clifton College, Bristol, erected a statue of former pupil Sir Douglas Haig in his uniform. In King's Lynn there is a memorial to those members of the Royal Naval Reserve 'whose lives were taken September 22nd 1914'.[48]

In many places unity and local loyalty were encouraged through interdenominational co-operation over a memorial, or the provision of non-denominational social facilities.[49] The Memorial Cross at Boughton Aluph, Kent, was on the village green, not in the church grounds. At the dedication, the rector explained that the site was where 'most of those whose names are inscribed spent their boyhood'.[50] In Clayton, West Sussex the parish war memorial is a roofed lichgate to a churchyard. According to the local vicar, this memorial was placed on the edge of church grounds so as to 'meet the views of those who would rather see a memorial outside the church instead of in it'.[51] In nearby Slinfold, near Horsham, there is a roll of honour in the church but the memorial cross was placed outside the boundary wall.[52]

There were disputes about locations. In Cockermouth ex-servicemen petitioned to have the memorial in the cemetery, but the choice was overturned by a majority at a public meeting who wanted it to be on Station Road.[53] However, often such rows could be resolved by multiplication, not division. In Durideer, Dumfriesshire, there are two memorials, one by the station, the other in the village square.[54] In Northrop, Flintshire, the parish church had a memorial but there was also a 'Heroes Memorial' gateway and names were added to family gravestones.[55] Arguments about memorials tended to be parochial and particularistic and often personal.

Often buildings were seen as practical and supportive of stabilizing interactions. A survey of European nations indicated that the British were most disposed towards utilitarian memorial projects, such as the provision of a nursing home in Cambridge for disabled veterans. Such schemes were often those most favoured by the ex-servicemen themselves.[56] However, such proposals were usually dismissed by local elites. The playwright Sir Arthur Pinero, for example, objected to the construction of a social club in his local village as 'the commemoration of the dead should not make a mere excuse for demands by the living for something they would like to have'.[57] Of course, these sentiments did not always apply when these elites thought the community needed some new facility, such as new hospitals or hospital facilities. There were hospitals or wards built in St Anne's-on-the-Sea, Teddington, Watford and Woolwich. Newport, on the Isle of Wight, presented funds to the District Nursing Association, while 'the Milkmen of the Thames Valley', among others, gave a bed with a plaque commemorating fallen colleagues to the Richmond Royal Hospital.[58] Other memorials included convalescent homes and a water pipe to a school and a fireplace in a surgery in Dudley, Tyneside, and a bus stop at Skelton, Cumbria.[59] In Wadhurst ex-servicemen voted for a memorial building and a sports field and in Battle 200 men called for a the provision of a club rather than a cenotaph.[60] Wealdstone erected a memorial clock tower.[61] This was one of 185 such clock towers in the country, along with many sports fields and 9 chalk figures.[62] Memorial cottages were promoted as practical, 'touching, significant and beautiful'.[63] A former soldier from Abington suggested, through his local newspaper, 'that a much better and more substantial form of memorial would be the erection of a number of semi- or self-contained cottages to accommodate a number of disabled heroes'.[64] While there were concerns about secularization expressed in Barcombe and in North Chapel, both in Sussex, village halls were seen 'as an opportunity for the reform of leisure activity and for promoting social harmony in small communities'.[65] Memorial halls were built in Lacey Green and Loseby Row, Buckinghamshire and Kirby, Cleveland.[66] The village hall in Loughton, Buckinghamshire, includes a plaque of names while in Steep, Hampshire, there is a village hall and a memorial in the parish church.[67]

The Home Shrine

There were numerous personal memorials. A woman, born in 1913, recalled that her mother in Northrop had a display case in which she kept pictures of her two dead sons and commemorative bronze medallions for each and messages of sympathy from the King.[68] Nick Mansfield's grandmother never visited her son's grave on the Continent. Her memorial was in her unused front room:

> On one side was a faded sepia postcard of a smooth-faced teenager, her son Walter, self-conscious in ill-fitting khaki, contained in a coloured, embossed mount of generals, allied flags, battleships and aeroplanes; on the other, a crude oil painting of a sunlit and flowered war cemetery, hawked door-to-door by a penniless woman artist in the early 1920s who filled in name, rank and number to order.[69]

At the country house in Mells, Somerset, the Horners erected a statue of their son Edward, 1888–1917, riding a bronze horse by Alfred Munnings and an epitaph which refers to the 'eager valour' of their son to join up in 1914 and describes how he 'fell' defending a French village. It concludes 'This in the morning of his youth he hastened to rejoin his friends and comrades by a swift and noble death'.[70]

The discussions about how the dead should be remembered reveal different understandings of the war. Philip Gibbs, a Liberal war correspondent, felt that memorials should be 'warnings of what war means in slaughter and ruin, in broken hearts and agony'.[71] More frequently memorials included Christian images as a means of uniting the dead and the living in a shared, familiar notion.[72] The people of Shoreham cut a 100ft-long cross into a hillside overlooking the village. It was visible and accessible to people in a way that placing a memorial in a church would not have been. In Papa Stour and North Yell, in Shetland, the dead are memorialized in stained glass windows in churches.[73] The Sams family paid for an 8ft-high alabaster angel to be placed in Emberton church. On the angel is a quotation from Revelation 21:4: 'And God shall wipe away all tears from their eyes and there shall be no more death neither sorrow nor crying neither shall there be any more pain for the former things are passed away'. Jesus Christ was represented on some memorials and on some his sacrifice was equated with that of the members of the armed forces. Gilbert Ledward's shrine for Stonyhurst

College, a Catholic school, included figures from the armed services surrounding the crucified Christ, the Lower Peover memorial depicts soldiers kneeling before a crucifix and the stained glass window in Bampton reminded those who looked up at it that soldiers could have committed themselves to Christianity prior to death and thus would enjoy redemption.[74] Cornhill War Memorial depicts the Archangel St Michael using his sword to repel two beasts which are fighting one another while also 'leading in Brotherhood and Love'.[75] The memorial cross in the churchyard of St Michael and All Angels, Little Bredy, Dorset, shows a carved figure of Jesus holding a lamb, and the following words are inscribed below: 'I will seek out my sheep and deliver them out of all places where they have been scattered. To the glory of God in everlasting memory and praise of those who gave their lives for us in the Great War'.[76] The analogy of Jesus as shepherd and the representation of soldiers as sheep may have encouraged comforting associations of the soldiers as innocents who, like Jesus, suffered for humanity. On the George Heriot's School War Memorial, Edinburgh, there is a pelican. This refers to the story of how, in time of need, the mother pelican wounded herself in order to feed her chicks with her own blood. The bird features in early Christian iconography to show how Jesus gave his life for his followers and continues to do this through the Communion wine. There is also a line from Horace: '*Dulce et decorum est pro patria mori*'. Tredegar War Memorial makes the request to 'Sanctify the ties that bind us to the Unseen'.[77] In Newcastle the patron saint of the Northumberland Fusiliers, St George, commemorates triumph and patriotism.[78] These examples indicate how Christian themes were intertwined with notions of nation and community in order to comfort and reassure, not to challenge.

The terminology used on the memorials is also of interest. In many places, the dead are not referred to as the far too shocking 'killed' but as 'the fallen'. This phrase dates from the seventeenth century and was used during the war itself, but came into its own as a euphemism for the war dead in the years after the Armistice.[79] Others describe the deaths of local men as sacrifices 'willingly' undertaken. Churchers College, Petersfield, Hampshire, refers to the dead as those who 'laid down their lives that England might live'.[80] The idea that the dead had freely given so as to protect the freedom of others was echoed elsewhere.

The war was not only fought for liberty but also for justice. In Emberton, Buckinghamshire, the memorial was erected 'by the families of the fallen in the Great War 1914–1918 in token of their undying love for those who willingly and with thanksgiving yielded up their lives in the service of their God, King and Country and in the cause of Liberty and Justice *Dulce et decorum est pro patria mori*'.[81] In Frithville, Lincolnshire, Captain S.V. Hotchkin, the local MP who unveiled the memorial in 1920, informed those attending that 'it is your duty to fight for right and justice, for your land and country'.[82] On the Tomb of the

Unknown Warrior in Westminster Abbey the legend reads: 'For King and country; for loved ones home and empire; for the sacred cause of justice and the freedom of the world'. In 1918, in the commemorative tome *For Remembrance: solider poets who have fallen in the war*, Arthur St John Adcock developed the notion of a tribute to 'These men, these boys, who died that Freedom might live [who] knew why they made the great sacrifice'. He went on to suggest that they 'have trodden instinctively and worthily in a beaten track; their courage, chivalry, love of justice, are theirs by inheritance, the ideas that led them are the common ideals that led the best of our race through the past'.[83]

The Royal Artillery Memorial at Hyde Park Corner announced that 'their glory will abide for ever' and quotes Shakespeare's *Henry V*, 'here was a Royal fellowship of death'. On opening a Freemasons' Memorial Hall the King expressed his 'earnest hope that this hall may stand forever as a monument to that public spirit and comradeship which unite Freemasons in seeing that the names of their Brethren who made the supreme sacrifice in the Great War should never be forgotten'.[84] Because duty could be understood in many ways, memorials could unify all those who agreed that sacrifices had been made.

Many memorials naturally make reference to the restoration of peace. The Masonic Peace Memorial Hall in London (now Freemasons' Hall) in its name, and in Bermondsey the unveiling speech referred to the 'men of peace, they had no wish for war'.[85] Worcester Labour Club has a board with an image of two clasped hands and the words 'These warr'd in hope to end all war. To record proudly the names of the members of this club who served their country'.[86] The West London Co-operative Society Roll of Honour is in remembrance of 'those who made the great sacrifice. God make us better men and women and give us peace in our time. They served for freedom'.[87] A synagogue in Bradford has a decorated plaque which explains that those named 'gave their lives for justice, liberty and peace in the Great War, 1914–1918'.[88] In Balcombe the Victory Hall, decorated with a fresco depicting peace and social harmony, was dedicated to all 200 villagers who served.[89] In Bristol a cenotaph was built 'sacred to the memory of Bristol's sons and daughters who made the supreme sacrifice. They died that Mankind might learn to live in peace'. There are also references to 'valiant hearts' and 'knightly virtue' of the dead who 'gave to save mankind'.[90] The memorials, by explaining that the dead had all fought for the same reason, to bring peace, offered an explanation with which many people could agree.

The formal proclamation of peace in London. (Credit: Mrs C.S. Peel, *How We Lived Then 1914–1918* (John Lane, London, 1929), p. 173)

Excited crowds gather in front of Buckingham Palace hoping to see the royal family on Armistice Day. (Credit: *How We Lived Then 1914–1918* (John Lane, London, 1929), p. 172)

Muted Armistice Day celebrations at the Barnbow National Filling Factory near Leeds. (Credit: *The Story of Barnbow* (1919), p. 57; TNA, MUN 5/155)

The Cenotaph in the early 1920s.
(Credit: Thomas Moult, *Cenotaph: a book of remembrance* (Jonathon Cape, London, 1923))

At the end of the war Spanish Influenza had become a major killer among soldiers and civilians alike. Unusually the virus particularly affected the young and healthy. In this cartoon by E. Noble a monster representing an influenza virus hits a man over the head as he sits in his armchair. (Credit: pen and ink drawing by E. Noble, *c.* 1918; Wellcome Collection)

The Peace Day procession at Hampton, Middlesex. (Credit: Richmond Local Studies and Archives, ref LCF8728)

This *Punch* cartoon reflected the feelings of many people during the General Election campaign of December 1918 when promises to hang the Kaiser were made by politicians. (Credit: *Mr Punch's History of the Great War* (Cassell, London, 1920), p. 276)

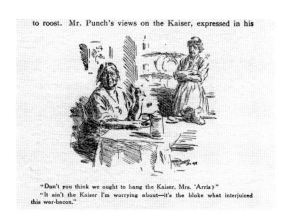

to roost. Mr. Punch's views on the Kaiser, expressed in his

"Don't you think we ought to hang the Kaiser, Mrs. 'Arris?"
"It ain't the Kaiser I'm worrying about—it's the bloke what interjuiced this war-bacon."

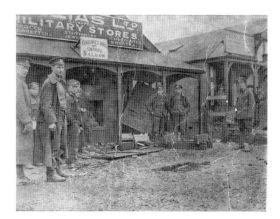

The Kinmel Park riots of March 1919 was the worst mutiny on British soil during the twentieth century. However, it was successful as it saw Canadian troops at the camp rapidly being sent home. (Credit: Michael E. Hanlon, Roads of the Great War blog http://roadstothegreatwar-ww1.blogspot.co.uk/2014/04/the-kinmel-park-incident-of-1919.html)

Women who played a part in the Allied victory were thanked at a special garden party at Buckingham Palace. Many lost their jobs in the return to peace. (Credit: Mrs C.S. Peel, *A Hundred Wonderful Years* (John Lane, London, 1929), p. 243)

CONTRASTING TYPES AMONGST THE GUESTS AT THE ROYAL GARDEN PARTY.

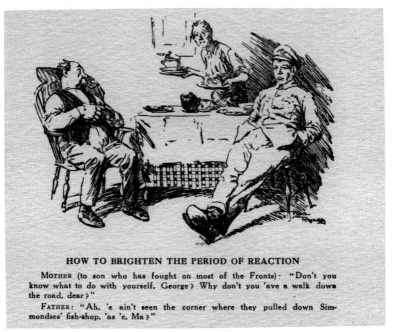

HOW TO BRIGHTEN THE PERIOD OF REACTION

MOTHER (to son who has fought on most of the Fronts): "Don't you know what to do with yourself, George? Why don't you 'ave a walk down the road, dear?"

FATHER: "Ah, 'e ain't seen the corner where they pulled down Simmondses' fish-shop, 'as 'e, Ma?"

After their wartime experiences many soldiers found it hard to readjust to life as civilians, as this cartoon suggests. (Credit: *Mr Punch's History of the Great War* (Cassell, London, 1920), p. 287)

Residents at St Dunstan's Home for Blinded Soldiers learn to play the banjo, May 1919. (Credit: Wellcome Collection (Wellcome Library 812125i))

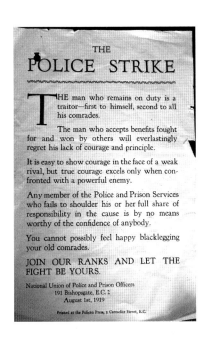

THE POLICE STRIKE

THE man who remains on duty is a traitor—first to himself, second to all his comrades.

The man who accepts benefits fought for and won by others will everlastingly regret his lack of courage and principle.

It is easy to show courage in the face of a weak rival, but true courage excels only when confronted with a powerful enemy.

Any member of the Police and Prison Services who fails to shoulder his or her full share of responsibility in the cause is by no means worthy of the confidence of anybody.

You cannot possibly feel happy blacklegging your old comrades.

JOIN OUR RANKS AND LET THE FIGHT BE YOURS.

National Union of Police and Prison Officers
191 Bishopsgate, E.C.2
August 1st, 1919

Printed at the Pelican Press, 2 Carmelite Street, E.C.

On 31 July 1919, a small number of men of the Metropolitan Police went on strike. Out of a force of 18,200 men only 1,156 participated in the strike, all of whom were instantly dismissed. The strike was absolutely crushed, and along with it the police union. The sacked men never got their jobs back. This is a leaflet produced by the union. (TNA, MEPO 3/1786)

Headlines in the *Manchester Guardian* relating to the police strike in Liverpool. (Credit: Proquest/ *Manchester Guardian*, 4 August 1919)

LAWLESSNESS AT LIVERPOOL.

TROOPS FIRE OVER PILLAGING CROWDS.

RENEWAL OF DISORDER LAST NIGHT.

WARSHIPS DESPATCHED: TANKS ARRIVE.

300 ARRESTS: 74 HOSPITAL CASUALTIES.

ENGLAND EXPECTS

(With Mr. Punch's best hopes for the success of the National Industrial Conference.)
BOTH LIONS (together): "Unaccustomed as I am to lie down with anything but a lamb, still, for the sake of the public good."

Although often successful locally, national attempts to get unions and employers to work together for the common good failed as both sides had very different objectives. (Credit: *Mr Punch's History of the Great War* (Cassell, London, 1920), p. 282)

The Galloway car was built as a way of keeping skilled female engineers from the dole queue. Priced at £550, the car 'made by ladies for others of their sex' was designed to be economical and easy to maintain. (Credit: Douglas Scott/Scottish Museum of Transport, Glasgow)

The American divorcée Nancy Astor, portrayed by John Singer Sergeant in 1909, was the first woman elected to the House of Commons to take her seat there. She succeeded her husband as MP for Plymouth Sutton. (Credit: The Athenaeum/Wikipedia)

The French tennis star Suzanne Lenglen proved to be a role model for a new generation of women. (Credit: Library of Congress/Wikipedia)

The fashions of 1919 were very different to that of the pre-war era. Dresses were simpler and hem levels higher than would have been thought wise in 1914. (Credit: Mrs C.S. Peel, *A Hundred Wonderful Years* (London, John Lane, 1929), p. 242)

Although puttees were invaluable in keeping mud from the trenches off soldiers' trousers, there was little call for them in peacetime Britain. (Credit: *Gloucestershire Evening Post*, 26 October 1919)

An advertisement for Vauxhall Cars. (Credit: *Tatler*, 6 October 1919)

The medal index card for Percy Toplis, 'The Monocled Mutineer'. In real life he was a cold-blooded murderer, who was killed in a gun battle with police near Penrith in June 1920. (Credit: Ancestry/The National Archives)

Ypres immediately after the Armistice. (Credit: William Pulteney, *The Immortal Salient* (London, 1925))

In front of Lloyd George, Georges Clemenceau and the other Allied delegates Johannes Bell signs the Peace Treaty on behalf of Germany in the Hall of Mirrors at Versailles on 28 June 1918. The painting is by Sir William Orpen. (Credit: Wikipedia/Imperial War Museum (Art.IWMM ART 2856))

Crystal gazing: a popular way of attempting to contact the fallen after the First World War. (Credit: Emile Boirac, *The Psychology of the Future* (Kessinger Publishing, London, 1920))

David Lloyd George was the Prime Minister until 1922. He led a Conservative-dominated coalition which had a large Parliamentary majority. (Credit Wikipedia/Vernon Kellogg, *Facing Starvation in Belgium* (Doubleday, New York, 1918), p. 39)

Chapter 8

Ain't Misbehavin'

In 1919–20 there were fears that men, brutalized by war and disillusioned by the lack of support for veterans, were turning to crime. The vicious racecourse war between the Birmingham Gang and the Anglo-Italian Sabinis and their allies might be seen as evidence of this. Police and journalists' accounts of Glasgow street gangs began to be laced with references to American crime and gangsters. *The Times* blamed the war for the increase in use of cocaine arguing that: 'We have all been living furiously . . . The apostle of the cocaine cult finds many disciples, for he offers a new release from time and circumstances.'[1] These concerns were meshed with alarm over the latest dance crazes. These conspicuous exhibitions could be a symptom of trauma, an expression of longing, of relief and of joy and a challenge to the old order. The *Daily Mail* reported the shocking news that 'Dancing without gloves has become the mode, because the cost of gloves has risen to impossible figures, and smoking was never so common when sitting out.'[2] There was a sense of feverish liberation as women shortened their hair and their skirts and left their corsets at home so they could more easily dance the knee-knocking, bottom-jerking routines demanded by the dangerous new sounds of Jazz.

In June 1919, the Lawn Tennis Championships resumed at Wimbledon, and the *Graphic*'s correspondent wrote that: 'The leap with which lawn tennis has regained its pre-war position has not been beaten by any rival . . . Here we have the Wimbledon of 1914 only more so.'[3] The star of the tournament was undoubtedly the French player Suzanne Lenglen, who easily defeated the British champion Mrs Lambert Chambers in the women's single final: 'In the opinion of the members of the Wimbledon committee there are not more than six men who could play her with any hopes of success.' The *Sheffield Evening Telegraph* noted that 'Off the court Mlle. Suzanne Lenglen is just a happy, laughing girl. On it she is the living embodiment of ruthless efficiency.'[4] And John Montgomery commented that:

> Her robust almost acrobatic movements and her masterly accomplishment of the game prompted thousands of young English girls to take up not only tennis, but also rowing, running, cycling and swimming. In moderation, the pre-war young lady had enjoyed all these recreations, but only gently, and very discreetly and modestly clothed. Now Mlle Lenglen actually wore short skirts, and with the development of the popular picture

papers, she could be seen . . . leaping in the air, free and unrestricted, hitting out at the ball – an elegant, modern girl, heralding the approach of a new deal for women.[5]

As we have seen, women were expected to return to their pre-war place in British society. Suzanne Lenglen was a role model for an alternative approach.

High society too resumed its pleasures. The first event was a great Victory Ball at the Royal Albert Hall on 28 November 1918 which was attended by 4,000 guests. The *Illustrated London News* pronounced it 'a great success'. The highlight was 'a procession consisting of characters representing the Allies or otherwise symbolic of the war.'[6] However, the London Season was slow to resume, partly because many men were still in uniform. Organizers were reluctant to put on balls and the like before the peace treaty was signed. There were also concerns about setting the right tone. However, by April 1919 the magazine could happily report that: 'London is every day becoming more like its pre-war self, and Society is showing an unmistakable desire to enjoy a Season as similar as possible to those of half-a-dozen years ago.' Debutantes were still waiting to be presented at Court, but the magazine hoped that 'some form of royal substitution for the unavoidably postponed honour will be found by the courteous kindness so characteristic of the King and Queen, who have the happiness of their subjects so close at heart.'[7] *The Times* said that there was a backlog of nearly 12,000 young ladies, who had either come out or had recently been married, awaiting presentation: 'It is difficult to see how the Lord Chamberlain's Department can cope with so many.'[8]

The great leisure pursuit in the years immediately after the Armistice was dancing. For the young, it was one of the few ways of meeting members of the opposite sex and to forget the difficulties of everyday life for a few hours. The *Daily Mail* reported in February 1919 that: 'People are dancing as they have never danced before in a happy rebound from the austerities of war . . . But the dancing is not quite the same as it was in the dim old days before 1914.'[9] The centre of the craze was London. Kate Meyrick, who was a partner in one of the first nightclubs, remembered that: 'Everyone . . . young and old alike had caught the dancing craze: almost any place with a respectable band and a decent floor was bound to make money.'[10] And in the *Bystander*, a magazine firmly aimed at Society, Freddie See invited readers to 'see dance mad London . . . It looked good to see so much evening garb again. A lot of London girls in pretty frocks is a sign that takes a lot of beating.'[11]

It wasn't only the upper classes who took to the dance floor. Dance halls up and down the country attracted huge Saturday night crowds. The most spectacular venue was undoubtedly the 'Palais de Danse', which opened in Hammersmith,

West London, in October 1919.[12] It claimed to be the 'Largest & Most Luxurious Dancing Palace in Europe' with 'Two First Class Jazz Bands' and '80 Lady and Gentlemen Instructors'.[13] Somewhat oddly the style inside the former skating rink was Chinese: 'Tall black-lacquered columns decorated with Chinese lettering signifying good luck, supported the pagoda-like structure that formed the ceiling.'[14] The *Daily Mail* described the varied mix of participants: 'Women dressed as men, men as women, youths in bathing drawers and kimonos, matrons moving about lumpily and breathing hard. Bald obese perspiring men. Everybody terribly serious: not a single laugh or the palest ghost of a smile.'[15] The floor was never empty. If dancers arrived alone, a steward would find them 'a sixpenny partner'. No alcohol was served, but dancers could recover over tea and buns. Admission at lunchtime was 2*s* 6*d*, comparable to the cost of a 'dansant' at a West End hotel, but without the formality.

Most dancers were not terribly adept. The philosopher C.E.M. Joad later wrote of his experiences on the dance floor that:

> You shuffled around the room in what a contemporary wit called 'a form of country walking slightly impeded by a member of the opposite sex' and you called it a foxtrot. You slid around a little faster and called it a one-step . . . eventually the foxtrot and the one-step merged into a uniform shuffle which presented no difficulty to anybody.[16]

For the more enthusiastic there were a range of lessons and dancing masters available for beginners and those who thought themselves more advanced. Newspaper classified columns were full of advertisements for such institutions. In Manchester, for example, Miss Frances Vesey offered lessons in 'Operatic, classical, mime, and ballroom, fox trot, hesitation, 1920 Tango, latest novelty, pasa-doble' and Lawrence Tiller offered all of the above as well as 'special children's classes'.[17] The work was tiring but remunerative.

Dancing was particularly important to women. It was a chance to forget the workaday world for a few hours each week, the chance to look your best and, for some, the opportunity for romance. And at a time when there were increasing constraints on the sort of work that women could undertake, dance could lead to freelance work as teachers, or less salubriously as dance hostesses. The *Manchester Guardian* described how three girlfriends had clubbed together to open a dancing academy in Scarborough. They provided:

> dancing lessons until noon, their pupils ranging from officers with one leg to children just learning to talk . . . In the afternoon dancing in the hall and a rest until dinnertime. Dancing in the evenings and big money

every Saturday. They had a grand time of it, kept their good looks, and wore out eight pairs of dancing shoes each.[18]

There was extra spice on the dance floor with the arrival of black musicians from America bringing the new music of Jazz with them. The new music was received rapturously by audiences, less so by commentators concerned about the origins of Jazz and who was playing it. The *Daily Mail* was disturbed by the 'jungle' elements of the dances and of the primitive rituals of 'negro' orgies.[19] The syncopated rhythms were not like anything anybody on the dance floor had heard before. The first musicians had arrived during the war and found a ready audience for their music. The money was good. The *Bystander* grumbled in January 1919 that 'The Prime Minister hardly earns in a year what a black Jazz bands rakes in a season.'[20] The nightclubs of London vied to bring bands across the Atlantic. The Original Dixieland Jazz Band, for example, began their London residency at the Rector's Club, but moved to the much larger Hammersmith Palais, where their leader Nick La Rocca confessed that they were 'musical anarchists'. This was not anything that could be said about any dance band before the First World War. Dalton's Club was also proud of its Jazz band, under Gus Haston, who became a major draw.[21]

Jazz spread almost instantly across the dancefloors of Britain, although the vast majority of musicians let alone their audiences could never have heard a real Jazz player. Instead, the music known as Jazz became a mildly syncopated faster dance. In April, Webb's Music Stores in Banbury offered 'How to Jazz: A Simple Guide to the 1919 Dances with eight explanatory diagrams of foot positions.'[22] Over the Easter holidays Blackpool hoped to attract trippers to Jazz dances, Jazz afternoon teas 'and at all public dances the "jazz" and "foxtrot" will be introduced'.[23]

The dance phenomena and in particular Jazz had their critics. Canon Drummond protested in *The Times* that this modern form of dance reflected 'a lowering of morals and a sickness in the pulse of the country'.[24] Had the music been Anglo-Saxon, perhaps, it would have not have had the bad press that it did have, or indeed have had the same appeal to dancers from all social backgrounds. Lord Rochester, a prominent Methodist, claimed that 'Dancing has been known to lead to impurity of thought, desire and practice.'[25] Which of course is its purpose.

Within the YMCA there was considerable debate about allowing mixed dancing at their clubs. The general consensus was that it should be permitted under 'proper supervision', although Captain J.S. Redmayne of the Association's headquarters thought that by allowing such activities 'It may have the effect of keeping many nice women away and attracting others whose presence is less desirable.'[26] In this, as in so many other ways, the YMCA was out of touch with what potential members increasingly wanted.

A great post-war novelty was the nightclub, which appeared in London immediately after the Armistice. They were different from traditional venues for dancing and socializing for the upper and middle classes in that they were neither gentlemen's clubs nor were they restaurants with dance floors. Freddie See in the *Bystander* described being taken by a girlfriend to 'a real night-dance':

> A wide flight of stairs soft carpeted led us down into the midst of a gay scene. It was a warm luxurious scene too. My mind went back to Continental gambols of ages ago. It cheered me to walk into the place. Diana had surrendered a couple of bits of paste-board on entering that made us component parts of this world of life and light and laughter. For they were taking things merrily these dancers. They laughed and smiled and chattered as they danced . . . The music played by a collection of dusty rag-time artists was the most wonderfully seductive I have ever heard.[27]

Clubs soon gained, rightly or wrongly, a reputation for licentious behaviour and the attention of the authorities.[28] Certainly they proved a magnet for disapproving stories in the popular press. Reading between the lines, initially at least, some were little more than attractive drinking clubs where it was possible to dance. But they met the need for something that was a little livelier than the existing venues, attracting men and women from the fast set, as well as people from the theatrical and other fields who wanted a drink after hours and were prepared to pay extortionate prices to do so. At the Rector's Club in Tottenham Court Road decanters of whisky were on offer in the gentleman's cloakroom.[29] The wartime restrictions on pub opening hours were only partly relaxed in 1921, so bars closed promptly at 10pm. Occasionally there were police raids to ensure that the law was being obeyed, but as the police were being paid off, these didn't mean much. Eventually, Sergeant George Goddard of the Vice Squad was discovered in 1928 to have £24,000 in various bank accounts, a house worth £1,700 and an expensive car, all on a sergeant's salary of £6 15s a week. In his defence, he claimed that he had made the money selling sweetmeats at the British Empire Exhibition at Wembley.[30]

One of the first clubs to open was Dalton's Club, which was in a basement off Leicester Square: 'At the end of a long, narrow passage you came to the ballroom, a lengthy apartment with a low ceiling. The bandstand was at one end . . . it held far more people than you would ever have supposed it capable of accommodating, which was a valuable advantage for club purposes'.[31] It was co-owned by Kate Meyrick, who was the estranged wife of an Irish doctor. In her memoirs she wrote that, in order to support her family, at the end of 1918 she replied to a newspaper advertisement 'Fifty pounds wanted for partnership to support tea dances'. She went into partnership with Dalton Murray, who dealt with the business side. It is, however, difficult to believe that somebody who claimed to be so innocent and naive would go into such a trade.[32] From its opening in April 1919, Dalton's Club was an immediate success.[33] Murray and Meyrick were meeting a pent-up demand for entertainment of almost any kind: 'Dalton's Club became so crowded each afternoon and evening that there was hardly room to dance, while late arrivals could never get a table.'[34] 'Dance Instructresses' were employed: professional dancing partners who were paid a small wage that was augmented by tips. According to Kate Meyrick, some of these girls took home up to £80 per week and ended up marrying aristocrats. But most existed, at best, on the fringes of prostitution.[35]

The dancing partners soon attracted the attention of the police. In December 1919, Murray and Meyrick appeared at Bow Street Magistrates Court, where they were charged with 'permitting the club to be used as a habitual resort of prostitutes'. Mr Muskett, for the prosecution, graphically described the club as 'a dancing hell and an absolute sink of iniquity. It was a noxious fungoid growth on our social life.' The police, it was claimed, had seen 292 women of 'this class' leave the premises. In his defence, Dalton said: 'yes, I know what they are, and I would like to turn them out. What can I do? I am always on the watch to see that there is no kissing or cuddling or anything else going on.' The Club was closed and Dalton Murray fined £50 and Mrs Meyrick £25.[36] She later recalled: 'the shame and ignominy I suffered when I heard my innocent venture described in court as "a hell of iniquity". The girls who were declared as being so bad all went to other clubs or dance halls. I was left to start life afresh, robbed – for ever, as I thought – of my good name.'[37] However, she soon became involved in a new venture Brett's, another basement club on the Charing Cross Road.

In the popular mind, certainly in the popular press, nightclubs were associated with drugs, which would be used to lure the best of British womanhood to a grim end. However, the truth was rather different. The recreational use of narcotics before the First World War was largely restricted to members of the small Chinese communities of Limehouse, Liverpool and Cardiff and a few bohemian free spirits seeking relief from jaded lives. The police noted a fascination of the rich with Chinatown.[38] Although there was legislation to inhibit sale of opium in 1908, London byelaws passed in 1909 and an international agreement about its danger agreed in 1912, until the war it could be purchased over the shop counter. The drug could be smoked fairly openly in Limehouse and seaman's lodging houses and a derivative, laudanum, was used to relieve rheumatic pain. Cocaine was given to patients by dentists and morphine was prescribed as a painkiller by doctors. In *The Sign of Four* (1890), Sherlock Holmes is noted as injecting a 7 per cent solution of cocaine.

It is difficult to know much drug taking went on among the armed forces during the First World War. Drugs must have been used at least occasionally by soldiers and a small number of men became addicted to morphine as the result of medical treatment. At the inquest into the death of John Hall, an airman who died of a morphine overdose in 1921, the pathologist Sir Bernard Spilsbury said that morphine-taking had not been uncommon among wartime fliers. Both Harrods and the respectable chemists Savory & Moore were prosecuted in February 1916 for sending cocaine and morphine to the front, without recording the details of the men to whom the drugs were sent. In advertisements Harrods suggested that its supplies were 'A useful present for friends at the front'.

On 4 July 1914, immediately prior to the outbreak of war, the *East End Advertiser* reported the trial of Kwong Tai for unlawfully selling opium for 18*s* 6*d* for a 4oz tin. He was fined 20*s* with 2*s* costs. In 1918 Walter Gibson, a shipping merchant, died of an overdose of morphine and his Limehouse dealer, from whose establishment there had been five convictions for opium smoking in 1917, was sentenced to one month's hard labour and deportation from Britain. In 1920, after the 1919 local anti-Chinese riots, Tam Kow, who was suspected of trafficking in opium, was deported after having been caught in possession of opium and opium smoking utensils. Lillian Wyles, a police inspector in the division covering Limehouse between 1919 and 1922, recorded in her autobiography that the local Chinese smuggled opium and that 'I was many times invited to smoke a pill of opium by a bowing obsequious Chinaman . . . I never succumbed to the temptation'.[39] Annie Lai, who prepared, smuggled and sold opium, recalled that: 'The local police were alright with us. Well they would use a little discretion sometimes – probably got a couple of bob now and again . . . somebody'd get the word to say there was going to be raids, that night. It was never the local police. It was the CID from Scotland Yard.'[40] Within a month of the Armistice, the *Daily Express* endeavoured to shock its readers that:

> Anxiety in connection with the war has driven many people to see the false solace of drugs . . . Drugs are hawked in London on the streets and in notorious cafes. Anybody who knows the ropes can buy heroin, cocaine, morphia or any of the preparations known as 'chandoo' or 'pop'. Haschish, the drug of the Assassins, the *Cannabis Indica* of the pharmacopoeia, is available in cigarette form, in the compressed tablet, or in dark green treacly liquid.
>
> The dope fiends of London seek only one thing – the feeling of well-being, of exhilaration, the elimination of time and space. War has increased the nervous tension of the individual to an unheard-of degree. Men and women alike have craved for a change from the normal to the fantastic and rare.[41]

As with so much of the crime reporting of the *Express* and its rivals, the story was largely bunkum. Headlines included 'Yellow Peril in London' (*Daily Express*),

'White Girls Hypnotised by Yellow Men' (*Evening News*) and 'Chinatown's Lure of Pretty Clothes' (*East End News*).[42] The film *Broken Blossoms* (1919) was based on a short story set in Limehouse and had several scenes featuring drug addicts and drunkards. Undoubtedly, there was a slight surge of interest in narcotics and their effects, but legislation and firm police action quickly stamped out the problem. As well as attacks on the habit itself, in the same breath the press also attacked permissiveness, youth (especially independent-minded young women) and foreigners who were behind the craze.

The use of narcotics was exposed with the death of a young actress, Billie Carleton, at a Victory Ball in November 1918 supposedly of cocaine poisoning. Her death, and the circumstances surrounding it, led to a flurry of ever more lurid press stories. The *Daily Express* reported that she had been led astray by a circle of hashish-eating friends and reminded readers of supposed German plans to subvert Britain with addiction. It ran a series of articles exposing the 'Vice Trust' which controlled the trade, as well as prostitution, gambling and nightclubs. Its profits came from women, who were both its agents and its victims: 'The woman drug fiend is almost invariably a missionary of her vice … You will find the women dope fiend in Chelsea, in Mayfair, and Maida Vale. An obscure traffic is pursued in certain doubtful teashops. The sale of certain beauty specifics is only a mask for the illicit trade in certain drugs.'[43]

Observers claimed that cocaine was largely used by young women on the edge of respectability such as chorus girls and nightclub hostesses. These girls were poorly paid and poorly fed and the stimulant allowed them to perform energetically and vivaciously at least during a show, as well as offering a hint of fashionable decadence. Cocaine use may have been encouraged by a shortage of bottled stout during the war, which, apparently, was the traditional pick-me-up of chorus girls in calmer days. The journalist Sidney Felstead explained the attraction:

> Midnight suppers and early-morning dances, bodily lassitude and sleeplessness, all banished by 'dope'. What wonder that a woman succumbs to the mystery of this all-healing drug, the lure of a few grains of cocaine discreetly obtained by some male acquaintance. In the beginning at any rate, a sniff of cocaine represents to her mind, no more danger than would a brandy and soda to one of her man friends. The day of reckoning does not come into calculation.[44]

Special attention was paid to the supposedly decadent habits of the upper classes, the class of people, as Felstead noted, 'which lives without apparent means of support, and as such find themselves with a great deal of time on their hands . . . Idlers, all of them, typical specimens of that erratic world which is always willing to try something "new".[45] Most people tried narcotics because it was something new and rather daring. There was also an aspect of snobbery: drugs were both expensive and unlikely to be indulged in by the lower classes. Philip Ziegler, the biographer of Diana Cooper, observed that her friend Katherine Asquith's preferences were shaped as much by class as by chemistry: 'to reduce oneself to a stupor with morphia was risky, perhaps immoral, but to drink a whisky and soda would have been common – a far worse offence'.[46]

The police cracked down on the people who distributed the drugs. Opium dens were raided, street dealers rounded up and the men behind them ruthless pursued, particularly the dominant figures in London's drugs world; Eddie Manning and Brilliant Chang. Manning was a black Jamaican. The CID described him as being:

> without doubt . . . a scoundrel of the lowest possible type and for years past has been earning his living by selling cocaine etc to prostitutes and others in the West End and has also has opium smoking parties at his flat. He has been exceedingly cunning and would never venture into the street with drugs in his possession.[47]

Manning seems to have arrived in Britain from America just before the First World War probably as a musician in a Jazz orchestra. In 1920, he was gaoled for sixteen months for shooting two men in a 'low class restaurant' in Newport Street. By then he was already one of the metropolis' top drug dealers. In January that year, a former Army officer, Eric Goodwin, died of an overdose of heroine, while waiting at Manning's flat, presumably to buy more drugs. Manning was also implicated in the deaths of two prostitutes, Freda Kempton and Maud Davis, to whom he had also supplied cocaine.[48]

Manning moved from Soho to Regent's Park Road in Primrose Hill, where he entered into partnership with a Greek woman, Zenovia Iassonides. She and her husband ran a cafe – the Montmartre – in Soho to which women were said to flock for drugs. When the police raided Madam Iassonides, they found Manning 'in possession of an opium pipe, cocaine morphine, a hypodermic syringe and needles and ¾lb of opium, a set of apothecary's scales, a revolver, also a number of indecent photographs'. Manning received six months for possession and Iassonides was deported. Manning spent his last years in Parkhurst prison, having been sentenced to three years for receiving stolen goods, where he died of a heart attack in 1931.[49]

More mysterious was Brilliant Chang, the Western educated son of a Chinese merchant, whose exotic appearance and personality made him the centre of attention in the media and which eventually destroyed him. It is now impossible to separate the real man from the racist myths about him. In the early 1920s he was an exotic figure on London's nightclub scene, immaculately dressed and with a charisma which attracted women, fear and rumour in equal parts. The nightclub owner Kate Meyrick described how his 'snake-like eyes and powerful personality used to fascinate nearly all the women he met – and all too often to their downfall' and refused him access to her club.[50] A reporter from the *Sunday Express* described meeting him:

> It was at a night club. A dance had just finished, and the little tables were crowded. Suddenly the curtain covering the door was pushed aside, and 'Brilliant' Chang stood at the entrance. He paused a moment, silhouetted against the dark curtain, while his eyes searched the room. A murmur ran round the tables. 'There's the rich young Chink!' Half a dozen girls rose to greet him. Nodding slightly, he advanced and spoke to one of them. The others, shrugging their shoulders, sat down again.[51]

His last few years were sad ones. He retreated to Limehouse, where his Western manners and dress stood out and where he was hated by the local Chinese community for the difficulties he had caused them. Evidence about him was passed to the police. The restaurant he ran was raided and he was found with cocaine in his possession. Chang was sentenced to eighteen months in prison and finally deported. Although it is almost certain that Brilliant Chang was a dope dealer of some kind, it is likely that he was not the mastermind that Meyrick and countless other writers claimed. His crime was to be an exotic figure in an otherwise drab world and to fit the racist stereotype of a scheming oriental.[52]

The drugs craze was sometimes used as evidence that the country was engaged in a period of unprecedented lawlessness.[53] In January 1920, General Sir Nevil Macready, Commissioner of London's Metropolitan Police, told *The Times* that 'crime accompanied by violence is prevalent throughout the Metropolitan Police district, especially in the inner areas'.[54] In an editorial the newspaper put the surge in crime down to: 'The disregard of the sacredness of human life inevitably created and fostered in thousands of uncontrolled minds by the war, the unemployed by which the war in many cases has been followed, and the mischievous effect of some of the melodramatic plays produced in the cinema theatres, have all had something to do with it.'[55]

On the surface, at least, *The Times* and its rivals had a point. As we have seen, the year 1919 saw a great increase in industrial militancy and revolutionary sentiment, which must have been unsettling to its readers. The newspapers were full of stories about violent and disturbing crime. In the issues of *The Times* for 21 January 1920 a dozen crimes were reported. They included: 'the murder of an old man by a burglar at Bolton and two post office raids, one a "hold up" by armed men and the other a particularly impudent safe robbery, in which as in many recent crimes,

the thieves escaped in a motor car'.[56] Other crimes discussed included the murder
of Miss Shore, 'the victim of the Hastings train outrage', Mrs Buxton, who was
killed at the Cross Keys Public House in Chelsea, a ship's captain in Fowey held
up at gunpoint (the gun turned out to be just a toy) and £10,000 worth of jewels
stolen from Lady Loughborough's flat in Grosvenor Square. And in St Helens a
man was arrested for trying to break into the home of the town's chief constable,
by impersonating a policeman.[57]

The years 1919 and 1920 saw an increase in hangings for murder: 13 in 1919
and 24 in 1920, with another 8 in 1921. Only in 1945, another immediate postwar
year, were there more hangings than had occurred in 1920.[58] They mainly related
to crimes within the family. Sir Nevil Mcready felt that:

> another result of the war would be an increase in the number of women
> murders. Before the war, he said, when a man quarrelled with his wife, or
> the woman he lived with, he 'just clip her under the ear' and everything
> would be all right again the next day. But now, after four years of life-
> taking, he would hit her over the head with an iron bar or anything that
> happened to be handy, and there would be no next day for her.[59]

There seems little evidence that returning servicemen were more prone to
murder than other men. One exception, however, was that of Henry Gaskin,
who strangled and battered his wife Elizabeth in woods on Hednesford Hill,
Staffordshire. During the war Gaskin had been a sapper in the Royal Engineers,
having been released from prison to join up in 1916. The *Birmingham Post*
reported the case:

> Following marital problems, Gaskin, a former soldier, and his wife
> Elizabeth (23) had decided to separate. They had lived at Bridgtown,
> Cannock, Staffordshire but in the winter of 1918, she had moved out of
> the house and gone to stay with her parents at nearby Hednesford. On
> Wednesday 19 February, a young girl called at the parents' house with a
> message for Lizzie from Gaskin. It was a note arranging a meeting for
> later that afternoon. Lizzie left home and was never seen alive again. She
> failed to return home that night, and the next morning Lizzie's mother
> called to see Gaskin. He admitted arranging the meeting but claimed that
> he had failed to keep the appointment and had no idea what had become of
> his wife. The police were called but an initial search failed to uncover her
> body. A week later Gaskin broke down and led the police to her mutilated
> and dismembered corpse. At his trial, held at Stafford Assizes on 11 July,
> the court heard how Gaskin had met his wife as arranged then returned

to his house. He asked her to come home for good, but she refused, and instead asked him for a divorce so that she could marry her new lover. Gaskin became irate and grabbed her by the throat, strangling her. He then hid the body until the next morning when he wheeled it in a barrow to a sight near the local gasworks where he set about dismembering it. The short trial ended when the jury took just thirty-four minutes to convict him of the crime. Stafford Gaol no longer housed a scaffold so Gaskin was taken to Winson Green prison, Birmingham, where he was hanged by John Ellis and William Willis.[60]

Another ex-serviceman was involved in a series of brutal murders in the summer of 1920. Percy Toplis, known to history as the 'Monocled Mutineer', was a psychopath whose exploits entranced the newspaper reading public. He had a long career as a petty criminal and confidence trickster with a habit of impersonating Army officers. Unusually for the period, Toplis was armed. According to the *Sunday Post*: 'And when a man of that breed carries a gun he shoots to kill. Toplis was the nearest approach to the American "gun man" we have had in this country.'[61] On 25 April 1920, the corpse of Sidney George Spicer, a young Salisbury taxi driver, was discovered with a bullet wound to the head under a hedge at Thruxton Down, near Andover. Spicer's grey Darracq five-seater was later found abandoned in Swansea. Evidence accumulated indicating Toplis as the perpetrator. An intense and heavily publicized hunt was raised for him even before a verdict of wilful murder was returned on 26 May. During his 6 weeks on the run, sightings of him were reported from 107 different places. At the start of June he shot and gravely wounded a policeman and gamekeeper who together challenged him with being in unlawful occupation of a lonely shooting lodge in Banffshire. He then fled south as an even more desperate fugitive. On the evening of 6 June, he was ambushed and shot dead by police outside Plumpton church in Cumberland. Toplis was found by armed detectives. The subsequent inquest heard that the Inspector Richie hid behind a building until Toplis was close. He then told Toplis to 'Stop, Pull up!', but instead Toplis ran off. Inspector Richie reported, 'Still running he turned round, and at a range of about five yards fired twice direct at the police. He was turning around to fire a third time when [Sergeant] Bertram fired, and Toplis fell, being so close that he fell into my arms'. A witness, Charles Norman Parry, said that there was an exchange of shots and concluded 'that, had the police not fired, Ritchie would have been killed, as he was so close to him'.[62]

Despite countless stories in the press, the official *Criminal Statistics* suggest that there was little or no increase in overall crime during the immediate postwar period. The introduction to the 1922 edition noted that: 'In spite of the prevalence of unemployment and of other conditions conducive to such crimes, crimes against property have shown no tendency to increase, but are actually fewer than formerly. An exception is certain crimes against property committed with violence. In particular, shop-breaking has much increased.'[63]

Other increases were for 'sexual crimes', notably bigamy, and housebreaking, which the report attributed 'to trade depression and part to the greater facilities to commit crimes afforded to persistent offenders by the modern tendency to milder sentences'. Surprisingly, considering the coverage in the press, crimes of 'violence against the person' remained slightly below the level of 1913, 965 in 1919 and 1,107 in 1920 compared to 1913's figure of 1287.[64]

Some of the police's toughest customers were gang members. There had always been gangs in most British cities made up of ruffians and other hard men, who terrorized local neighbourhoods. The membership of these gangs was fluid, with members coming and going and even associating with several gangs at the same time. There seems to have been a resurgence in the immediate postwar period.[65] In March 1919 *The Times* reported on the first Grand National meeting at Aintree. Despite the biting wind and snow: 'It was a joyful and memorable event in accordance with the best traditions of the great festival.'[66] In June the Derby was similarly affected by bad weather, but punters had the satisfaction of seeing a 33-1 outsider, Grand Parade, beat the favourite, Panther. There were immense crowds. Continuing liquor restrictions meant that they were much soberer than perhaps had been the case at pre-war meetings.[67] These events provided good prospects for gangsters. Writing of the Elephant Boys in South London, Brian Macdonald recalled: 'Among the new industries supported and controlled by the Elephant Gang were night-clubs, protection rackets, extortion, gambling, dog- and horse-racing pitches, horse-thieving, car-thieving and beatings. Complementing these activities were receiving, safe-breaking, smash and grab, burglary, hijacking, jump-up, robbery and wage grabs. Families developed their own specialities. Individuals loaned themselves out to organisations in London and beyond.'[68]

Racecourses had always attracted the rougher element, but before the war they had largely been kept in check. But in the immediate postwar period the presence of gangs and the violence they brought with them threatened the sport's future. It was now relatively easy for gang members to arrive at meetings in charabancs or by car or motorcycle. They were drawn to racetracks, where there was money to be made from providing 'protection' to bookmakers and the chance to pick the pockets of, and intimidate, cash-rich punters. There were also ever changing alliances with the racecourse police, who sometimes relied on gang members to maintain order and, with local police forces, for information about their rivals.

North of the River Thames was the no less enterprising Anglo-Italian Sabini Gang, led by Darby Sabini.[69] Sabini was acknowledged to be the sharpest in the business: 'Darby was a first class organiser and had a sweet set up all around the

London horse-racing courses . . . [his] strength was in his organisation and his ability to attract hard men to support him and stay with him'.[70] One story of the Sabinis, told by a man who was a bookie's runner in 1920, is that when they went to Lambeth New Cut the whole market cleared for fear of them.[71] Arthur Harding took part in the racecourse wars. He recalled his brush with the Sabini gang and the police in:

> There was a gang of bookmakers from Hackney who were in the protection racket. They all had the police straightened up but they were having trouble with the Italian mob . . . Hymie Davis, the big Aldgate bookmaker, had trouble with the Darby Sabini gang and he paid me to look after him. They said they were going to do him at Kempton Park and he asked us to come. So we got together a team and went down to Brighton. Altogether there must have been about sixty of us . . . When we got to Brighton the Italians were already in the top ring. Harry Boy Sabini was keeping a book outside. Our mob were all in a booth, sixty-handed. Then the police came in and started battering them about with their truncheons. Not me, I was too wise for that. I was watching the performance from afar. Several of them were pinched and they were given twelve-month sentences for stealing glasses from a pub. I got a gold watch and a chain from Hymie Davis as a reward, but I couldn't help him. By that time Darby Sabini lived in Brighton and he had the local police all tied up.[72]

In 1920, gangs caused trouble at several meetings. Racegoers were 'seriously troubled by the presence of large numbers of undesirable rogues – some of them aliens – who were not afraid to carry their pre-war practices of picking on the innocent public to the extreme lengths of intimidation and personal violence'.[73] 'White Knight', the racing correspondent of the *Leeds Mercury*, wrote that if this was not unchecked:

> [it] will soon put an end to the racing boom. The undesirables appear to have been in great force during the three days of the Bibury Club meeting, at Salisbury last week, and there were numerous complaints by visitors of being "held up" and robbed by the gangs. It was also reported that motor cars had been stopped and boarded by the bandits and the occupants robbed in broad daylight. One unfortunate individual, who only goes racing occasionally, stated that he has been victimised on three occasions recently, having been held-up twice and been welshed once to the tune of £40.[74]

Matters appear to have really got out of hand at the Salisbury meeting:

> George McCarthy, North Kensington was charged with damaging cups and tumblers in marquee on the racecourse in order to distract attention from the operations of the gang in adjacent refreshment tent. They raided the till, but the cashier was too prompt tor them, and cleared out first with the cash. The gang escaped arrest. Several persons the police stated, were injured by flying cups, and McCarthy was remanded, it being intimated that a further charge would probably be brought against him.
>
> A Bethnal Green man named George Hunt was charged with attempting to obtain an umbrella by fraud. Seeing a constable coming from the paddock with an umbrella he claimed it as his own. Actually, it belonged to the Chief Constable of Wiltshire, and the constable promptly ran the men in. He was discharged, his defence being that he merely offered the constable half-a-crown for it.[75]

Amazingly, despite the presence of the Chief Constable, there seem to have been no police officially on duty at Salisbury. The Club used their own stewards, who were unable to control the crowd.

There were similar incidents at a number of other meetings during the summer of 1920. The violence threatened to get out of hand, but was controlled by firm and effective police action: 'an extra force of police armed with ash clubs were employed at Goodwood . . . the activities of these racecourse ruffians were effectively and sternly checked and punished'. Similar action was taken at meetings in Brighton and Lewes.[76] However, the racecourse ruffians returned the following year, causing chaos at meetings at Alexandra Palace and Bath and a mass fight between the Sabini and Brummagen gangs at Epsom on Derby Day.[77] It took considerable effort by the police and the racecourse authorities over several years to control the gangs and to imprison many of their leaders.

Some postwar developments had long roots, stretching back to well before the war. The changes to women's lives which were attributed to the war since at least the 1890s, and gambling and criminal violence were not novelties either. However, to those who had witnessed the conflict, whether in the forces or in Britain, 1919 seemed to be a year of change. Vera Brittain explained that:

> the older generation held up their outraged hands in horror at such sacrilege, not understanding that reckless sense of combined release and anti-climax which set my contemporaries, who had lived a lifetime of love and toil and suffering and yet were only in their early twenties, dancing in the vain hope of recapturing the lost youth that the war had taken.[78]

The interest in the dance floor and the race track can be seen as a light-headed means of coping with hideous memories and the fear of a fatal dose of the flu. They were also seen as evidence that the war had destroyed certainties about the English race, social class and the roles fit for men and women.

Chapter 9

Looking Forwards

After the Armistice how did people think about the First World War that had just ended? Many, of course, remained traumatized by the event, either because they were still directly suffering the effects on their bodies or in their minds, or because members of their family had fallen. We discuss them and their experiences elsewhere in this book. For everybody else, again as we have seen, the Armistice brought pride, that Britain had emerged victorious, and great relief. It would be wrong, as some writers have suggested, to assume that the immediate postwar period exploded in a riot of Jazz dancing and street protests. People adjusted to the new circumstances of the peace as best they could. At a personal level people tried to make sense of the war through numerous reminiscences. In addition, they looked forward to how technology, developed for wartime, could be used in peacetime.

Over the months following the Armistice life began to return to a semblance of pre-war normality. One of the first signs that life was returning to normal was the abandonment of rationing. The U-Boat campaign of early 1917 had nearly brought Britain to its knees as tens of thousands of tons of food were sunk by German submarines. Previous rather desultory attempts to curb consumption, particularly of bread, were replaced in early 1918 by the introduction of rationing for certain goods, notably bread, bacon and fats, such as butter and lard. One American visitor to London in the summer of 1918 found that 'British cooking is not the most skilful in the world, and the result of the restrictions is to make eating rather a monotonous and uninteresting experience.'[1] Although under central guidance, rationing was very much the responsibility of local authorities. The historian Jay Winter suggested that: 'The general rule was that the worse off a section of society was before 1914, the greater were its gains in life expectancy in wartime'. He felt that a paradox of the war was that 'because of armed conflict, this country became a healthier place in which to live'. Life expectancy for men increased from 49 years of age in 1911 to 56 years in 1921, female mortality rates declined during the First World War and there were striking gains in infant survival chances. These changes can all be related to a decline in nutrition-related diseases. As increased supplies arrived from North America, rationing, except for butter, meat and sugar, was abandoned in May 1919.[2] The last two items to be rationed were bread and sugar, something which continued until mid-1920. The prosperity of the immediate postwar period led to the introduction of new types of food catering for middle-class households with enough disposable income to buy snacks, such as chewing gum and particularly crisps. Crisps were developed by Frank Smith who packaged the produce cooked by his wife in greaseproof paper bags selling them from his pony and trap around North London. He also included a twist of salt for flavouring. They quickly became immensely popular and within a year a factory was under construction in Brentford.[3]

Some wartime changes proved popular either with the public or with business and there seemed little popular pressure to reverse them. The dairy trade, for example, decided in April 1919 to maintain the one delivery a day to homes that had become the norm during the war. *The Times* grumbled that in summer at least a second delivery was essential, as suburban homes lacked suitable places to store milk: 'There is no cellar and milk placed in the usual cupboard-larder quickly turns sour if the air is at all sultry.'[4]

The immediate post-war period saw an explosion in publication of books about the war. Memoirs in their dozens were published, some from the commanders in the field, but many from former ordinary soldiers. They were overwhelmingly patriotic in nature. In September 1919 Hodder & Stoughton, which was by no means the largest or most prestigious publisher, issued:

> a new volume of tales of the 'Old Contemptibles' by Boyd Cable, and 'The History of the Guards Division' by Colonel A Murray CB . . .' The Story of the Fourth Army: In the Hundred Days August 8–November 1918' in two volumes . . . 'A Treasury of War Poetry of the Great War' edited by Professor G Herbert Harrison. . . . 'Tanks 1914–1918: the Log Book of a Pioneer' by Lieutenant Colonel Sir Albert Stearn in which the full story of the tanks is told for the first time.[5]

This extract lists perhaps a quarter of the books published by Hodder & Stoughton on the war during the autumn of 1919. Other publishers were equally prolix. Unfortunately, few were of literary merit so, almost without exception, they have long been forgotten. Collier and Lang thought many books concerned 'the squabbles of autobiographical generals over their own and each other's mistakes' concluding that almost everything was 'pretty heavily bespread with bunk'.[6]

The pages of the *Times Literary Supplement* (*TLS*) for the period contained many reviews and listings for hundreds of books about the war. Many of the books on the war reviewed in the *TLS* in 1920 and 1921 were German accounts. This perhaps reflects a long-supressed wish to discover how the enemy had fared. But then, as now, there is nothing publishers like more than leaping on a bandwagon in the hope of making a quick buck. The *TLS* declared in September that: 'There is nothing in the autumn lists to support the assertion recently made by an author that publishers no longer find a profitable market for war books.'[7] Yet, the author was right, there were far fewer titles published in 1920, and even fewer still in 1921. The disillusionment that many people increasingly felt about the war, particularly as the hopes of 1919 and 1920 were dashed by economic uncertainties, surfaced in books towards the end of the 1920s, when in the words of another memoirist, Charles Carrington: 'Every battle [was] a defeat, every officer a nincompoop, every soldier a coward.'[8]

There were those for whom the war had been the greatest event in their lives. They had found comradeship and purpose in the services, which seemed to dissipate in the postwar uncertainties. Such feelings contributed to the growth of fascism on the Continent, but were much less political in relatively stable Britain. From the mid-1920s most regiments and other units organized annual dinners for veterans to meet old comrades and reminisce about their wartime experiences. Attendees shared a nostalgic view of the war years of their own special world and theirs alone.[9] Almost as soon as the war was over, attempts were made to set up clubs for officers of particular regiments. This was after all the high point of the gentlemen's club with dozens in London alone and with most other towns and cities each having two or three. Probably the best known of the postwar creations is Buck's Club, which was established in June 1919 by Captain Herbert Buckmaster for his fellow officers of the Royal Horse Guards. It is still trading. Even while the war was on, he wrote to potential members that:

> We are starting directly after the war, a small club, in London in the neighbourhood of St James's Street consisting to start with, of three rooms, 1) an American bar 2) a writing or reading-room 3) a card room. All kinds of drink will be procurable, also oysters and sandwiches . . . Tea for those that like it will be procurable in the afternoon.[10]

Toc H, established in 1920, had loftier aims than cocktails. It had its origins in Talbot House, founded by the charismatic Revd Philip 'Tubby' Clayton in 1915 as a social club in Poperinghe which lay a few miles behind the front line in Belgium. Talbot House called itself 'Everyman's Club' because, uniquely, men of all ranks and none were welcome to use the facilities and, particularly to worship in the attic chapel.[11] After the war Clayton was driven to set up such an establishment in London. He envisioned: 'a cosy house with a good ABC [cafe] downstairs and upstairs, lecture room, library, games rooms and "grousing" room, together with a London Territorial Lethe chamber, where warlike reminiscences may merge wholly into imaginative art'.[12] The response was overwhelming, and Toc H was founded in 1920, with a clubroom 'Mark I' in South Kensington, but it soon expanded all over Britain. Clayton was astute enough to try to make sure that the movement was open to all men, not just ex-servicemen. Several local Marks, or chapters, however tried to restrict membership to veterans and prevented conscious objectors from joining. Initially too, 'Fellowship' was seen by the older generation as being service in the war, and it was hard to get young people involved. But, as Tresham Lever wrote: 'the awful disillusionment that followed the Armistice had antagonised the older and the younger generations, led to the cult and pursuit of ease and pleasure, and rendered the lesson of service [to the less fortunate] exceedingly hard to learn'.[13]

In 1919 what historians have called the first modern charity was born. This was the Save the Children Fund, originally the Fight the Famine Council, which was as much a political movement as it was a charity. Its founder, Eglantyne Jebb, once said of the Fund that:

> it must seek to abolish, for good and for all, the poverty which makes children suffer and stunts the race of which they are the parents. It must not be content to save children from the hardships of life – it must abolish these hardships; nor think it suffices to save them from immediate menace – it must place in their hands the means of saving themselves and so of saving the world.[14]

Among many of the liberal middle classes there was much sympathy for the plight of Germany. The Save the Children Fund raised considerable sums – far more than they had expected – despite their publicity clearly linking the continuing British naval blockade of Germany with starving children. Founded at a meeting at the Royal Albert Hall in May 1919, it soon circulated a hard-hitting leaflet protesting at the continuing blockade on Germany. Titled 'Our blockade caused this', the text read: 'All over Europe millions of children are starving to death. We are responsible. How can you stop it? Write to Lloyd George and say you will not stand it, raise the blockade everywhere.' Another leaflet was headed 'A starving baby'.[15] The response was overwhelmingly positive. The initial appeal raised £10,000, including a donation from a small girl who wrote rather optimistically: 'I have taken half-a-crown out of my money box and am sending it to you so that you can feed all the starving children.' By the end of 1919, Miss Jebb had been granted an audience with Pope Benedict XV. Dr Hector Munro, who accompanied her, later recalled: 'When she spoke everything else seemed to lose its importance and one agreed to whatever she wished.' It was a feeling that many people in authority came to share.[16]

Save the Children had an initial appeal to the liberal middle class, letters seeking their support appeared in the left-leaning press, such as the *Manchester Guardian*, but not *The Times* which was mildly hostile to the whole idea. The appeals stressed: 'the sense of fellow-feeling conveyed by such aid as we may be able to render to meet the awful suffering is perhaps as valuable as the actual relief'.[17] While others reported graphically on the distress to children. In Budapest, for example, 'Babies a few weeks old are wrapped in hard paper napkins which will only stand being washed twice. With a wretched substitute for soap and minimum of coal, washing of their persons or their clothes are dangerously limited, and rubber sheets are not to be had.'[18] At the time of the second postwar Remembrance Day commemorations, when feelings among many people were still raw, in November 1920, newspaper adverts for the charity included the chilling refrain: 'another helpless child is DEAD – another and another while you read. Think of your responsibilities – it is within your responsibilities to save such lives.'[19]

The Fund was also organized differently to other charities of the time. Most charities raised their funds through subscribers who expected a say in the running of the charity in return for their donations. Now donors gave directly, leaving the organization of the Fund to a small group of professional managers.[20] This provided the model for subsequent charities. As a result, Save the Children was less deferential, but also very much more successful than its competitors.

The immediate postwar period saw the growing use of technology which had developed during the First World War, and which would have a great impact over the decades. Cinema projectors, for example, increasingly showed films at a steady speed rather than with the jerky motions that pre-war audiences had experienced and soon there were successful experiments with talking pictures.[21] On a much smaller scale, Rawlplugs, which had actually been developed before the war, were launched in 1919. In 1920, in an article for 'home craftsmen' on the construction of an 'clothes-airer for use in the kitchen', the *Birmingham Gazette* said that there were made 'of fibre and provide the best and easiest method of fastening things to any kind of wall without damaging it'.[22]

Pioneering intercontinental flight attracted attention, although few passengers, while motor vehicles had a greater immediate impact and there was also great interest in radio communications. In each case the industries had been boosted by wartime developments in performance and reliability and could build on the pent-up demand for goods

Aviation in 1914 was still very much at an experimental stage. By 1918 it had become a key component of the war effort. On the outbreak of war 4 squadrons of the Royal Flying Corps were sent to France, with 105 officers, 63 aeroplanes, and 95 lorries. Left at home were 116 aircraft (described as 'mainly junk') and a few hundred officers and airmen. By the time of the Armistice the new Royal Air Force boasted 188 squadrons scattered across the globe, with 22,467 aircraft and 103 airships on strength, and 27,000 officers and 264,000 other ranks.[23] It was widely acknowledged that the air services had played a key role in the Allied victory. And the chivalric heroism of 'aces' such as Billie Bishop, Albert Ball and

Manfred von Richthofen had entranced civilians at home, more used to reading about the deaths of thousands of men daily in the mud of Flanders.

This romance carried on into the immediate postwar period with a number of record-breaking flights that spanned the continents attracting huge public interest. The best known of these was the first non-stop west to east transatlantic flight by John Alcock and Arthur Brown. Their flight took 16 hours from Newfoundland, ending when their plane crashed into a bog in Connemara. They were both knighted for their exploits deserving the honour, for, according to Cecil Lewis, the trip: 'was a triumph of endurance and navigating skill, for the wireless broke down almost immediately, and the machine encountered fogs and storms almost the whole way across'.[24]

A few weeks earlier, Harry Hawker and Kenneth Mackenzie-Grieve had attempted the same flight, but their aircraft had crashed mid-Atlantic and after an uncomfortable couple of hours they were rescued by a Danish steamer. Unfortunately, it was unequipped with wireless so could not send details of their rescue. Their fate transfixed the public at home. To many, when it was found that they were alive and well, the placards 'HAWKER SAFE' 'seemed of immeasurably more significance than the Versailles treaty'. Their journey home from Scotland turned into a triumphal parade: 'At every stop along the line great crowds gathered to greet them, and the jubilation at King's Cross on their arrival recalled scenes at Victoria when the first trainloads of lightly wounded came in from the 'Somme Victory' of 1916.'[25]

Closer to home there was keen interest in the commercial possibilities of civil aviation. In January 1919, the *Spectator*, hardly a revolutionary journal, discussed the possibility that 'London and provincial centres may be linked up for newspaper delivery and carriage of copy and photographs.'[26] The problem was that the demand was not yet there. Describing the transatlantic flights, Graves and Hodge pointed out: 'in spite of public enthusiasm for the fliers themselves [the problem] was that they had more scientific than commercial value, and more sporting value than scientific. No freight could be carried . . . A great deal of organisation and much mechanical improvement were needed before Atlantic flights could become commercially viable.'[27]

Flights over England and the near Continent were very different: there were enough people willing to find out. One such person was Cecil Lewis, who had served with distinction in both the RFC and RAF. On discharge, he joined a couple of pilot friends:

> We bought a couple of Avros from the Aircraft Disposal Board and fitted the rear cockpit to take two passengers and roped in some good Air Mechanics . . . and set off light-heartedly to make the great BP

air-minded . . . When the weather was good we did quite well; but the public was cautious – particularly up north. Flying was still something of a miracle: 'on the ground you know where you are, but in the air where are you.' To fill up the time, we gave exhibitions, impersonated Providence at garden fetes, dropping balloons and confetti on the crowd below, while the children sang 'All the good things around us are sent from Heaven above.'[28]

Among the passengers and his colleagues carried were the newly-weds Robert Hamilton and Nora Standen who flew from their wedding at Chorleywood to a honeymoon in Fowey.[29] The business folded as winter approached. However, the ever adaptable Lewis was soon offered a post training pilots in the embryonic Chinese Air Force.

There were also considerable amounts of war surplus materiel available very cheaply with tens of thousands of ex-servicemen who had considerable experience in operating and maintaining the equipment. The more imaginative of these could see the potential to develop their fields profitably in the peacetime world. As mentioned earlier, Frank Smith, late of the Army Service Corps, used ex-Army deep fat fryers to make his crisps, honing skills learnt while cooking for the troops during the war. It was easy enough to buy war surplus materiel, as *Flight* magazine advised readers: 'Many bargains for those who have the understanding to acquire discreetly should be going in the disposal of "overs" which the Ministry of Munitions from time to time are offering in the open market.' Items currently available included 'engines galore, new and second-hand aeroplanes, spares, tanks, tyres, miles of aeroplane linens in various stages, suitable for shirtings, linings and whatnot'.[30] Unfortunately, as Cecil Lewis pointed out, most items were unsuitable for civilian purposes: 'Fighting machines must sacrifice everything to performance, commercial machines to safety.'[31]

This elemental truth was lost on the companies who tried to start commercial passenger and freight services. One of first operations was Aircraft Transport and Travel, which began to fly freight between Folkestone and Ghent a few days after the Armistice in DH9 bombers. The first passenger services were between London and Paris closely following railway lines except the short hop over the Channel. A fewer of the braver British delegates to the Peace Conference at Versailles travelled this way. However, commercial flights between the two capitals did not begin until 15 July 1919, when Colonel W.N. Pilkington flew with Captain Jerry Shaw from Hendon to Le Bourget. Regular flights, however, did not begin until the end of August, when the fare was 15 guineas, the equivalent of a first-class fare by train and ferry. Passengers were soon offered a limousine service to the airfield and a lunchbox containing six sandwiches, fruit and chocolate for 3s, although they had to provide their own drink.[32]

Much of the success of these early services was due to the carefree confidence of the pilots who flew through bad weather with only the crudest of instruments. Sir Frederick Sykes, the civil servant responsible for the development of civil aviation, was a regular passenger. He described one flight from Paris in which after 2½ hours above a snow storm his pilot decided that they should be over England. They came down through thick cloud. Suddenly obstructions came into view and the aircraft crashed into a Belgian dyke. They got to the coast, where Sykes found a freighter to take him to England, and the pilot was left to see whether the wreckage could be salvaged. On another occasion over London the aircraft he was flying in barely missed St Paul's Cathedral when it suddenly loomed up ahead in the low cloud and fog.[33]

Accidents were in fact fairly rare. Far more serious were the attempts by Britain's erstwhile ally the French to put their competitors out of business. The French government offered generous subsidies to French companies and this coupled with serious fare-cutting policies almost put the British companies out of business by February 1921.[34] In 1920 Churchill declared 'civil aviation must fly by itself' but in March 1921 government help was provided to Handley Page to reopen its London–Paris service. Further subsidies followed and in April 1924 the government financed the formation of Imperial (later British) Airways.

The return to peace led to a release of pent-up demand for cars. The numbers of vehicles licensed increased fivefold from 89,000 in 1910 to 475,000 by the end of 1920. In 1919 there were 110,000 private cars on the road, which had nearly doubled to 187,000 a year later.[35] In part this pressure was met by the sale of war surplus materiel. Unlike aircraft, cars provided for the military could easily be converted for civilian use. Indeed, an advertisement from 1917 made that point: 'An important of this uninterrupted manufacture [of staff cars] is that Vauxhall cars will be ready for sale *immediately* war work ceases.'[36]

The Ministry of Munitions had regular auctions of surplus mechanical transport. One at the Wormwood Scrubs depot in September 1919 offered 'A Leyland workshop, Rover Ambulance, Clement-Talbot Wagonette', while among the lots at an auction the following week was a 'Rolls Royce Touring Car Aluminium Body in green, upholstered in red leather, spare rims etc (used for King's Messenger work only)'.[37] By the end of the year the Ministry had disposed of 12,000 lorries and lorry chassis, 11,000 motorcycles and nearly 7000 'cars, ambulances and light vehicles'.[38] There was also a large number of automobile manufacturers, many in effect hand-making cars to customers specifications.[39] In their advertising, they made much of their war work. The assumption being that purchasers were likely to have had experience of their machines during the war:

the 1920 Wolseley Fifteen embodied 'the results of our war experience in aero engines and naval gun mechanism, superadded to the excellences of design which made the pre-war Wolseley famous'.[40]

These motor cars were not cheap and, by today's standard, performance was sluggish at best. The Wolseley Fifteen '4-seat touring body' model was £800, with a supplement of £200 for one with 'enclosed saloon body'. The supercar of the day – the Hispano-Suiza H6 with a maximum speed of 85mph – cost £2,300, for which *The Times* motoring correspondent wrote: 'you get a machine in the design and manufacture of which it is plain that cost has been the least consideration. . . . [it has] speed, power and flexibility, all three to an unusual degree'.[41] Far more popular was the Ford Model T: 40 per cent of all cars registered were Fords. Other cheap models were the Morris Cowley (cost £315) or Morris Oxford with an electric starter (£360 for the two-seater or £390 for the four-seater). Even so, cars were beyond the pockets of most families.[42]

The experience of driving was vastly different from today. There were complaints about the dust from people who drove to Goodwood races in July 1919 and many a puncture was caused by broken beer bottles thrown by thoughtless passengers from open charabancs.[43] The Ministry of Transport was established in 1919 and took over responsibilities for major roads from local county councils, although it would be a few years before roads began to improve. It could also be difficult to obtain petrol in rural areas. Fuel was sold in cans by garages (many of which doubled as the village blacksmith). The first petrol pump was opened at Aldermaston in 1919 on the Berkshire stretch of the Bath Road, one of Britain's busiest.[44] One thing that hasn't changed is traffic jams. The first roads specifically designed for the motor car were not built for a decade or so, and in cities cars had to fight for road space with horse-drawn vehicles. There had been a brief experiment with traffic signals in 1868 but the first traffic lights were not introduced until the first electric signals appeared on the streets of London in 1929.[45]

Motorcycles offered an alternative to the car: they were cheaper to buy and run, the tax was lower and the machine was fairly easy to maintain. Thousands of war surplus machines made their way onto the roads in 1919, followed by new models from British and foreign manufacturers. As with cars, the immediate postwar models were little different from those used in France or even those built before the war. However, they offered speed (and thrills) at a modest price. A 2.5hp Royal Enfield light weight model was on sale for £65 at the 1920 Motorcycle Show. Sidecars, to accommodate the whole family, cost an extra £95. It was not until 1925 that more cars were sold than motorbikes.[46]

Anybody who had reached the age of 14 could obtain a licence to drive a motorcycle, and 16 for one to drive a car. There were no driving tests. The argument being that most accidents were caused by bad drivers, 'road hogs' as they were called. One simply learnt on the roads, but with so little motorized traffic it did not really present a problem. The maximum speed limit was set at 20mph: a limit that was almost universally ignored. It was not until 1931 that it was raised to 30mph.[47] It was relatively unusual for a car's owner to drive himself (and it was almost always a he because there were relatively few women drivers). A chauffeur/mechanic was employed in most well-to-do households. An exception was Sir Stanley Reed, the editor of *The Times of India*, who provided a testimony for Vauxhall which they used in their advertising: 'I do not keep a driver and look after the engine entirely myself, but have never found that the car offers any difficulty to the intelligent owner–driver.'[48]

As with any new technology, it was not long before the criminal fraternity sought to benefit from the automobile. At the mundane level, Sidney Felstead described how easy it was to steal a car to order. Having received a commission from a man in Hammersmith for a particular model: 'The following afternoon he took a walk into Cavendish Square, where he found a luxurious coupé standing before the house of a famous specialist. What could be easier than to jump in, turn on the self-starter, and drive down to his friend who had his £50 all ready waiting.'[49]

Felstead was told that it was 'most profitable to steal cars not easily recognizable . . . [but] it is not really safe to steal anything but Fords . . . [which are] all alike as the proverbial two peas'.[50] But what really attracted criminals was speed, which meant that it was easy to evade police in pursuit, in Felstead's words: 'Not even the redoubtable Sherlock Holmes could have hoped to catch a criminal who vanished into thin air immediately he had achieved his purpose.' The murderer Percy Toplis travelled across large areas of England and Scotland during the late spring of 1920 by motor car and motorbike. His exploits would not have been possible even a decade before.

Motor cars were soon used in heists. On 21 January 1920, *The Times* reported a 'particularly impudent safe robbery, in which, as in many recent crimes, the thieves escaped in a motor car'. The safe at Bermondsey Dockhead Post Office was broken into containing nearly £1,000 in cash, stamps and postal orders. The vehicle was described as being a Ford 'painted chocolate'.[51]

The police could not easily give chase. They had few cars, and those that they had were elderly and slow. And, in addition, they were often restricted to their areas of jurisdiction, which was a real problem when there were 191 police forces across England and Wales alone.[52] In London action was finally taken in September 1920. General William Horwood, the Commissioner of Metropolitan Police, announced a greater use of motor vehicles: 'On land, on sea, and certainly not least in the air, great developments are at hand, and the police cannot afford to be left behind in the race.' Detectives were to be issued with motorcycles: 'Now the divisional detective inspectors can cover the ground as swiftly as their chiefs and can take a man with them in the side-car.' Their main use was to get to break-ins before the burglars had fled the scene.[53]

Sidney Felstead applauded the work of the new Flying Squad, as the motorized police quickly became known:

> Inside of eighteen months there have been quite 500 criminals brought to justice, most of them habitual offenders, whose profession is anything from burglary to pocket-picking. Matters have reached such a stage indeed, so highly efficient has the Intelligence Department at the yard become, that the Flying Squadron is able to arrest criminals just as they are about to commit a crime.[54]

Motor vehicles, that is lorries, cars and motorcycles, were of course not new in 1919. Tens of thousands had played a significant role in supporting the British Army during the war, becoming much more efficient in the process. Over the four years, engines, braking and lights had all greatly improved. In 1914, the Army had 80 lorries on its books, by the Armistice the number had grown to nearly 47,000. In addition, by November 1918 the Army had acquired 34,000 motorcycles, 11,000 cars and 12,000 light vans. Even so, the bulk of carrying of shells and other supplies was still performed by horses, mules and donkeys. As a result, animal feed was the single biggest item imported into France during the war.[55] The war had led to huge improvements in the efficiency of lorries. It was also easy and cheap to buy war surplus machines in the years after the Armistice. It was not surprising that many ex-servicemen set up small haulage companies, many of whom had learnt to drive while in the Army. Early lorries in service before 1914 had an economic range of about 40 miles, which limited them to taking goods to and from railway freight yards. Prices were slashed as one- or two-lorry firms sought to gain traffic from the railways and each other. Their popularity grew. The number of licensed goods vehicles increased tenfold from 143,877 in 1910 to 650,148 in 1920 and 1,524,061 in 1925.[56] The service offered, particularly when compared with the railway companies, was often better, with quicker journeys and fewer goods stolen or broken. When the railways were largely immobilized by the General Strike in 1926, it was noted how much more traffic managed to get through by road. This had not happened in the previous great railway strikes in 1911 and 1919.

One phenomenon of the late wartime and the immediate postwar periods was spiritualism. There was a veneer of pseudo-science to it, which made it attractive to the more gullible intellectual. Grieving mothers and widows went to seances and spiritual healers in order to receive messages from their loved ones from beyond the grave. The movement, in the words of the historian David Cannadine, offered the 'private denial of death'.[57]

Spiritualism was also in part a response to a feeling that the Church, in its various forms, had been too closely identified with the war and thus at odds with its central message of peace. And, indeed, why would God unleash such devastation on his believers? It wasn't just soldiers who lost their faith in the trenches. People at home stayed at home rather than going to church, let down by their priests who clearly did not believe what they preached. It also harked back to half-forgotten pre-Christian beliefs in ancestor worship, ghosts that many potential believers must have been comfortable with.[58]

And for many who grieved, the fact that there had not been a funeral at home, which would ordinarily lead to acceptance that a loved one had died, meant that there could not be closure. Despite the telegram from the War Office, many were unable to accept their husband's or son's death. The service records at The National Archives are full of letters from relatives seeking more information from the Army about their loved ones' deaths. And newspaper small ads often included appeals for information about missing men: 'Will anyone taken prisoner at or near Gommecourt on July 1st kindly COMMUNICATE with Mrs Peach, 24 Elm Avenue, Nottingham who desires news of her son 2/Lieut E J Peach 1/7 Sherwood Foresters, seconded MGC, last seen July 1st in action at Gommecourt.'[59]

Spiritualism began in the pre-war era, but came to prominence during the First World War and the inter-war period. Most towns had a spiritualist church where travelling mediums would hold seances weekly or monthly. A typical one was in Preston, where at the meeting on 6 November 1919, the speaker was Ernest Oaten of Manchester and the general public were cordially invited. The small ad in the *Lancashire Daily Post* concluded: 'Now you critics come with your Questions'.[60]

The movement reassured believers that their sons and husbands had not died in the conventional sense and also there was no need to grieve because the deceased were much happier than they had been on Earth. According to a Lancashire spiritualist, the Revd Vale Owen writing in a Sunday newspaper, immortality was given over to a kind of vaguely pious lotus-eating in a snug suburban heaven and the spirits he found there were: 'just as natural as we are. They are simply bubbling over with the joy of life and humour is not absent from their composure.'[61]

The two greatest proponents of spiritualism during and after the war were the creator of Sherlock Holmes, Sir Arthur Conan Doyle, and the physicist Sir Oliver Lodge. Both of whom grieved for much-loved sons who had fallen during the war. Conan Doyle later wrote that: 'Evidence of the presence of the dead appeared in his own household, and the relief afforded by posthumous messages taught him how great a solace it would be to a tortured world if it could share in the knowledge which had become clear to himself.'[62] In 1916, Lodge published a bestselling book, *Raymond or Life and Death with Examples of the Evidence of the Survival of Memory and Affection after Death*, which described his son's life in a paradise which

Raymond called Summerland, where he felt 'brighter and lighter and happier altogether'. And where the departed smoked cigars and called for whisky and soda. Both the cigars and the whisky were manufactured in laboratories 'out of essences and ether and gasses'.[63]

It was easy for critics to point out spiritualism's failings. In 1919 a letter writer to the *Courier* suggested that: 'Mothers and friends of fallen soldiers [are] resorting to table-rapping, creakings, automatic writing through the medium of the planchette, Ouija, heliograph etc in the hope of once more communicating with their loved ones.' The author of the letter accused mediums of being aggressive 'quacks' that preyed on the delusional and were, even, mouthpieces of the Devil himself.[64]

Communication was through a medium or clairvoyant, somebody supposedly with psychic powers. Conan Doyle took the magician Harry Houdini to see Eva, one-such clairvoyant apparently able of bringing the dead to life. However, Houdini was unconvinced, for Eva had been unable to produce nothing more lifelike than a huge inflatable rubber doll. And Barbara Cartland was less than convinced by a medium who announced that she was an incarnation of an Egyptian princess and demanded a large flask of brandy before she started work.[65]

But for a few people spiritualism provided succour in a way that conventional religion could not. Florence Billington met a spiritualist in Leeds:

> He came to lunch with his wife, and while we were having a cup of tea, this man told me that he could see a very young boy in khaki standing behind me. 'He says he was killed in the war – have you any idea who that is?' I said, 'Yes I know who he is.' He said, 'Well, this young man is showing an awful lot of love towards you. He's here for you and he wants me to tell you that he loved you with all his heart and soul and had hoped to make his life with you, if he could have done.' On occasion since, I have felt his spirit visit me: that he was thinking of me and was somewhere near.[66]

If spiritualism has faded as its inconsistencies were exposed in the media, many of the developments of the immediate postwar period remain with us today, whether they be ones which have obviously transformed our lives like the motor car and civil aviation, or whose impact has been more subtle such as Rawlplugs and potato crisps.

Conclusion

The war had been the most traumatic event in British history. It was not referred to as the Great War for nothing. Over 700,000 men, who in other circumstances might have grown old in Britain, had been killed. At least another 1½ million were in some way physically or mentally affected by the war. Society had been turned upside down in order to beat the enemy. By 1918 when there seemed little prospect of Allied victory, just endless stalemate in the killing fields of the Western Front, there was a widespread sense of war-weariness. Once the Armistice was declared the sense of victory as an opportunity to build something better soon faded. Those in positions of authority wasted the chance to create a better society, choosing instead to reconstruct Britain along cherished patterns. In that they had general support of the electorate in England, Wales and Scotland if not in southern Ireland.

Much was made subsequently of the 'lost generation' of brilliant minds and athletic bodies who lay in Flanders' fields, and the young women at home who were fated to remain spinsters because there were no men for them to marry. However, the 1921 census showed that Great Britain's population had in fact not declined. On census night England, Wales and Scotland had a population of 42,767,530, an increase of 4.7 per cent over 1911, with 20,430,623 males and 22,336,907 females.[1]

The choice in Britain was not between chaos and revolution. Internationally, the Treaty of Versailles did not lead to a satisfactory conclusion to the First World War. The Treaty satisfied no one, both the Germans and the British came to the conclusion that it was grossly unfair, although for different reasons. The twenty years between 1919 and 1939 appears to be a pause between two titanic battles with Britain and France on one side and Germany on the other. Despite the ideological differences, notably the rise of communism and fascism, some have referred to the wars in Europe between 1914 and 1945 as the 'Second Thirty Years' War'.

At home the Conservative-dominated coalition chose return to traditional economics and to dismantle the State apparatus built up to win the war. Governments took the 'Geddes Axe' to public expenditure in 1922, came off the Gold Standard in 1926, failed to deal with the Great Depression and mass unemployment and offered little support to ex-servicemen existing on pitiful pensions. The nationalism and appeal to cultural superiority which had bolstered the war effort were seized on by politicians such as Stanley Baldwin and, in particular, 'Jix' Willam Joynson-Hicks, the Home Secretary between 1924 and 1929. During his time in office, with various degrees of success, Jix opposed nightclubs, revisions to the Church of England Prayer Book, and the lowering of the voting age for women from 30 to the same age as men, 21. In 1945, Labour Prime Minister Clement Attlee, admittedly with the advantage of hindsight, made a better effort to deliver homes, to provide full employment and to create a comprehensive welfare state.

Despite the huge impact they made on society, British losses were not as devastating as elsewhere. In contrast to much of Europe, Britain had not been invaded. The only fighting on British shores had taken place in the air over its cities, and this caused little direct damage. The revolutionary war in Ireland had relatively little impact on the mainland and eventually led to the creation of the Irish Free State, a self-governing state with Dominion status within the Empire. Victory enabled the British to see themselves as peaceful, civilized, tolerant and generous. Nevertheless, people of all classes sought justice which was often understood as a return to a version of pre-war conditions. But it was not possible. Too much had changed. The immediate postwar years were a time of great uncertainty. Many felt that revolution was just around the corner. There were huge numbers of strikes across the whole of industry spreading even to the police, and mutinies in the forces raised doubts about the loyalty of the Army as well as the police. In Ireland, an imaginative revolutionary leadership under Michael Collins and Eamon De Valera defeated the unimaginative British military and the civil authorities in Dublin Castle. Yet, the Irish initially achieved little more than had been offered in devolved powers by the British government in 1914 and the new State proved to be a peculiarly conservative one.

There was no revolution in part because there was no co-ordination between the strikers. But more importantly there was no thirst for revolution among the working classes. Of more concern for most union members was the need to find work and for those in employment to maintain wartime gains. The Labour leadership was antipathetic to direct action. The trade-union movement leaders were not revolutionary figures. They focused on improving conditions for their members by ensuring wages kept pace or ahead of inflation and ensuring that members in the forces could return to their pre-war jobs. Certainly, there were national strikes – the Railway Strike of September 1919 was particularly notable – but most industrial action was local and locally organized within a particular industry. The cotton weavers of Oldham were not interested in the struggles of the woollen workers of Halifax across the Pennines. Those who sought to be revolutionary leaders were isolated. Their greatest success – preventing a shipload of arms being sent to Poland for the fight against the new Soviet Union – was built on the support of the Labour leadership. While they claimed that they stopped a war against Russia, the disillusioned servicemen needed little persuasion to make their feelings clear. Although slowly a notion of class identification was becoming more important, working people were rarely united. Women who had gone into the fields, the factories and the offices during the war were expected to give up these jobs to returning veterans and to return to domesticity or domestic service. However, they had made gains. The franchise was extended, some new posts arose and as new factories opened, women found employment there. The role of women in society had changed, although it took time for this to be realized. Most of all they had more confidence. The triumph of the vivacious French teenager Suzanne Lenglen at Wimbledon over a staid British opponent was, perhaps, a sign of this.

The lack of revolutionary fervour might also have been because there were reassuringly familiar distractions. In the spring of 1919 the King was at Royal Ascot to see his horse win and debutantes began to attend grand balls as the Season restarted. Moreover, Ministers took care to diffuse potentially difficult situations. Winston Churchill abandoned a carefully thought out, but impractical, scheme to demobilize the forces to minimize potential unemployment. This was replaced by a simple plan so that the men who had served longest were discharged first. When, during the summer of 1919, there were protests from workers about the shortage of beer, the government restored production to near pre-war levels and increased the strength of the beer itself. Initially, there was no plan for a national war memorial. The provision of a temporary cenotaph at the Peace Day parade in July 1919 was a last-minute idea. Its immediate and overwhelming popularity caught the authorities by surprise. Fifteen months later, on Armistice Day 1920, the permanent memorial was opened by the King. The government was more sure-footed when it called for the 2-minute Silence at 'the eleventh hour of the eleventh day'. This was also a last-minute decision, but one that had immense and immediate effect as Britain literally stopped for 2 minutes.

People focused on their families, on caring for the thousands of men wounded psychologically and physically who gained support from institutions such as the Star and Garter Home for incurable ex-servicemen or Queen Mary's Hospital in Sidcup, which pioneered plastic surgery. They grieved, they built local war memorials and they placed photographs on display and treasured memories of the deceased in their homes. But, of course, it was not possible to turn the clock back. Britain had changed too much and people, particularly the young, also developed new attitudes, rebuilt their communities and looked forward to new consumer goods, new music and new fashions.

The immediate postwar period had a sour, unsettled feeling about it: an unfortunate mixture of loss, exhaustion and pessimism. It was a feeling that hardly dissipated for two decades. Traditional values had lost much of their force, imperial power was under threat and there was no new relationship between management and workers. However, there remained a hope that, with a bit of tweaking, the condition of the people could be improved. Indeed, this occurred, if patchily in London and the South East, less so in the industrial heartlands of Wales and Northern England.

However, it took the election of a Labour government after a second world war in 1945 to really kick-start the changes to society and the economy that were largely frozen between the wars. In 1965, reflecting on the period 1914–45, the historian A.J.P. Taylor concluded that 'In the Second World War the British people came of age. This was a people's war. . . . Traditional values lost much of their force. Other values took their place. Imperial greatness was on the way out; the welfare state was on the way in.'[2]

It definitely helped that Attlee's government had learnt from the mistakes made by its predecessors. It was perhaps more important that, in contrast to the desire in 1918 to return to a supposedly Edwardian golden age, the electorate in 1945 had no desire to return to the inter-war world.

Appendix

How Much was that Worth?

It is almost impossible to compare the worth of money a hundred years ago and now. Food and books, for example, cost much less today in proportion, while rail tickets and housing cost more. However, historians very roughly assume that a penny today would be worth a pound in 1914. Because of inflation the pound sterling lost about half its value during the war. As a result, wages and prices rose accordingly. So, a pound in 1919 might buy £120 worth of goods today.

The pre-decimal currency consisted of pounds (£), shillings (*s*) and pence (*d*); 12*d* made up a shilling and there were 20*s* to the pound. In addition, there were also farthings (a quarter penny) and halfpennies in circulation. The First World War saw the introduction of pound and 10*s* Treasury notes (that is bank notes) and the withdrawal of gold sovereign and half-sovereign coins. Prices of goods aimed at the middle and upper classes were often priced in guineas, which was worth 21*s*.

Notes

Introduction: When the War was Over, Why was There No Revolution?

1. http://news.bbc.co.uk/1/hi/health/4350050.stm.
2. On the wider cultural pessimism see Samuel Hynes, *A War Imagined: the First World War and English Culture* (Pimlico, London, 1990), pp. 312–29. The argument has been refuted by Jay Winter, *Sites of Memory, Sites of Mourning: the Great War Experience in European Cultural History* (Cambridge University Press, Cambridge), 1995, pp. 200–1.
3. Stephen Graham, *Europe: Wither Bound? Being Letters of Travel from the Capitals of Europe* (Thomas Butterworth, London, 1921), p. 11.
4. Dan Weinbren, '"From gun carriage to railway carriage": the fight for peace work at the Woolwich Arsenal 1919–22', *Labour History Review*, 63, 3, 1998, pp. 277–97.
5. Ewen A. Cameron, 'Politics, ideology and the Highland land issue, 1886 to the 1920s', *Scottish Historical Review*, 72, 1, 193, April 1993, pp. 75, 79.
6. Adrian Gregory, *The Last Great War. British Society and the First World War* (Cambridge University Press, Cambridge, 2008), pp. 267, 270. This conclusion echoes views expressed in the 1960s. See A.J.P. Taylor, *English History, 1914–1945* (Clarendon Press, Oxford, 1965), pp. 186–8; C.L. Mowat, *Britain Between the Wars* (Methuen, London, 1968), p. 43.
7. The National Archives of the United Kingdom (henceforth TNA), CAB 24/96 CP327.
8. Ministry of Labour, 'Report from the Ministry of Labour's Special Intelligence Branch on the Situation in the Coal Miners' Strike', 24 July 1919, TNA, HO 144/1534/387000, www.nationalarchives.gov.uk/pathways/firstworldwar/aftermath/p_labour.htm (accessed 24 July 2017).
9. Home Office Directorate of Intelligence, 'Report on Revolutionary Organisations in the United Kingdom', Cabinet Papers, CP 1830 of 2 September 1920, TNA, CAB 24/111.
10. Vera Brittain, *Testament of Youth: An Autobiographical Study of the Years 1900–1925* (Victor Gollancz, 1933, this edn Penguin, Harmondsworth, 1994), p. 429; Virginia Woolf, 'Mr Bennett and Mrs Brown', 1924, in *A Woman's Essays:*

Selected Essays, Volume 1, ed. and introd. Rachel Bowlby (Penguin, London, 1992), pp. 70–1.

11.   Gerardo Chowell, Luís M.A. Bettencourt, Niall Johnson, Wladimir J. Alonso and Cécile Viboud, 'The 1918–1919 Influenza Pandemic in England and Wales: Spatial Patterns in Transmissibility and Mortality Impact', *Proceedings: Biological Sciences*, 275, 1634, 7 March 2008, p. 507.

12.   Quoted in Christopher Andrew, *Her Majesty's Secret Service: The Making of the British Intelligence Community* (Viking Penguin, New York, 1986), p. 228.

13.   Walter Long to Lloyd George, 9 January 1919, Parliamentary Archives, Lloyd George MSS F/33/2/3 quoted in Andrew, *Her Majesty's Secret Service*, p. 232.

14.   Duke of Northumberland, 'The real meaning of nationalisation', *National Review*, 74, 1919, p. 69.

15.   Millicent Garrett Fawcett, *The Women's Victory and After. Personal Reminiscences, 1911–1918* (Sidgwick, London, 1920), p. 106, https://archive.org/details/womensvictoryaft00fawcuoft (accessed 17 July 2017).

16.   Juliet Nicolson, *The Great Silence, 1918–1920: Living in the Shadow of the Great War* (John Murray, London), p. 226.

17.   William Gallacher, *Revolt on the Clyde. An autobiography* (Lawrence and Wishart, London, 1936), p. 234.

18.   Richard Dawson, *Red Terror and Green; the Sinn Fein-Bolshevist Movement* (E.P. Dutton & Co., New York, 1920), pp. 217, 224, 261, https://archive.org/stream/redterrorgreensi00daws#page/222/mode/2up (accessed 3 March 2018); MacLean linked land raids, strikes and the Irish struggle. See *Stornaway Gazette*, 29 November 1918, 6 December 1918 and 13 December 1918, cited in James Hunter, 'The Gaelic connection: The Highlands, Ireland and Nationalism, 1873–1922', *Scottish Historical Review*, 54, 158, 2 October 1975, p. 201.

19.   Sandison Family Papers, D1/123/12/4, Sandison, 4 August 1918 and D1/123/13/5, Sandison, 26 January 1919 in the Lerwick, Shetland Archives quoted in Linda K. Riddell, 'Shetland and the Great War', University of Edinburgh, Ph.D. (2012), pp. 222, 251.

20.   *Shetland News*, 21 November 1918, in Riddell, 'Shetland and the Great War', p. 252.

21.   *Shetland Times*, 1 March 1919; 8 March 1919, in Riddell, 'Shetland and the Great War', p. 252.

22.   Arthur Henderson, *The Aims of Labour* (Headley Bros, London, 1918), pp. 9–10.

23.   Arthur Henderson, 'The industrial unrest: a new policy required', *Contemporary Review*, 115, January–June 1919, p. 364.

24.   Keith Middlemas (ed.), *Thomas Jones' Whitehall Diary I* (Oxford University Press, London, 1969), p. 100.

25.   Margaret Cole (ed.), *Beatrice Webb's Diaries, 1912–1924* (Longmans, London, 1952), pp. 134, 136, 164.

26. Middlemas (ed.), *Thomas Jones*, pp. 96–103; Kenneth O. Morgan (ed.), *Lloyd George: Family Letters, 1885–1936* (Oxford University Press, London, 1973), p. 190; Keith Middlemas, *Politics in Industrial Society: The Experience of the British System Since 1911* (Andre Deutsch, London, 1979), p. 145.

27. Élie Halévy, *The Era of Tyrannies: Essays on Socialism and War* (1938; Anchor, New York, English edn, 1965), p. 80; Walter Kendall, *The Revolutionary Movement in Britain, 1900–1921: the Origins of British Communism* (Weidenfeld & Nicolson, London, 1969), p. 195.

28. Stuart Hall and Bill Schwarz, 'State and society, 1880–1930', in Mary Langan and Bill Schwarz, *Crises in the British State 1880–1930* (Hutchinson, London, 1985), p. 7.

29. Chanie Rosenberg, *1919: Britain on the Brink of Revolution* (Bookmarks, London, 1995).

30. Jay Winter, *The Experience of World War I* (Oxford University Press, Oxford, 1994), p. 7.

31. Arthur Marwick, *The Deluge: British Society and the First World War* (The Bodley Head, London, 1965). See also Arthur Marwick, 'The impact of the First World War on British society', *Journal of Contemporary History*, 3, 1, 1968, pp. 51–63; B.B. Gilbert, *British Social Policy 1914–1939* (Batsford, London, 1970), p. 1.

32. George Lansbury, *Daily Herald*, 4 January 1919.

33. Keith Jeffrey and Peter Hennessy, *States of Emergency. British Governments and Strikebreaking Since 1919* (Routledge & Kegan Paul, London, 1983), p. 6.

34. *Labour Leader*, 13 March 1919.

35. *Herald*, 22 March 1919.

36. James E. Cronin, 'The British State and the Structure of Political Opportunity', *Journal of British Studies*, 27, 3, July, 1988, pp. 208–9.

37. Jose Harris, 'Political Thought and the Welfare State 1870–1940: An Intellectual Framework for British Social Policy', in David Gladstone (ed.), *Before Beveridge: Welfare Before the Welfare State* (Civitas, Trowbridge, 1999), p. 43.

38. Joan Smith, 'Labour tradition in Glasgow and Liverpool', *History Workshop Journal*, 17, 1984, pp. 44, 49.

39. On the divisions between unions see Chris Wrigley, 'The state and the challenge of labour in Britain, 1917–20', in Chris Wrigley (ed.), *The State and the Challenge of Labour: Central and Western Europe 1917–1920* (Routledge, London, 1993).

40. Stephen Humphries, *Hooligans or Rebels? An Oral History of Working-class Childhood and Youth 1889–1939* (Blackwell, Oxford, 1981), p. 187.

41. Gallacher, *Revolt on the Clyde*, pp. 233–4.

42. Peter Hart, '"Operations abroad": the IRA in Britain 1919–23', *English Historical Review*, 115, 460, February 2000, p. 102.

43. *Nottinghamshire Free Press*, 14 March 1919, cited in Martyn Ives, *Reform, Revolution and Direct Action Amongst British Miners. The Struggle for the Charter in 1919* (Brill, Leiden, 2016), p. 136.

44. Report cited in Ives, *Reform, Revolution*, p. 137.

45. *Ibid.*, pp. 183, 190–3.

46. *Ibid.*, pp. 140, 142, 287, 309.

47. Parliamentary Papers 113 HC Vol. 113 5s c2348, 20 March 1919, http://hansard.millbanksystems.com/commons/1919/mar/20/government-decision#S5CV0113P0_19190320_HOC_353 (accessed 17 July 2017).

48. *Labour Leader*, 8 March 1919.

49. MFGB Report of Proceedings at a Conference of the Industrial Triple Alliance 23 July 1919, p. 8, cited in Ives, *Reform, Revolution*, p. 194.

50. Martin Crick, *The History of the Social Democratic Federation* (Ryburn, Keele University, Staffordshire, 1994), p. 284; *The Times*, 27 May 1919.

51. A.L. Morton and George Tate, *The British Labour Movement* (Lawrence and Wishart, London, 1979), p. 279.

52. *The Times*, 1 February 1919.

53. *The Times*, 2 April 1919.

54. Chris J. Wrigley, 'The state and the challenge of labour', pp. 262–3; Chris J. Wrigley, 'Counter-revolution and the "failure" of revolution in interwar Europe', in David Parker (ed.), *Revolutions and the Revolutionary Tradition: In the West 1560–1991* (Routledge, London, 2002), p. 182.

55. Gregory, *The Last Great War*, pp. 267, 270.

56. John Foster, 'Prologue: what kind of crisis? What kind of ruling class?', in John McIllroy, Alan Campbell, and Keith Gildart (eds), *Industrial Politics and the 1926 Mining Lockout* (University of Wales Press, Cardiff, 2004), p. 27; Alan Campbell, *The Scottish Miners 1874–1939. Volume Two: Trade Unions and Politics* (Ashgate, Aldershot, 2000), p. 169.

57. Adam R. Seipp, *The Ordeal of Peace: Demobilisation and the Urban Experience in Britain and Germany, 1917–1921* (Ashgate, Farnham, 2009), p. 163.

58. Hall and Schwarz, 'State and society, 1880–1930', pp. 24, 26–7; Bill Schwarz and Martin Durham, 'A safe and sane labourism: socialism and the state, 1910–24', in Mary Langan and Bill Schwarz, *Crises in the British state 1880–1930* (Hutchinson, London, 1985), pp. 127, 145–6; Martin J. Daunton, 'How to pay for the war: state, society and taxation in Britain, 1917–24', *English Historical Review*, 111, 443, September 1996, pp. 885.

59. Ralph Miliband, *Parliamentary Socialism. A Study in the Politics of Labour* (Merlin, London, 1961, 2nd edn 1972), p. 62.

60. Rodney Lowe, 'Hours of Labour: Negotiating Industrial Legislation in Britain, 1919–39', *Economic History Review*, 35, 2, May 1982, pp. 254–71.

61. V.I. Lenin, 'Imperialism and the split in the Labour movement', in *Imperialism – the Highest Stage of Capitalism* (1916; this edn, Resistance Books, Sydney, 1991), p. 128.

62. John Foster, 'British imperialism and the labour aristocracy', in Jeffrey Skelley (ed.), *The General Strike, 1926* (Lawrence & Wishart, London, 1976), pp. 20, 33.

63. Middlemas, *Politics in Industrial Society*, pp. 371–3. For the view that those within the civil service who favoured corporatism were outmanoeuvred by the Treasury see Rodney Lowe, 'The Ministry of Labour 1916–1924. A graveyard of social reform?', *Public Administration*, 52, 1974, pp. 415–38.

64. Ross McKibbin, *The evolution of the Labour Party 1910–1924* (Oxford University Press, London, 1974), p. 240.

65. Simon Webb, *1919 Britain's Year of Revolution* (Pen & Sword, Barnsley, 2016), p. 4.

66. *Punch*, 2 July 1919, pp. 28–9, available at https://archive.org/stream/punchvo-1156a157lemouoft#page/n593/mode/2up (accessed 17 July 2017).

Chapter 1: Demobilization and the Return to Civilian Life

1. Robert Graves and Alan Hodge, *The Long Week-End* (Harmondsworth, Penguin, 1971).

2. *Ibid.*, p. 7.

3. John Bourne, 'The British working man in arms', in Hugh Cecil and Peter Liddle (eds), *Facing Armageddon: The First World War Experienced* (Pen & Sword, Barnsley, 1996), pp. 336–7.

4. Ian Beckett, 'The Soldier's Documents of the Great War and the Military Historians', *Archives*, 23, 1, 1998, p. 66.

5. The most prominent mutiny in the British Army during the First World War was at the Etaples training camp in the summer of 1917. It was largely caused by oppressive discipline.

6. Winston S. Churchill, 'Demobilisation. Note by Mr Churchill', 21 February 1919, Memorandum GT6874. TNA, CAB 24/75/74.

7. Max Arthur, *We Will Remember Them: Voices from the Aftermath of the Great War* (Weidenfeld & Nicolson, London, 2009), pp. 109–10.

8. *Ibid.*, p. 110.

9. Frank Richards, *Old Soldiers Never Die* (Faber & Faber, London 1933), p. 317.

10. Quoted by Stephen Richard Graubard, 'Military Demobilization in Great Britain following the Great War', *Journal of Modern History*, 19, 4, 1947, pp. 300–1. Much to the despair of some of his courtiers George V had sworn not to touch alcohol until British victory.

11. Arthur, *We Will Remember*, p. 111. The Sherwood Foresters was the county regiment for Nottinghamshire where there were many coal mines.

12. Graubard, 'Military Demobilization', p. 302. *Manchester Guardian*, 6 January 1919.

13. Arthur, *We Will Remember*, p. 122.

14. Philip Gibbs, *The Realities of War* (Heinemann, London, 1920), p. 445.

15. Frank P. Crozier, *A Brass Hat in No Man's Land* (Cape, London, 1930), p. 237.

16. Richards, *Old Soldiers*, pp. 315–16. J.C. Dunn, *The War the Infantry Knew: 1914–1919: A Chronicle of Service in France and Belgium* (Jane's, London, 1987), p. 572.

17. Dunn, *The War the Infantry Knew*, pp. 580–4.

18. Arthur, *We Will Remember*, pp. 107–8.

19. *Ibid.*, p. 109.

20. Crozier, *A Brass Hat*, p. 236.

21. Arthur, *We Will Remember*, pp. 122–3.

22. *Ibid.*, p. 123.

23. Crozier, *A Brass Hat*, p. 238. Controversially he called for senior officers to suffer the same punishment as their men who had mutinied and noted: 'This was not done in 1919.'

24. Alf Drury quoted in Robert A. Leeson, *Strike. A Live History, 1887–1971* (George Allen & Unwin, London, 1973), p. 64.

25. Joy Cave (ed.), *I Survived Didn't I? The Great War Reminiscences of Private 'Ginger' Byrne* (Leo Cooper, Barnsley, 1993), p. 105.

26. They are listed in Dave Lamb, *Mutinies 1917–1920* (Solidarity, Oxford and London, 1977).

27. This paragraph is based on an article by Phil Carradice, 'The Kinmel Camp Riots of 1919', www.bbc.co.uk/blogs/wales/entries/cfb526c8-186d-3afe-b3e0-095c8898f868.

28. Graves and Hodge, *The Long Week-End*, p. 22.

29. *The Times*, 8 January 1919.

30. TNA CAB 24/73. *Report on Revolutionary Organisations in the United Kingdom*, 13 January 1919. Sir Basil Home Thomson, the Head of the Criminal Investigation Department at New Scotland Yard since 1913, wrote the reports for the Home Secretary to circulate to a select circle.

31. Basil Thomson, *Queer People* (Hodder & Stoughton, London, 1922), p. 276.

32. Quoted in Gerard DeGroot, *Blighty: British Society in the Era of the Great War* (Longman, London and New York, 1996), p. 269.

33. Rowland Feilding, *War Letters to a Wife* (Medici Society, London, 1929), pp. 376–7.

34. John Collier and Iain Lang, *Just the Other Day: An Informal History of Great Britain Since the War* (Hamish Hamilton, London and New York, 1932), p. 59; Arthur, *We Will Remember*, p. 129.

35. Graubard, 'Military Demobilization', p. 304.

36. *Ibid.*, p. 310.

37. Jonathan Mein, Anne Wares and Sue Mann (eds), *St Albans: Life on the Home Front 1914–1918* (Hertfordshire Publications, Hatfield, 2016), pp. 236–7. Tresham Lever, *Clayton of Toc H* (John Murray, London, 1971), pp. 96–7.

38. Cave (ed.), *I Survived*, p. 108.

39. Clothier, 'British Demobilization', p. 6; Graubard, 'Military Demobilization', p. 299. A private received £5 war gratuity, corporal £6 and sergeant £7, rising to £720 for a field marshal (source http://wargratuity.wordpress.com (accessed 12 November 2017). W.R. Garside, *British Unemployment 1919–1939: A Study in Public Policy* (Cambridge University Press, Cambridge, 2002), pp. 35–6.

40. Graves and Hodge, *The Long Week-End*, p. 23.

41. Gibbs, *The Realities*, p. 447.

42. Graves and Hodge, *The Long Week-End*, p. 23.

43. Arthur, *We Will Remember*, p. 135.

44. Brittain, *Testament of Youth*, p. 122.

45. Edith Wharton, *A Son at the Front* (Schribber's New York, 1923), pp. 187–8.

46. David R. Lewis (ed.), *Remembrances of Hell – The Great War Diary of Writer, Broadcaster and Naturalist – Norman Ellison* (Airlife, Shrewsbury, 1997), p. 98.

47. Graves, *Goodbye*, p. 235. 'The habit of continuous obscene language, which a long and miserable war had always induced, persisted for four or five years more and had even spread to the younger women'. Graves and Hodge, *The Long Week-End*, p. 22.

48. Robert Roberts, *The Classic Slum* (Penguin, Harmondsworth, 1978), p. 228; www.lancashireinfantrymuseum.org.uk/the-accrington-pals-and-the-benedictine-connection-or-a-bene-and-ot (accessed 20 November 2017).

49. Richard Van Emden and Steve Humphries, *All Quiet on the Home Front: An Oral History of Life in Britain During the First World War* (Hodder Headline, London, 2003), p. 305.

50. Arthur, *We Will Remember*, p. 132.

51. Van Emden and Humphries, *All Quiet*, pp. 307–8.

52. David Butler and Gareth Butler, *British Political Facts 1900–1994* (Macmillan, London, 1994), pp. 326, 337. Such couples were not unknown before 1914, when social workers began to refer to 'unmarried wives'.

53. Based on an article in the *Lost Cousins Newsletter*, November 2017, www.lostcousins.com/newsletters2/midnov17news.htm#Nevergiveup (accessed 20 November 2017). Thanks to Sue Palmer and Pater Calver for permission to reproduce it.

54. Arthur, *We Will Remember*, pp. 113–14.

55. William Carr, *A Time to Leave the Ploughshares: A Gunner Remembers 1917–18* (Robert Hale, London, 1985), p. 173.

56. Maude Onions, *A Woman at War: Being Experiences of an Army Signaller in France in 1917–1919 – '807' Unit 3, W.A.A.C., L Signals, A.P.O.3, France* (C.W. Daniel, London, 1929), pp. 54–5.

57. *Evening Standard*, 26 May 1920.

58. Arthur, *We Will Remember*, p. 90.

59. Talbot House, *The Pilgrim's Guide to the Ypres Salient* (Herbert Reiach, London, 1920), p. 48. To hire a car and driver for a day cost about 400 Francs (roughly £7).

60. Arthur, *We Will Remember*, p. 91.

61. Morgan (ed.), *Lloyd George: Family Letters*, p. 102.

62. *The Times*, 13 October 1919.

63. Graves and Hodge, *The Long Week-End*, p. 23.

64. Joanna Bourke, *Dismembering the Male. Men's Bodies, Britain and the Great War* (Reaktion Books, London, 1996), pp. 193, 23.

65. Lewis (ed.), *Remembrances of Hell*, p. 98.

66. Patricia Bell and Freddy Stitt, 'George Herbert Fowler and County Records', *Journal of the Society of Archivists*, 23, 2, 2002, pp. 252–3; Mein, Wares and Mann (eds), *St Albans*, p. 238.

67. Van Emden and Humphries, *All Quiet*, pp. 301–2.

68. *Ibid.*, p. 309. This caused great concern among editorial writers, but Britain was not noticeably a more violent place in 1920 than in 1910.

69. Graves, *Goodbye*, p. 235.

70. Cecil Lewis, *Sagittarius Rising* (Penguin, Harmondsworth, 1977), p. 209.

71. Jeremy Paxman, *Great Britain's Great War* (Viking, London, 2013), p. 283.

72. Gibbs, *The Realities*, p. 449.

73. Quoted in Suzie Grogan, *Shell Shocked Britain: the World War's Legacy for Mental Health* (Barnsley, Pen & Sword, 2014), p. 68.

74. *The Times*, 2 July 1919, p. 2.

75. *The Times*, 13 February 1920.

76. Arthur, *We Will Remember*, pp. 200–1.

77. Carol A. Lockwood, 'From solider to peasant? The Land Settlement scheme in East Sussex, 1919-1939, *Albion*, 30, 3, 1998, p. 444; Leah Leneman, 'Land settlement in Scotland after World War I', *Agricultural History Review*, 37, I, pp. 52–64.

78. Clothier, 'British Demobilization', p. 9.

79. Geoffrey Moorhouse, *Hell's Foundations: A Town, its Myths and Gallipoli* (Sceptre, London, 1992), pp. 114–16.

80. Mein, Wares and Mann (eds), *St Albans*, p. 238.

Chapter 2: A Range of Struggles

1. David Fitzpatrick, *The Two Irelands 1912–1939* (Oxford University Press, Oxford, 1998), pp. 90–3.

2. *Sheffield Independent*, 14 February 1921; John Tanner, '"The only fighting element of the working class"? Unemployed activism and protest in Sheffield, 1919–24', *Labour History Review*, 73, 1, April 2008, p. 135.

3. *The Times*, 13 August 1921.

4. *Shetland Times*, 12 April 1919, cited by Riddell, 'Shetland and the Great War', p. 247.

5. *Manchester Evening News*, 3 May 1920. On the rally see Seipp, *The Ordeal of Peace*, pp. 203–4.

6. *The Times*, 28 January 1919.

7. Michael McCarthy, 'The Broadford Soviet', *The Old Limerick Journal*, No. 4, September 1980, pp. 37–40. See also See D.R. O'Connor Lysaght, 'The Story of the Limerick Soviet' (April 1919), *People's Democracy*, Limerick, 1979, available, https://libcom.org/library/1919-story-limerick-soviet (accessed 3 March 2017); Rayner Lysaght, 'The Munster Soviet Creameries', *Irish History Workshop Journal*, No. 1, 1981; J. Kemmy, 'The Limerick Soviet', *Saothar: The Journal of the Irish Labour History Society*, 2, 1976.

8. Ingrid Henriksen, Eoin McLaughlin and Paul Sharp, 'Contracts and cooperation: The relative failure of the Irish dairy industry in the late nineteenth century reconsidered', *European Historical Economics Society Working Paper*, 71, 2015.

9. Gerald Noonan, *The IRA in Britain, 1919–1923: 'In the Heart of Enemy Lines'* (Liverpool University Press, Liverpool, 2014), p. 153.

10. Peter Hart, '"Operations abroad"', p. 72.

11. Ray Wilson and Ian Adams, *Special Branch. A History: 1883–2006* (Biteback Publishing, 2015, electronic edn).

12. Tom Gallagher, *Glasgow, the Uneasy Peace: Religious Tension in Modern Scotland, 1819–1914* (Manchester University Press, Manchester, 1987), pp. 90–1. However, Iain D. Patterson, 'Irish Republican activities in Scotland', *Scottish Historical Review*, 72, 1, 193, April 1993, p. 47, suggested that the figure of 3,000 is 'probably an overestimate', p. 47, and Hart, '"Operations abroad"', pp. 73, 79, put the figure at 'perhaps a thousand men' across Scotland and England. Wales had no IRA units.

13. The impact of this activity has been categorized as 'highly marginal'. See Patterson, 'Irish Republican activities', p. 46.

14. James E. Handley, *The Irish in Modern Scotland* (Cork University Press, Cork, 1947), p. 299.

15. James Gillogly, *Decoding the IRA* (Mercier Press Ltd, Cork, 2008), p. 194.

16. William O'Brien, *The Irish Revolution and How it Came About* (Allen & Unwin, London, 1923), p. 423.

17. Leah Leneman, 'Lowland land settlement in the twentieth century: a forgotten segment of modern Scottish history', *Scottish History Review*, 67, 2, 184, October 1988, p. 165.

18. James Hunter, 'The Gaelic connection', p. 201.

19. Leah Leneman, *Fit for Heroes? Land Settlement in Scotland After World War I* (Aberdeen University Press, Aberdeen, 1989), pp. 88–90; Ewen A. Cameron, *Land for the People?: The British Government and the Scottish Highlands, c.1880–1925* (Tuckwell, East Linton, 1996), pp. 166–90; James Hunter, *The Making of the Crofting Community* (John Donald, Edinburgh, 1976), pp. 271–7.

20. Quoted in Iain J.M. Robertson, 'Governing the Highlands: the place of popular protests in the Highlands after 1918', *Rural History*, 8, 1, April 1997, p. 120.

21. Iain J.M. Robertson, *Landscapes of Protest in the Scottish Highlands After 1914. The Later Highland Land Wars* (Ashgate, Farnham, 2013), p. 144.

22. *Evening Star*, 27 October 1919, Wal Hannington, *Unemployed Struggles 1919–36. My Life and Struggle Among the Unemployed* (Lawrence and Wishart, London, 1977), pp. 3–8.

23. House of Commons Debate, 8 June 1920, Hansard, Vol. 130 cc225-6, http://hansard.millbanksystems.com/commons/1920/jun/08/soviet-committees-great-britain#S5CV0130P0_19200608_HOC_212 (accessed 12 November 2017). See also the article on the Arborfield History Society website www.arborfieldhistory.org.uk/WW1/WW1_Motor_Depot.htm.

24. L.J. Macfarlane, 'Hands off Russia. British Labour and the Russo-Polish war, 1920', *Past and Present*, 38, 1967, p. 143.

25. Carole Fink, *Defending the Rights of Others: The Great Powers, the Jews, and International Minority Protection, 1878–1938* (Cambridge University Press, Cambridge, 2006), p. 222.

26. Van Emden and Humphries, *All Quiet*, pp. 293–5.

27. *The Times*, 4 November 1919, p. 13.

28. Arthur, *We Will Remember*, p. 96.

29. Sir E. Wild, ll4 HC 5s, 2778, 15 April 1919. He was the West Ham Upton MP 1918–22. http://hansard.millbanksystems.com/commons/1919/apr/15/aliens-restriction-bill#S5CV0114P0_19190415_HOC_297 (accessed 3 March 2017).

30. The story of the 1919 riots is told in Jacqueline Jenkinson, *Black 1919: Riots, Racism and Resistance in Imperial Britain* (Liverpool, Liverpool University Press, 2009), pp. 1, 217–16.

31. Alex King, *Memorials of the Great War in Britain: The Symbolism and Politics of Remembrance* (Bloomsbury, London, 1998), p. 156; *The Times*, 14 June 1919.

32. Riddell, 'Shetland and the Great War', pp. 236–7.

33. Jacqueline Jenkinson, 'Black sailors on Red Clydeside: rioting, reactionary trade unionism and conflicting notions of "Britishness" following the First World War', *Twentieth Century British History*, 19, 1, pp. 29–60; Jacqueline Jenkinson, 'The 1919 race riots in Britain: their background and consequences', University of Edinburgh, Ph.D. (1987), pp. 126, 270–1 available,

www.era.lib.ed.ac.uk/handle/1842/6874; Jenkinson, *Black 1919*; Rozina Visram, *Asians in Britain: 400 Years of History* (Pluto, London, 2002), p. 199; Neil Evans, 'The South Wales Race Riots of 1919', *Llafur*, 3,1, 1980, pp. 5–29; Colin Holmes, *John Bull's Island; Immigration and British Society, 1871–1971* (Macmillan, London, 1988), pp. 140–57; Peter Fryer, *Staying Power: The History of Black People in Britain* (Pluto, London, 1984), pp. 304, 299; *The Times*, 30 May 1919.

34.   Brad Beavan, 'Challenges to civic governance in post-war England: the Peace Day disturbances of 1919', *Urban History*, 33, 3, 2006, pp. 369–92.

35.   Neil G. Orr, 'Keep the Home Fires Burning: Peace Day in Luton, 1919', *Family and Community History*, 21, 1999, pp. 17–22.

36.   *Herts Advertiser*, 26 July 1919, quoted in Mein, Wares and Mann (eds), *St Albans*, p. 228.

37.   Nuala C. Johnson, 'The spectacle of memory: Ireland's remembrance of the Great War, 1919', *Journal of Historical Geography*, 25, 1, 1999, pp. 47, 51.

38.   *The Times*, 27 June 1919.

39.   *Walton Times*, 25 April 1919; 'The Labour situation 26 April 1919', TNA, GT 7172 CAB 24/78.

40.   *Comrades Journal*, September 1919, in Paul Burnham, 'The radical ex-Service-men of 1918', in Nick Mansfield and Craig Horner (eds), *The Great War: Localities and Regional Identities* (Cambridge Scholars, Newcastle, 2014), p. 44.

41.   *Berkshire Chronicle*, 3 September 1920 and *Liverpool Post and Mercury*, 5 August 1920, cited in Burnham, 'The radical ex-Servicemen', p. 45.

42.   Alastair Reid, 'Dilution, trade unionism and the state in Britain during the First World War', in S. Tolliday and J. Zeitlin (eds), *Shopfloor Bargaining and the State* (Cambridge University Press, Cambridge, 1985), pp. 45–74.

43.   Susan Kingsley Kent, *Making Peace: The Reconstruction of Gender in Interwar Britain* (Princeton University Press, Princeton, 1993), p. 113.

44.   Orr, 'Keep the Home Fires Burning', p. 21.

45.   *Daily Sketch*, 28 June 1919, quoted in Martin Pugh, *Women and the Women's Movement in Britain 1914–1959* (Macmillan, London, 1992), p. 82.

46.   *Manchester Guardian*, 26 March 1919.

47.   *Manchester Guardian*, 20 March 1919; *Manchester Guardian*, 13 March 1919; *Manchester Guardian*, 29 March 1919.

48.   Cheryl Law, *Suffrage and Power: The Women's Movement 1918–1928* (I B. Tauris, London, 1997), p. 68.

49.   Van Emden and Humphries, *All Quiet*, p. 309.

50.   Hugh A. Clegg, *A History of British Trade Unions Since 1889 Volume II, 1911–33* (Clarendon Press, Oxford, 1985), p. 568. In 2016, by contrast, 322,000 days were lost to industrial action in 101 stoppages, www.ons.gov.uk/

employmentandlabourmarket/peopleinwork/workplacedisputesandworking-conditions/articles/labourdisputes/latest (accessed 12 November 2017).

51. Seipp, *The Ordeal of Peace*, pp. 156–7.
52. *Kentish Independent*, 29 August 1919.
53. 4 February 1919, TNA, CAB 23/9.
54. Ron Bean, 'Police unrest, unionisation and the 1919 strike in Liverpool', *Journal of Contemporary History*, 15, 4, October 1980, p. 633.
55. *Daily Express*, 27 September 1919. Emphasis in original.
56. *Daily Mail*, 27 September 1919.
57. *Daily Chronicle*, 29 September 1919.
58. Anne Olivier Bell (ed.), *The Diary of Virginia Woolf, Vol. 1 1915–1919* (Hogarth Press, London, 1977), p. 303. Entry for 1 October 1919.
59. The text is quoted in Gregory Blaxland, *J.H. Thomas* (Frederick Muller, London, 1964), pp. 131–2.
60. *The Times*, 3 October 1919.
61. *Railway Review*, 10 October 1919.
62. *Daily Express*, 29 September, 3 October 1919.
63. Laura Beers, 'Is this man an anarchist? Industrial action and the battle for public opinion in interwar Britain', *Journal of Modern History*, 82, 1, March 2010, p. 48.
64. Clegg, *A History of British Trade Unions Since 1889*, p. 291.
65. For the view that public opinion favoured the strikers see Chris Wrigley, *Lloyd George and the Challenge of Labour: The Post-war Coalition 1918–1922* (Harvester Wheatsheaf, Hemel Hempstead, 1990), p. 222; Philip Bagwell, *The Railwaymen: The History of the National Union of Railwaymen, Volume 1* (George Allen & Unwin, London, 1963), pp. 395–6.
66. Ruth Dudley Edwards with Bridget Hourican, *An Atlas of Irish History* (3rd edn, Routledge, Abingdon, 2005), p. 96.
67. Charles Townsend, 'The Irish railway strike of 1920: industrial action and civil resistance in the struggle for independence', *Irish Historical Studies*, 22, 1979; Philip Ollerenshaw, 'Business boycotts and the partition of Ireland', in Brenda Collins, Philip Ollerenshaw and Trevor Parkhill (eds), *Industry, Trade and People in Ireland 1650–1950: Essays in Honour of W.H. Crawford* (Ulster Historical Foundation, Belfast, 2005), pp. 205–27.
68. *The Times*, 25 November 1918.
69. *A Century of Home Ownership and Renting in England and Wales*, part of the 2011 Census Analysis by the Office for National Statistics, available, http://webarchive.nationalarchives.gov.uk/20160105160709/http://www.ons.gov.uk/ons/rel/census/2011-census-analysis/a-century-of-home-ownership-and-renting-in-england-and-wales/short-story-on-housing.html (accessed 3 March 2017).
70. *Woolwich Pioneer*, 11 June 1920.

71. Beavan, 'Challenges', pp. 388–9.
72. Dennis Hardy and Colin Ward, *Arcadia for All: The Legacy of a Makeshift Landscape (*Mansell, London, 1984), pp. 76–91.
73. Chris Kempshall, 'New Anzac-on-Sea', www.eastsussexww1.org.uk/new-anzac- (accessed 12 November 2017).
74. Philip Abrams, 'The failure of social reform, 1918–1920', *Past & Present*, 24, April 1963, p. 43.
75. Peter Malpass, *Housing and the Welfare State: The Development of Housing Policy in Britain* (Palgrave Macmillan, Basingstoke, 2005), p. 32. See also Adam Tooze, *The Deluge: The Great War, America and the Remaking of the Global Order, 1916–1931* (Allan Lane, London, 2014), p. 359.
76. Neville Macready, 2 August 1919. See TNA, MEPO 3/1786.
77. Bean, 'Police unrest', p. 634 cites Liverpool City Council leader Alderman Stanley Salvidge's recollections of a conversation with Lloyd George in S. Salvidge, *Salvidge of Liverpool. Behind the Political Scene 1890–1928* (Hodder & Stoughton, London, 1934), p. 177.
78. TNA, CAB 23/12, 3 October 1919.
79. Chris Wrigley, 'The state and the challenges of labour in Britain, 1917–20', in Chris Wrigley (ed.), *Challenges of Labour: Central and Western Europe, 1917–1920* (Routledge, London, 1993), pp. 262–88.
80. Aneurin Bevan, *In Place of Fear* (William Heinemann, London, 1952), pp. 40–1.
81. TNA, HO 45/346578.
82. Quoted in Pete Brown, *Man Walks Into A Pub* (Headline, London, 2003), p. 155.
83. *Sheffield Evening Telegraph*, 23 May 1919.
84. Rodney Lowe, 'The failure of consensus in Britain: the National Industrial Conference, 1919–1921', *Historical Journal*, 21, 3, September 1978, p. 671.
85. Arthur J. McIvor, 'Employers, the government and industrial fatigue in Britain, 1890–1918', *British Journal of Industrial Medicine*, 1987, 44, pp. 724–32.
86. R.S.F. Schilling, 'Industrial Health Research. The work of the Industrial Health Research Board, 1918–44', *British Journal of Industrial Medicine*, July 1944, 1, 3, p. 145.
87. Keith Laybourn, 'Waking up to the fact that there are any unemployed': Women, Unemployment and the Domestic Solution in Britain, 1918–1939', *History*, 88, 292, pp. 606–23, October 2003.
88. Bill Schwarz, 'Conservatism and "caesarism", 1903–22', in Mary Langan and Bill Schwarz, *Crises in the British State 1880–1930* (Hutchinson, London, 1985), p. 53.
89. The Ministry of Reconstruction, *Reconstruction Problems*, No. 1, 1918.
90. R.H. Tawney, 'The abolition of economic controls 1918–1921', *Economic History Review*, 13, 1943, pp. 9, 11.

91. George Orwell, *The English People* (Collins, London, 1947), in Peter Davison, *The Collected Works of George Orwell, Volume 12* (Secker and Warburg, London, 1998), p. 210.
92. Nicolson, *The Great Silence*, p. 227.
93. Bean, 'Police unrest', p. 645.
94. *Ibid.*, p. 646.
95. Quoted in *Ibid.*, p. 651.

Chapter 3: Economic Reconstruction

1. Peter Clarke, *The Keynesian Revolution in the Making* (Clarendon Press, Oxford, 1988), p. 31; David Greasley and Les Oxley, 'Discontinuities in competitiveness: the impact of the First World War on British industry', *Economic History Review*, 49, 1996, pp. 82–100; J. Ellis Barker, 'Britain's true wealth and the unimportance of the war debt', *The Nineteenth Century and After*, 83, May 1918, pp. 926–9.
2. Taylor, *English History*, p. 1.
3. J.F. Martin, 'The government and control of the British coal industry 1914–18', Loughborough University, M.Phil. (1981), p. 165.
4. The Financial Secretary to the Ministry of Munitions, Sir Worthington Evans, House of Commons Debate, 25 April 1918, Hansard, Vol. 105, cc1181.
5. J.A. Dowie, '1919–20 is in need of attention', *Economic History Review*, 28, 1975, pp. 439–50.
6. Edward V. Morgan, *Studies in British Financial Policy 1914–25* (Macmillan, London, 1952), p. 131.
7. John Maynard Keynes, *The Economic Consequences of the Peace* (Macmillan, London, 1919), pp. 11–12.
8. Barry Eichengreen (ed.), *The Gold Standard in Theory and History* (New York and London, 1985), pp. 6–7, 105.
9. TNA, T 172/643; J.M. Keynes, 'Memorandum on the Probable Consequences of Abandoning the Gold Standard', 17 January 1917.
10. Russell Ally, 'War and Gold. The Bank of England, the London Gold Market and South Africa's Gold, 1914–19', *Journal of Southern African Studies*, 17, 2, June 1991, p. 25.
11. In the end Germany defaulted on most reparations, because the demands were unrealistic. See Niall Ferguson, 'The balance of payments question: Versailles and after', in Manfred F. Boemeke, Gerald D Feldman and Elizabeth Glaser (eds), *Versailles: A Reassessment after 75 Years* (German Historical Institute, Washington and Cambridge University Press, Cambridge and Washington, 1998), p. 424.
12. Peter Cline, 'Reopening the case of the Lloyd George coalition and the post-war economic transition 1918–1919', *Journal of British Studies*, 10, 1, November 1970, pp. 164.

13. *Interim Report of the Committee on Currency and Foreign Exchanges After the War, 1918*, Cmd 9182, paragraph 15.

14. TNA, CAB 27/71 FC 1st Minutes, 24 July 1919.

15. John Maynard Keynes, *A Tract on Monetary Reform* (Macmillan, London, 1923), pp. 9–10.

16. Susan Howson, *Domestic Monetary Management in Britain, 1919–38* (Cambridge University Press, Cambridge, 1975), p. 11.

17. S.N. Broadberry, 'The emergence of mass unemployment: explaining trends in Britain during the trans-World War I period', *Economic History Review*, 43, 1996, pp. 271–82.

18. Martin Daunton, *Just Taxes: The Politics of Taxation in Britain 1914–1979* (Cambridge University Press, Cambridge, 2002), pp. 5, 12–13; Daunton, 'How to pay', p. 888.

19. Tawney, 'The abolition', pp. 13–14.

20. W.H. Hamilton and H.G. Moulton, J.M. Clark (eds), *Readings in the Economics of War* (University of Chicago Press, Chicago, 1918), p. 562.

21. Tawney, 'The abolition', pp. 9, 11.

22. TNA, CAB 24/67 GT 6401, 18 October 1918.

23. Derek H. Aldcroft, *The Inter-War Economy: Britain, 1919–1939* (Batsford, London, 1970), p. 18; Emil Davies, *The Case for Railway Nationalisation* (Collins, London, 1913), p. 51.

24. Pete Brown, *Man Walks Into a Pub: A Sociable History of Beer* (Macmillan, London, 2003), p. 147. The average strength of a pint of beer today is about 4 per cent ABV.

25. Annemarie MacAllister, 'The enemy within: the battle over alcohol', http://theconversation.com/the-enemy-within-the-battle-over-alcohol-in-world-war-i-30441 (accessed 19 November 2017).

26. Quoted in Kerrie Holloway, 'The Bright Young People of the Late 1920s: how the Great War's Armistice influenced those too young to fight', *Journal of European Studies* (2015), 45: 4, p. 319.

27. Brown, *Man Walks Into a Pub*, pp. 147–8, 152.

28. *Ibid.*, p. 153.

29. TNA Cabinet Memorandum February 10 1918, GT 3643, CAB 24/42.

30. S. Webb and B. Webb, *The Decay of Capitalist Civilization* (3rd edn, George Allen & Unwin, London, 1923), pp. 164, 167.

31. Martin Pugh, '"Class traitors": Conservative recruits to Labour 1900–30', *English Historical Review*, 113, 450, February 1998, p. 55.

32. TNA Cabinet Memorandum February–March 1919, G 237, CAB 24/75.

33. Lowe, 'The Ministry of Labour', pp. 415–35. See also George C. Peden, 'The Treasury as the Central Department of Government, 1919–1939', *Public Administration*, 61, 4, 1983, pp. 380–2.

34. Peden, 'Treasury, pp. 235–50. See also Kathleen Burk, 'The Treasury: From Impotence to Power', in Kathleen Burk (ed.), *War and the State: The Transformation of British Government* (Allen & Unwin, London, 1982), pp. 84–107.

35. Morgan, *Studies in British Financial Policy*, p. 122; Parliamentary Papers 1927 XI, Report of the Committee on National Debt and Taxation, p. 33; TNA, CAB 27/71 FC 3rd Minutes, 20 August 1919.

36. Howson, *Domestic Monetary Management*, p. 14.

37. George C. Peden, 'The Road to and from Gairloch: Lloyd George, Unemployment, Inflation, and the 'Treasury view' in 1921', *Twentieth Century British History*, 4, 3, 1993, pp. 224–49; George C. Peden, *Keynes and his Critics: Treasury Responses to the Keynesian Revolution 1925–1946* (Oxford University Press, Oxford, 2004), p. 6.

38. Robert W.D. Boyce, *British Capitalism at the Crossroads, 1919–1932: A Study in Politics, Economics and International Relations* (Cambridge University Press, Cambridge, 1998), p. 383 n. 102.

39. William A. Thomas, *The Finance of British Industry 1918–1976* (Methuen, London, 1978), p. 54.

40. Andrew McDonald, 'The Geddes Committee and the Formulation of Public Expenditure Policy', 1921–2, *Historical Journal*, 32, 3, 1989, p. 645.

41. *Ibid.*, p. 646.

42. Gail Braybon, *Women Workers in the First World War* (Croom Helm, London, 1981), p. 59.

43. R.M. Titmuss, *Essays on the Welfare State* (George Allen & Unwin, London, 1958), p. 86.

44. *Daily Herald*, 11 January 1919; 18 January 1919; and 25 January 1919.

45. Munitions Council Daily Report, 12 December 1919, TNA, MUN 4/3412.

46. TNA, CAB 24/112 MWR, 9 October 1920; TNA, MUN 4/6738; G. Carr, 'Engineering workers and the rise of labour in Coventry 1914–1939', University of Warwick, Ph.D. (1978), p. 119; Ian G. Hunter, 'Working class representatives in elective local authorities on Tyneside 1883–1921', University of Newcastle, M.Litt. (1978), p. 293.

47. 'The Report of the Women's Employment Committee for the Ministry of Reconstruction', PP, xiv, 1918, Cd 9239, 60. See also Deborah Thom, *Nice Girls and Rude Girls: Women Workers in World War I* (I.B. Taurus, London, 2000), p. 189.

48. David Kenyon, *First World War National Factories. An Archaeological Architectural and Historical Review, Research Report Series No. 76* (Historic England, Portsmouth, 2015).

49. Munitions Council Daily Report, 20 December 1918, TNA, MUM 4/3413.

50. House of Commons Debate, 13 February 1919, Vol. 112 c309W.

51. 'Area No 2 List of Large Firms Requiring Work', 16 April 1919, quoted in Seipp, *The Ordeal of Peace*, p. 147.
52. 'Self-contained Works for a Self-contained Car', *The Light Car and Cyclecar*, 5 February 1921, p. 232. The cloth badge on the workers' overalls was in red, white and green, the colours of the National Union of Women's Suffrage Societies while the enamelled plaques distributed to agents for Galloway cars were green, purple and white, the colours of the Women's Social and Political Union.
53. Oxford Dictionary of National Biography entry for Dorothée Pullinger; www. gracesguide.co.uk/Galloway_Motor_Car_Co (accessed 14 December 2017).
54. Quentin R. Skrabec Jr, *The Metallurgic Age: The Victorian Flowering of Invention and Industrial Science* (McFarland and Co., North Carolina, 2006), pp. 178, 190.
55. *Woolwich Pioneer*, 5 December 1919.
56. R.M. Lynne, 'The military railways of Kent, Part I', *Journal of the Railway and Canal Historical Society*, 24, 4, March 1982, pp. 69–73; R.M. Lynne, 'The military railways of Kent, Part II', *Journal of the Railway and Canal Historical Society*, 24, 5, July 1982, pp. 110–20 and R.M. Lynne, 'The military railways of Kent, Part III', *Journal of the Railway and Canal Historical Society*, 24, 6, November 1982, pp. 167–70.
57. Beveridge Collection Munitions V 43 Court case of 18 April 1916. TNA, MUN 5/18/202/2.
58. Lloyd George's remarks quoted in Peter Van Ham, *Western Doctrines on East-West Trade: Theory, History and Policy* (Palgrave Macmillan, Basingstoke, 1992), p. 53; *Woolwich Pioneer*, 26 September 1919; *Woolwich Pioneer*, 21 April 1921; *Kentish Independent*, 29 August 1919.
59. *Woolwich Pioneer*, 28 January 1921.
60. *Kentish Independent*, 26 April 1919.
61. TNA, MUN 4/6394.
62. TNA, MUN 4/6397; TNA, MUN 4/5329; Oliver F.G. Hogg, *The Royal Arsenal, its Background, Origin and Subsequent History. Volume II* (Oxford University Press, Oxford, 1963), pp. 9991–1000; Report of the Enquiry into the future of His Majesty's factories at Gretna and Waltham Abbey, Cd 667, 1920.
63. TNA, MUN 4/6402. Howard Williamson, *The Great War Medal Collections Companion* (Howard Williamson, Harwich, 2011), pp. 84–6. The medals were made by disabled ex-servicemen.
64. *Woolwich Pioneer*, 27 December 1918.
65. *Woolwich Pioneer*, 19 December 1919.
66. *Evening Standard*, 28 November 1919; *Daily Gazette*, 29 November 1919; *Daily Herald*, 5 December 1919;
67. *Woolwich Pioneer*, 5 October 1921; *Woolwich Pioneer*, 1 January 1921.

68. *Evening Standard*, 31 December 1919; *Railway Magazine*, May/June 1944 90, 551, p. 131; *Railway and Travel Monthly*, 1/17 15, 91, pp. 307–8; House of Commons Debate, 13 May 1924, Vol. 173 cc1141-2.

69. *Woolwich Pioneer*, 3 February 1922; *Woolwich Pioneer*, 24 February 1922.

70. Alan A Jackson, *London's Metropolitan Railway* (David & Charles, Newton Abbot, 1986), pp. 282–3; A.A. Jackson, 'The great government locomotive sales of 1919–27, *Railway World*, 47, 555, 1986, pp. 408–11.

71. Gilbert Slater, 'Unemployment in Woolwich', in John J. Astor and Sir Arthur Lyon Bowley, *The Third Winter of Unemployment: The Report of an Enquiry Undertaken in the Autumn of 1922* (P.S. King & Son, London, 1923), p. 321.

72. Bernard Mallet and C. Oswald George, *British Budgets, 1921/1922–1932/33* (Macmillan, London, 1933), pp. 556–9; George C. Peden, *British Economic and Social Policy: Lloyd George to Margaret Thatcher* (Philip Alan, Oxford, 1985), pp. 45–52.

73. Margaret Morris, 'In search of the profiteer', in Chris Wrigley and John Shepherd (eds), *On the Move: Essays in Labour and Transport History Presented to Philip Bagwell* (Hambleton, London, 1991), p. 185.

74. Martin J. Daunton, 'Payment and participation: welfare and state formation, 1900–1951', *Past and Present*, 150, February 1996, 1, pp. 178; Daunton, 'How to pay', p. 896.

75. J.C. Stamp, 'The special taxation of business profits in relation to the present position of national finance', *Economic Journal*, 29, 1919, pp. 407–27; J.-L. Robert, 'The image of the profiteer', in J. Winter and J.-L. Robert (eds), *Capital Cities at War* (Cambridge University Press, Cambridge, 1997), pp. 104–32.

76. 5 March 1919, Parliamentary Debates 5th Ser., Vol. 113, p. 461.

77. Nothing really changes, as present government policy suggests!

Chapter 4: Political Reconstruction

1. DeGroot, *Blighty*, p. 314.

2. Geoffrey Regan, *The Guinness Book of Military Anecdotes* (Guinness, London, 1992), p. 127.

3. Michael Childs, 'Labour grows up; the electoral system, political generations, and British politics 1890–1929', *Twentieth Century British History*, 67, 2, 1995, p. 129.

4. Schwarz, 'Conservatism', in Schwartz and Langan, *Crises in the British State*, p. 52.

5. J.M. McEwen, 'The Coupon Election of 1918 and Unionist Members of Parliament', *Journal of Modern History*, 34, 3, September 1962, pp. 294–5.

6. None of the Party's seventeen candidates (including the only woman to be endorsed by the Conservative-dominated Coalition, Christabel Pankhurst) were

elected and the Party was wound up in June 1919. See E. Sylvia Pankhurst, *The Life of Emmeline Pankhurst: The Suffragette Struggle for Women's Citizenship* (T. Werner Laurie, London, 1935), p. 163; June Purvis, 'The Women's Party of Great Britain (1917–1919): a forgotten episode in British women's political history', *Women's History Review*, 25, 4, 2016, pp. 638–51.

7. Men who had served were issued with a silver badge so that civilians would know that they were veterans.

8. Stephen R. Ward, 'The British Veterans' Ticket of 1918', *Journal of British Studies*, 8, 1, November 1968, p. 166.

9. Plaid Cymru followed, being formed in 1925.

10. Ward, 'The British Veterans', p. 167.

11. There appear to have been some errors. Lloyd-George loyalist George Lambert of South Molton did not receive the coupon while Josiah Wedgwood, who did not want one, was allocated it. Trevor Wilson, *The Downfall of the Liberal Party* (Collins, London, 1966), pp. 157–9. On the classification of candidates see F.W.S. Craig (ed.), *British Parliamentary Election Statistics 1918–1968* (Political Reference Publications, Glasgow, 1968), pp. 1–2.

12. *Manchester Guardian*, 20 November 1918.

13. Roy Douglas, *History of the Liberal Party 1895–1970* (Sidgwick & Jackson, London, 1971), pp. 130–1.

14. Chris Cook, *The Age of Alignment, Electoral Politics in Britain 1922–1929* (Macmillan, London and Basingstoke, 1975), p. 10.

15. David Butler and Donald Stokes, *Political Change in Britain: The Evolution of Electoral Choice* (2nd edn, Macmillan, London, 1974), pp. 156, 162.

16. Sandra Stanley Holton, *Feminism and Democracy: Women's Suffrage and Reform Politics in Britain, 1900–1918* (Cambridge University Press, Cambridge, 2003), p. 130.

17. Brian Harrison, *Separate Spheres. The Opposition to Women's Suffrage in Britain* (Croom Helm, London, 1978), pp. 215–220; Brian Harrison, 'Women in a men's house. The women MPs 1919–1945', *Historical Journal*, 29, 3, 1986, p. 654.

18. Laura Beer, 'Education or manipulation? Labour, democracy and the popular press in interwar Britain', *Journal of British Studies*, 48, 1, January 2009, pp. 134–5, 141–2.

19. Cook, *The Age of Alignment*, p. 6.

20. Miliband, *Parliamentary Socialism*, p. 65.

21. The number of Labour seats varies from source to source. It can be calculated as sixty if Kettering's Co-operative MP is included and so are two others MPs, Jack Jones in West Ham Silvertown and Brigadier General Sir O. Thomas in Anglesey, who joined the Labour ranks soon after being elected.

22. In 1919 Labour gained power in twelve London boroughs, emerged as the leading party in two more, tripled the number of seats held on the London County

Council and became the largest party in Bradford. Glamorgan, Durham and Monmouthshire became Labour counties. Labour won thirteen Urban District Councils in Wales, gained 45 per cent of the vote in Sheffield and made gains in Liverpool, Manchester, Salford, Swindon and elsewhere. See Matthew Worley, *Labour Inside the Gate: A History of the British Labour Party Between the Wars* (I.B. Tauris, London, 2005), pp. 29–30.

23. Childs, 'Labour grows up', pp. 123, 143. See also Robert C. Self, *Evolution of the British Party System: 1885–1940* (Routledge, Abington, 2014), pp. 141–4.

24. Ross McKibbin, *Parties and People, England 1914–1951* (Oxford University Press, Oxford, 2010), pp. 5, 13–14.

25. Worley, *Labour Inside the Gate*, p. 35.

26. *Ibid.*, p. 43.

27. Ben Pimlott, *Labour and the Left in the 1930s* (Cambridge University Press, Cambridge, 1977), p. 196.

28. Miliband, *Parliamentary Socialism*, p. 13.

29. *Ibid.*, p. 62.

30. Maurice Cowling, *The Impact of Labour 1920–1924: The Beginning of Modern British Politics* (Cambridge University Press, Cambridge, 1971), p. 11.

31. *The Times*, 27 October 1921.

32. Richard Toye, '"Perfectly Parliamentary?" The Labour Party and the House of Commons in the inter-war years', *Twentieth Century British History*, 25, 1, 2014, p. 10.

33. Wrigley, *Lloyd George and the Challenge*, p. 305.

34. J.H. Thomas quoted in *The Times*, 8 March 1924.

35. David Howell, '"I loved my Union and my Country": Jimmy Thomas and the politics of railway trade unionism', *Twentieth Century British History*, 6, 2, 1995, pp. 145–73.

36. J.H. Thomas, *When Labour Rules* (Collins, London, 1920), pp. 8, 11, 15, 19.

37. Andrew Thorpe, *A History of the British Labour Party* (Macmillan, Basingstoke, 1997), pp. 47–8.

38. Stuart Ball, Andrew Thorpe and Matthew Worley, 'Elections, leaflets and whist drives: Constituency Party members between the wars', in Matthew Worley (ed.), *Labour's Grass Roots. Essays on the Activities of Local Labour Parties and Members, 1918–45* (Ashgate, Aldershot, 2005), p. 10.

39. Paul Ward, *Red Flag and Union Jack: Englishness, Patriotism, and the British Left, 1881–1924* (Royal Historical Society and the Boydell Press, Woodbridge and Rochester, 1998), p. 152.

40. Stuart Macintyre, 'British Labour, Marxism and working-class apathy in the nineteen twenties', *Historical Journal*, 20, 2, 1977, pp. 479–96.

41. Quoted in Daunton, 'How to pay', p. 907.

42.   Lord Henry Bentinck, *Tory Democracy* (Methuen, London, 1918), pp. 2–3, cited in McEwen, 'The Coupon Election', p. 306.

43.   McEwen, 'The Coupon Election', p. 306.

44.   Michael Kinnear, *The British Voter: An Atlas and Survey Since 1885* (Batsford, London, 1968), p. 70.

45.   J.R. MacDonald, *Parliament and Democracy* (National Labour Press, London, 1920), pp. 3–4. The fact that MacDonald had opposed the war may have had something to do with his defeats.

46.   *Liberal Agent*, 25 April 1924, p. 26.

47.   *Daily Herald*, 5 December, 1919.

48.   J.R. MacDonald, *Socialism: Critical and Constructive* (Cassell, London, 1921), p. 283.

49.   *Ibid.*, p. 2; J.R. MacDonald, *Parliament and Revolution* (National Labour Press, Manchester, 1919), p. 8.

50.   *Labour Standard*, 21 March 1925, quoted in Catriona Macdonald, 'Following the procession: Scottish Labour, 1918–45', in Matthew Worley (ed.), *Labour's Grass Roots. Essays on the Activities of Local Labour Parties and Members, 1918–45* (Ashgate, Aldershot, 2005), p. 38.

51.   J.R. MacDonald, *A Policy for the Labour Party* (London, 1920), pp. 53, 62; MacDonald, *Parliament and Revolution*, p. 6; *Forward*, 21 December 1918, quoted in Macintyre, 'British labour', p. 485.

52.   MacDonald, *Parliament and Revolution*, p. 103. MacDonald, *Socialism: Critical and Constructive*, p. 234; J.R. MacDonald, 'The Review outlook', *Socialist Review*, 16, 1920, p. 9.

53.   Chris Wrigley and John Shepherd (eds), *On the Move: Essays in Labour and Transport History Presented to Philip Bagwell* (Hambledon Press, London, 1991), p. 180.

54.   Peter Clarke, *Lancashire and the New Liberalism* (Cambridge University Press, Cambridge, 1971), pp. 130, 143.

55.   Jon Lawrence, 'The transformation of British public politics after the First World War', *Past & Present*, No. 190, February 2006, p. 187.

56.   C.F.G. Masterman, 'The General Election and After', *Contemporary Review*, 115, 1919, pp. 123–4.

57.   *The Times*, 28 November 1918.

58.   Editorial, *Manchester Guardian*, 11 December 1918.

59.   *Manchester Guardian*, 3 June 1919.

60.   Lawrence, 'The transformation', p. 203. See also Jon Lawrence, 'Labour: The Myths It Has Lived By', in Duncan Tanner, Pat Thane and Nick Tiratsoo (eds), *Labour's First Century* (Cambridge University Press, Cambridge), 2000.

61.   *The Times*, 1 March 1921.

62. *The Times*, 23 October 1924.

63. *Labour Organiser*, April 1921.

64. Karen Hunt, 'Making politics in local communities: Labour women in inter-war Manchester', in Matthew Worley (ed.), *Labour's Grass Roots. Essays on the Activities of Local Labour Parties and Members, 1918–45* (Ashgate, Aldershot, 2005), p. 80.

65. Ball, Thorpe and Worley, 'Elections', in Worley (ed.), *Labour's Grass Roots*, p. 11; Worley, *Labour Inside the Gate*, p. 3.

66. Michael Savage, *The Dynamics of Working-class Politics: The Labour Movement in Preston 1880–1940* (Cambridge University Press, Cambridge, 1987), p. 194. Manchester's first generation of female Labour councillors were often active in the co-op or a union and few described themselves as 'housewives', Hunt, 'Making politics', p. 84.

67. *Catholic Times*, 8 September 1919.

68. K.Y. Stenberg, 'Gender, class and London labour politics 1870–1914', Ph.D., Minnesota (1993), p. ii.

69. David Thackeray, 'Women and Conservative Activism in early twentieth-century Britain', *Journal of British Studies*, 49, 4, October 2010, pp. 837, 838, 841, 842.

70. *Conservative Agents' Journal*, September 1920; *Conservative Agents' Journal*, April 1923. See also *Conservative Agents' Journal*, November 1919; *Conservative Agents' Journal*, September 1920 and *Conservative Agents' Journal*, November 1920.

71. Schwarz, 'Conservatism', in Schwartz and Langan, *Crises in the British State*, p. 55.

72. Jon Lawrence, 'Fascist violence and public order in inter-war Britain', *Historical Research*, 76, 172, May 2003, p. 243.

73. John Stubbs, 'The impact of the Great War on the Conservative Party', in Gillian Peele and Chris Cook (eds), *The Politics of Reappraisal 1918–1939* (Palgrave, Macmillan, London, 1975), p. 35.

74. Martin Pugh, *Electoral Reform in War and Peace 1906–18* (Routledge & Kegan Paul, London, Henley and Boston, 1978), p. 183.

75. *Daily Herald*, 5 January 1923; *Woman's Leader*, 12, 1920, p. 290, quoted in Helen McCarthy, 'Parties, voluntary associations and democratic politics in interwar Britain', *Historical Journal*, 50, 4, December 2007, p. 902; David Jarvis, 'The shaping of the Conservative electoral hegemony, 1918–1939', in Jon Lawrence and Miles Taylor (eds), *Party, State and Society: Electoral Behaviour in Britain Since 1920* (Scolar, Aldershot, 1997), p. 145.

76. Yearbook of the YMCA (1921), p. 99.

77. Lieutenant Colonel H.H. Wade, 'The appeal to reason', *The League*, 2, 1920, p. 129, quoted in McCarthy, 'Parties, voluntary associations and democratic politics', p. 899.

78. Item 3, Cabinet meeting, 7 November 1919, TNA, CAB 23/18/4.

79. Graves and Hodge, *The Long Week-End*, p. 27

80. Collier and Lang, *Just the Other Day*, pp. 18–19.

81. *The Times*, 28 June 1919, p. 13.

82. *Yorkshire Telegraph and Star*, 24 June 1919, p. 4; Graves and Hodge, *The Long Week-End*, p. 26.

83. *The Times*, 20 May 1919, p. 14.

84. Margaret Macmillan, *The Peacemakers* (John Murray, London, 2002), p. 478.

85. Collier and Lang, *Just the Other Day*, p. 22; Macmillan, p. 490.

86. Brian Bond, *Survivors of a Kind: Memoirs of the Western Front* (Continuum, London and New York, 2008), p. 25.

Chapter 5: Adjusting to Peace

1. DeGroot, *Blighty*, p. 314.

2. Noreen Branson, *Britain in the Nineteen Twenties* (Weidenfeld & Nicolson, 1975), p. 209.

3. Quoted in Thom, *Nice Girls and Rude Girls*, p. 187.

4. Statistics and quote from Gerry R. Rubin, 'Law as a Bargaining Weapon: British Labour and the Restoration of Pre-War Practices Act 1919', *Historical Journal* (1989) 32:4, p. 933.

5. Rubin, 'Law as a bargaining weapon', pp. 932–3. However, only half of male employees had been discharged.

6. R.H. Gummer *The Story of Barnbow: How the Shells were Filled* (J.D. Hunter & Sons, Leeds, 1919), p. 55.

7. Angela Woollacott, *On Her Their Lives Depend: Munitions Workers in the Great War* (University of California Press, Berkeley, 1994), p. 107.

8. Van Emden and Humphries, *All Quiet*, pp. 286–7.

9. Woollacott, *On Her Their Lives Depend*, p. 108.

10. Arthur, *We Will Remember*, p. 223.

11. Quoted in Thom, *Nice Girls and Rude Girls*, p. 195.

12. *The Times*, 3 May 1919.

13. Woollacott, *On Her Their Lives Depend*, p. 183.

14. Branson, *Britain in the Nineteen Twenties*, p. 211.

15. *Manchester Guardian*, 22 March 1918.

16. Woolacott, *On Her Their Lives Depend*, pp. 183–4.

17. Branson, *Britain in the Nineteen Twenties*, p. 211.

18. The Local Advisory Committee dealt with employment issues. In 1919 the building, Lesser Colston Hall, came into the ownership of the Corporation of Bristol.

19. Miss B.A. Sparks had an MA from Oxford, was the Principal at Colston's Girls School and later the Principal at Cheltenham Ladies College.

20. Leonard Broad was the manager of the Bristol Employment Exchange and a Sales Manager at the local Greenbank Chocolate Factory.

21. A few days earlier 500 servants and former servants met in Bristol and demanded the 8-hour day, no caps and aprons and increased pay. *Bristol Times and Mirror*, 7 February 1919; Ministry of Munitions, Demobilization and Resettlement Department (Intelligence and Record Branch) Daily Notes, 7 February and 12 February, TNA, MUN 4/5336. One report indicates that when asked 'What is it about domestic service that you don't like? Is it the caps and aprons?' the response was a loud 'Yes'. Manchester and Salford Women's Trades and Labour Council said the cap as regarded as the badge of slavery. *Manchester Guardian*, 26 February 1919. A Ministry of Reconstruction committee reported that while uniforms should be provided by employers, if required, 'We think that in many instances they will agree to dispense with caps', *Observer*, 16 March 1919.

22. The resentment about long hours, low pay and 'living in' was noted in Luton and Manchester in December 1918 and confirmed by surveys in Sheffield, Bradford, Coventry, Derby, Leeds, Newcastle, Rochdale and Nottingham in January 1919. See Ministry of Munitions, Demobilization and Resettlement Department (Intelligence and Record Branch), Daily Notes, 19 December 1918; 4 January 1919; 7 January 19191; 24 January 1919, TNA, MUN 4/5337, Munitions Council Daily Report 9 December 1918, TNA, MUN 4/3412.

23. These councils were named after Liberal MP John Henry Whitley who, in 1917, chaired a committee which reported on 'the Relations of Employers and Employees'. Following its deliberations it was agreed that each industry should have a statutory council to determine wages and conditions. It would be staffed by representatives of both employees and employers.

24. Nicolson, *The Great Silence*, p. 4.

25. Brian W. Harvey and Carol Fitzgerald (eds), *Edward Heron-Allen's Journal of the Great War* (Sussex Record Society, 2002), entry for 20 July 1918, p. 202.

26. Graves and Hodge, *The Long Week-End*, p. 35; Paxman, *Great Britain's Great War*, p. 281.

27. Branson, *Britain in the Nineteen Twenties*, p. 208.

28. Graves and Hodge, *The Long Week-End*, pp. 37–8.

29. *Spectator*, 20 November 1920, p. 7.

30. Nicolson, *The Great Silence*, p. 159.

31. *Aberdeen Press and Journal*, 28 March 1919, p. 6.

32. *Western Gazette*, 12 September 1919, p. 10. The story was reported in many newspapers.

33. Debate in the Commons, 5 July 1922, http://hansard.millbanksystems.com/commons/1922/jul/05/criminal-law-amendment-bill#S5CV0156P0_19220705_HOC_323 (accessed 2 March 2018).

34. Quoted in *Voices of the First World War*, Podcast 30 Women's War Services www.iwm.org.uk/history/podcasts/voices-of-the-first-world-war/podcast-30-womens-war-services (accessed 9 December 2017).

35. Statistics of the Military Effort of the British Empire during the Great War (HMSO, London, 1922), p. 237. The exact figure was officers 79,445, other ranks 1,583,180, total 1,662,625. In addition, tens of thousands of sailors and airmen had also been wounded in some way.

36. *The Times*, 16 March 1885.

37. See http://ezitis.myzen.co.uk/hoxtonhouse.html (accessed 4 December 2017).

38. Meaghan Kowalsky, '"The Honorable Obligation": The King's National Roll Scheme for Disabled Ex-Servicemen 1915–1944', *European Review of History* (2007) 14:4, p. 568.

39. *Report by the Joint War Committee and the Joint War Finance Committee of the British Red Cross Society and the Order of St John of Jerusalem in England on voluntary aid rendered to the sick and wounded at home and abroad and to British prisoners of war, 1914–19* (HMSO, 1921), pp. 230–1. Their hospitals particularly looked after officers.

40. Jerry White, *The Worst Street in North London, Campbell Bunk, Islington, Between the Wars* (Routledge and Kegan Paul, London, 1986), pp. 48–9, 73.

41. *Islington Gazette*, 2 September 1922.

42. http://ezitis.myzen.co.uk/queenmarysidcup.html (accessed 9 December 2017). The remarkable work of the Hospital is described in Nicolson, *The Great Silence*, pp. 51–5. Arthur, *We Will Remember*, p. 143.

43. Kowalsky, '"The Honorable Obligation"', pp. 570–1.

44. Peter Leese, 'Problems Returning Home: the British Psychological Casualties of the Great War', *Historical Journal* (1997), 40:4, p. 1056.

45. 22 January 1919, Letter from Sir Laming Worthington Evans to Sir Douglas Haig, TNA, PIN 15/3883.

46. Kowalsky, '"The Honorable Obligation"', pp. 571–3.

47. Nicolson, *The Great Silence*, p. 48.

48. Arthur, *We Will Remember*, p. 166.

49. Quoted in Leese, 'Problems Returning Home', p. 1059.

50. Richards, *Old Soldiers*, p. 318. As there was no National Health Service then Richards would have had to pay to visit a doctor, which he probably was unable to afford.

51. *Ibid.*, p. 321.

52. Richard S. Grayson, *Belfast Boys: How Nationalists and Unionists Fought and Died Together in the First World War* (Continuum, London, 2009), p. 155. Those helped where largely Protestant. The Comrades and its rival organizations merged to form the British Legion in 1921.

53. Monthly reports of the Ministry of Pensions, April 1919, August 1919. TNA, CAB 24/80/72, CAB 24/89/33.

54. Leese, 'Problems Returning Home', p. 1062.

55. *Ibid.*, p. 1057. See TNA, PIN 15/421. One feels that little changed over the subsequent century.

56. Reported in the *Spectator*, 5 July 1919.

57. George Mosse, 'Shell Shock as a Social Disease', *Journal of Contemporary History* (2000), 35:1, p. 101.

58. Ted Bogacz, 'War Neurosis and Cultural Change in England, 1914–22: the work of the War Office Committee of Enquiry into 'Shell Shock', *Journal of Contemporary History* (1989) 24:2, p. 231.

59. *Ibid.*, p. 247.

60. *The Times*, 12 January 1920.

61. Simon Wessely, 'The life and death of Private Harry Farr', *Journal of the Royal Society of Medicine* (2006), p. 99.

62. Quoted in A.D. Macleod, 'Shell shock, Gordon Holmes and the Great War', *Journal of the Royal Society of Medicine* (2004) 97(2), pp. 86–9.

63. *Ibid.* Bogacz, 'War Neurosis and Cultural Change', p. 235.

64. Bogacz, 'War Neurosis and Cultural Change', pp. 228, 251.

65. Graves and Hodge, *The Long Week-End*, p. 23.

66. Quoted in Joanne Bourke, 'Effeminacy, ethnicity and the end of trauma: the sufferings of "Shell Shocked" men in Britain and Ireland 1914–1939', *Journal of Contemporary History* (2000) 35:1, pp. 62–3.

67. Graves, *Goodbye*, pp. 235, 239.

68. www.iwm.org.uk/history/podcasts/voices-of-the-first-world-war/podcast-33-shell-shock (accessed 9 December 2017).

69. *Ibid.*

70. Bourke, 'Effeminacy, ethnicity and the end of trauma', p. 63.

71. Bogacz, 'War Neurosis and Cultural Change', p. 228; Bourke, 'Effeminacy, ethnicity and the end of trauma', p. 63. See also some very graphic footage available on YouTube www.youtube.com/watch?v=faM42KMeB5Q (accessed 6 July 2017).

72. Clive Emsley, 'Violent crime in England in 1919: post-war anxieties and press narratives', *Continuity and Change* (2008) 23:1, pp. 183–4, 187.

73. Quoted in *Ibid.*, p. 188.

74. Nicolson, *The Great Silence*, p. 189.

Chapter 6: Commemoration

1. There is no agreed figure for British losses during the First World War. The figure used here were published by the War Office in *Statistics of the Military Effort*, p. 237. In addition, another 196,710 men from the Empire were killed, and 1,662,625 wounded in some way.

2. Entry for 11 November 1918, unit war diary 18 Kings Royal Rifle Corps, TNA, WO 95/2635/4.

3. 11 November 1918, TNA, WO 95/2635/4. This must have been a fairly common feeling.

4. Graves and Hodge, *The Long Week-End*, p. 13. It took until 25 November for the German forces in East Africa to surrender.

5. Harvey and Fitzgerald (eds), *Edward Heron-Allen's Journal*, p. 271.

6. Lady Mary Cameron, *Merrily I go to Hell* (Brentano's, New York, 1931), p. 125.

7. James Munson (ed.), *Echoes of the Great War: The Diary of the Reverend Andrew Clark* (Oxford University Press, Oxford, 1988), pp. 258–9.

8. Olivier Bell (ed.), *The Diary of Virginia Woolf*, pp. 216–17.

9. Cameron, *Merrily I go to Hell*, pp. 125–6.

10. Geoffrey Moorhouse, *Hell's Foundations: A Town, its Myths and Gallipoli* (Sceptre, London, 1992), pp. 102–3.

11. Mein, Wares and Mann (eds), *St Albans*, p. 227.

12. Brittain, *Testament of Youth*, pp. 462–3.

13. It was in fact the third anniversary of the Battle of Delville Wood on the Somme, which saw some of most desperate fighting in the whole war,

14. See the deliberations in the Cabinet Committee on Peace Celebrations, TNA, CAB 27/52.

15. Quoted in Angela K. Smith (ed.), *Women's Writing of the First World War: An Anthology* (Manchester University Press, Manchester, 2000), p. 322.

16. *The Times*, 30 June 1919.

17. Munson (ed.), *Echoes of the Great War*, p. 286. Entry for 29 June 1919.

18. E.B. Osborn, 'The Lessons of the Pageant', *Illustrated London News*, 26 July 1919, p. 116.

19. *The Times*, 21 July 1919.

20. *The Times*, 21 July 1919.

21. *Illustrated London News*, 26 July 1919.

22. *The Times*, 18 July 1919, 21 July 1919.

23. Olivier Bell (ed.), *The Diary of Virginia Woolf*, p. 292, entry for 19 July 1919. Collier and Lang, *Just the Other Day*, p. 16.

24. Allan Greenberg, 'Lutyen's Cenotaph', *Journal of the Society of Architectural Historians* (1989), 48:1, p. 20.

25. *Illustrated London News*, 26 July 1919.

26. *The Times*, 21 July 1919. Letter from 'RIP'.

27. Gavin Stamp, *The Memorial to the Missing of the Somme* (Profile, London, 2006), p. 45.

28. *The Times*, 21 July 1919.

29. Eric Homberger, 'The Story of the Cenotaph', *Times Literary Supplement*, 12 November 1976, p. 1430.

30. Philip Gibbs, *The Pageant of the Years* (Heinemann, London, 1946), p. 261.

31. Olivier Bell (ed.), *The Diary of Virginia Woolf*, p. 292.

32. *Ibid.*, diary entry for 20 July 1919, p. 294.

33. Sir Percy Fitzpatrick, memorandum submitted to Lord Milner for the attention of the War Cabinet, 4 November 1919, paper CP45. TNA, CAB 24/92/46.

34. Cabinet meeting, 4 November 1919, item 4, TNA, CAB 23/18.

35. See, for example, *Daily Express*, 7 November 1919.

36. *Western Morning News*, 12 November 1919.

37. *Daily Express*, 12 November 1919; *The Times*, 12 November 1919; Nicolson, *The Great Silence*, pp. 144–5.

38. *The Times*, 12 November 1919.

39. Nicolson, *The Great Silence*, p. 270.

40. This account is based on text at www.westminster-abbey.org/our-history/people/unknown-warrior (accessed 21 November 2017). See also Gregory, *The Last Great War*, pp. 24–6, and Nicolson, *The Great Silence*, pp. 266–74.

41. Quoted in James McMillan, *The Way it Was 1914–1934* (William Kimber, London, 1979), p. 108.

42. Greenberg, 'Lutyen's Cenotaph', p. 11.

43. Gregory, *The Last Great War*, pp. 27–8. And now the Tomb has perhaps largely been forgotten.

44. Quoted in Greenberg, 'Lutyen's Cenotaph', p. 11.

45. Quoted by Gregory, *The Last Great War*, pp. 26–7. See also the teenage Evelyn Waugh's reaction, Nicolson, *The Great Silence*, p. 142.

46. Ian Nannestad, '"Bubbles", "Abe my boy" and the "Fowler war cry": singing at the Vetch Field in the 1920s', *Sport in Society*, 17, 3, 2014, pp. 325–6; *The Times*, 11 November 1921.

47. Hannington, *Unemployed Struggles*, pp. 77–8.

48. Bob Bushaway, '"Name upon Name", the Great War and Remembrance', in Roy Porter (ed.), *Myths of the English*, *Polity* (Polity, Cambridge, 1994), p. 160.

49. Susan R. Grayzel, *Women's Identities at War: Gender, Motherhood and Politics in Britain and France During the First World War* (The University of North Carolina Press, Chapel Hill and London, 1999), pp. 227–9.

50. Niall Ferguson, *The Pity of War* (Allen Lane, Penguin, London, 1998), p. 437.

51. Quoted in Adrian Gregory, *The Silence of Memory: Armistice Day 1919–1946* (Berg, Oxford and Providence, Rhode Island, 1994), p. 9. The idea of commemoration as a means to reinforce solidarity is considered in Daniel Sherman, *The Construction of Memory in Interwar France* (University of Chicago Press, Chicago and London, 1999), p. 7 and by Jay Winter, *Sites of Memory*, p. 27.

52. Barclay Baron (ed.), *Letters from Flanders* (Centenary Press, London, 1932), letter dated 10 November 1918, pp. 167–8.

53. T.A. Lowe, *The Western Battlefields: A Guide to the British Line* (Gale & Polden, London, 1920), p. ix.

54. Quoted in Voices of the First World War podcast no 50 'legacy', www.iwm. org.uk/history/podcasts/voices-of-the-first-world-war/podcast-50-legacy (accessed 21 November 2017).

55. The work of the Units is discussed at www.vlib.us/wwi/resources/clear-ingthedead.html (accessed 21 November 2017). The IWGC was renamed the Commonwealth War Graves Commission in 1960.

56. The previous paragraphs are based on text from the CWGC website www.cwgc. org/history-and-archives/the-world-wars (accessed 21 November 2017).

57. Lowe, *The Western Battlefields*, p. 61.

58. Talbot House, *The Pilgrim's Guide to the Ypres Salient*, p. 90.

59. The centre for the Somme front was Amiens, but the town had hardly suffered in comparison with Ypres.

60. See correspondence on TNA, WO 32/5853. Churchill's proposal was ignored by the Belgian authorities.

61. This is discussed in some detail in a War Office file, TNA, WO 32/5569. The British memorial was eventually built at the Menin Gate, which was opened in 1927.

62. Lieutenant Colonel Beckles Wilson to Belgian Foreign Minister, 5 July 19, TNA, WO 32/5569.

63. Talbot House, *The Pilgrim's Guide to the Ypres Salient*, p. 44.

64. H.M. Morton, *Evening Standard*, 26 May 1920.

65. David W. Lloyd, *Battlefield Tourism* (Bloomsbury, London, 1998), p. 102.

Chapter 7: Local Memorials

1. George L. Mosse, *Fallen Soldiers, Reshaping the Memory of the World Wars* (Oxford University Press, Oxford, 1990), pp. 6–7, 96.

2. See, for example, Henry V. Morton, *The Heart of London* (Methuen, London, 1925), p. 26 and Henry Wade, *The Duke of York's Steps* (1929, new edn Harper, New York, 1982), p. 72 and K.S. Inglis, 'Entombing Unknown Soldiers: from London and Paris to Baghdad', *History and Meaning*, 5, 2, Fall/Winter 1993, p. 23.

3. Bushaway, '"Name upon Name"', pp. 136–67, 148.

4. Hynes, *A War Imagined*, p. 270.
5. Winter, *Sites of Memory*, p. 28.
6. Catherine Moriarty, 'Private grief and public remembrance: British First World War memorials', in Martin Evans and Ken Lunn (eds), *War and Memory in the Twentieth Century* (Berg, Oxford, 1977), p. 137.
7. King, *Memorials*, pp. 209, 242; Winter, *Sites of Memory*, p. 98.
8. A. Calder, 'The Scottish National War Memorial', in W. Kidd and B. Murdoch (eds), *Memory and Memorials: The Commemorative Century* (Ashgate, Aldershot, 2004), p. 61.
9. Michael Howard, 'The First World War reconsidered', in Jay Winter, Geoffrey Parker and Mary Habeck (eds), *The Great War and the Twentieth Century* (New Haven, Connecticut, 2000), pp. 16–17. On the evolution of views about memorials see Mark Connelly, *The Great War, Memory and Ritual: Commemoration in the City and East London, 1916–1939* (Boydell and Brewer, Woodbridge, 2015), p. 31 and Dan Todman, *The Great War: Myth and Memory* (Hambleton, Continuum, London, 2005), p. 50.
10. Kate Tiller, *Remembrance and Community* (British Association for Local History, Ashbourne, 2013), p. 5.
11. Quoted in Gregory, *The Last Great War*, p. 255.
12. Winter, *Sites of Memory*, p. 85.
13. Gregory, *The Last Great War*, p. 253.
14. Quoted by Tiller, *Remembrance and Community*, p. 53.
15. Inglis, 'Entombing Unknown Soldiers', p. 589. Gregory, *The Last Great War*, p. 260. In the end a conventional war memorial was erected in the town park.
16. Or as likely that they did not have the financial resources to contribute. Inglis, 'Entombing Unknown Soldiers', pp. 590–2. Inglis suggests that the high success rate might have been due to a 'predominantly deferential working class', p. 591). Gregory, *The Last Great War*, p. 261.
17. J. Bartlett and K.M. Ellis, 'Remembering the war dead in Northop: First World War Memorials in a Welsh Parish', *Journal of Contemporary History*, 34, 2, 1999, p. 239.
18. Mein, Wares and Mann (eds), *St Albans*, pp. 230–5.
19. Winter, *Sites of Memory*, p. 104.
20. P. Gough and S. Morgan, 'Manipulating the metonymic: the politics of civic identity and the Bristol Cenotaph, 1919–1932', *Journal of Historical Geography*, 30, 2004, pp. 676–7.
21. The *Citizen*, Letchworth, 17 October 1919, quoted in Catherine Moriarty, 'The absent dead and figurative First World War memorial', *Transactions of the Ancient Monument Society*, 39, 1995, p. 15.
22. *Evesham Standard*, 5 November, 1921.

23. King, *Memorials*, pp. 85, 86, 87, 110.

24. http://www.iwm.org.uk/memorials/item/memorial/28749 (accessed 1 March 2017).

25. Connelly, *The Great War*, p. 76.

26. http://www.iwm.org.uk/memorials/item/memorial/30297 (accessed 1 March 2017).

27. http://www.iwm.org.uk/memorials/item/memorial/56732 (accessed 1 March 2017).

28. *Carlisle Journal*, 20 June 1919, in King, *Memorials*, p. 77.

29. http://www.scapaflow.co/index.php/history_and_archaeology/the_20th_century/war/war_memorials (accessed 1 March 2017).

30. http://www.iwm.org.uk/memorials/item/memorial/28749 (accessed 1 March 2017).

31. Suzanne Evans, *Mothers of Heroes, Mothers of Martyr: World War I and the Politics of Grief* (McGill-Queen's University Press, Montreal and London, 2007).

32. http://www.scapaflow.co/index.php/history_and_archaeology/the_20th_century/war/war_memorials (accessed 1 March 2017).

33. http://www.iwm.org.uk/memorials/item/memorial/27739 (accessed 1 March 2017).

34. Alan Borg, *War Memorials: From Antiquity to the Present* (Leo Cooper, London, 1991), p. 120.

35. *Burnley Express*, 11 December 1926.

36. *Yorkshire Post and Leeds Intelligencer*, 29 April 1925, available at http://www.yorkshireindexers.info/wiki/index.php?title=Barnbow_Factory_Memorial_Cross_Gates (accessed 1 March 2017). See also the Barnbow Roll of Honour, TNA, MUN 5/155.

37. http://www.iwm.org.uk/memorials/item/memorial/11888 (accessed 1 March 2017) and https://livesofthefirstworldwar.org/community/3690 (accessed 1 March 2017).

38. Recording of Mrs Olive Castle, held in the Imperial War Museum and cited in Janet S.K. Watson, *Fighting Different Wars. Experience, Memory and the First World War in Britain* (Cambridge University Press, Cambridge, 2004), p. 288.

39. http://www.iwm.org.uk/memorials/item/memorial/64691 (accessed 1 March 2017).

40. http://www.iwm.org.uk/memorials/item/memorial/50880 (accessed 1 March 2017).

41. http://www.iwm.org.uk/memorials/item/memorial/13366 (accessed 1 March 2017).

42. http://buckinghamshireremembers.org.uk/gateway.php?page=355 (accessed 1 March 2017).

43. Unveiling programme quoted in Moriarty, 'Private Grief and Public Remembrance', p. 65.

44. *Ibid*.

45. Moriarty, 'The absent dead', p. 35.

46. http://www.iwm.org.uk/memorials/item/memorial/2084 (accessed 1 March 20170.

47. Nick Mansfield, 'Class conflict and village war memorials, 1914–24', *Rural History*, 6, 1, 1995, p. 75.

48. http://www.iwm.org.uk/memorials/item/memorial/65102 (accessed 1 March 2017).

49. King, *Memorials*, pp. 110–11.

50. *Kentish Express and Ashford News*, 12 February 1921 in Moriarty, 'Christian iconography', p. 70.

51. West Sussex Record Office, PAR/294/4/5, cited in Moriarty, 'Christian iconography', p. 70.

52. Keith Grieves, 'Common meeting places and the brightening of rural life: local debates on village halls in Sussex after the First World War', *Rural History*, 10, 2, 1999, p. 181.

53. *Carlisle Journal*, 3 June 1919, in King, *Memorials*, p. 91.

54. Gladys Cuttle, *Durisdeer War Memorials, Dumfriesshire, and Parish Memories* (Penpoint, 2010). For images see http://www.edinburghs-war.ed.ac.uk/sites/default/files/pdf_War_Memorials.pdf (accessed 1 March 2017).

55. *Northop Parish Magazine*, May 1919, quoted in Bartlett and Ellis, 'Remembering the war dead', pp. 232, 239, 241.

56. Winter, *Sites of Memory*, p. 97; K.S. Inglis, 'The Homecoming: The War Memorial monument in Cambridge, England', *Journal of Contemporary History*, 27, 4, 1992, 583–605. See also King, *Memorials*, pp. 65–70, 75–85.

57. Quoted in Grieves, 'Common meeting places', pp. 176–7, 179.

58. Gregory, *The Last Great War*, p. 261.

59. Gregory, *The Silence of Memory*; King, *Memorials*, p. 68; *Newcastle Evening Chronicle*, 20 May 1992, cited in Davies, 'War memorials', p. 112.

60. Grieves, 'Common meeting places', p. 184.

61. The *Observer and Gazette*, 16 November 1923, in Moriarty, 'Christian iconography', p. 70.

62. Gregory, *The Last Great War*, p. 258.

63. W.R. Leatherby, 'Memorials of the Fallen: Service or Sacrifice?', *The Hibbert Journal*, 1918–19, Vol. 17, p. 621, quoted in Bushaway, '"Name upon name"', pp. 146–7.

64. *Cambridge Daily News*, 20 January 1919, in Mansfield, 'Class conflict', p. 77.

65. King, *Memorials*, p. 77; Jeremy Burchardt, 'Reconstructing the rural community: village halls and the National Council of Social Service, 1919–1939',

Rural History, 10, 2, 1999, p. 210; Mansfield, 'Class conflict', pp. 77–8; Grieves, 'Common meeting places', p. 175.

66. For a longer, but by no means complete, list of memorial halls see Mansfield, 'Class conflict', p. 77.

67. King, *Memorials*, p. 86.

68. Recollections of Isabella Millington cited in Bartlett and Ellis, 'Remembering the war dead', p. 241.

69. Mansfield, 'Class conflict', p. 75.

70. Quoted in W.J. Reader, *At Duty's Call. A Study in Obsolete Patriotism* (Manchester University Press, Manchester, 1988), pp. 131–2.

71. Gibbs, quoted in King, *Memorials*, p. 76.

72. Moriarty, 'Christian iconography', p. 69.

73. https://papastour21century.wordpress.com/about-papa-stour/the-papa-stour-kirk/war-memorial-window-2/ (accessed 1 March 1917).

74. Moriarty 'Christian iconography', p. 72.

75. *The Times*, 2 November 1920.

76. Moriarty 'Christian iconography', p. 65.

77. *Ibid.*, p. 63.

78. Davies, 'War Memorials', p. 112.

79. *Oxford English Dictionary*. See also ProQuest Historical Newspapers the *Guardian* and the *Observer*.

80. IMW WMIPA record no. 40539. See www.iwm.org.uk_www.iwm.org.uk/memorials/item/memorial/40359 (accessed 1 March 2017). Of course it could be of some debate about how willing these sacrifices were.

81. http://www.mkheritage.co.uk/mkha/mkha/projects/jt/tw/docs/85.html (accessed 1 March 2017).

82. *Boston Guardian*, 10 April 1920, press cutting IWM WMIPA, record No. 20508.

83. Arthur St John Adcock, *For Remembrance: Solider Poets Who Have Fallen in the War* (Hodder & Stoughton, London, 1918), pp. 11–12, available at https://archive.org/details/cihm_991629 (accessed 1 March 2017).

84. *The Times*, 20 July 1933.

85. Gregory, *The Last Great War*, pp. 268–9.

86. http://www.iwm.org.uk/memorials/item/memorial/38729 (accessed 1 March 2017).

87. http://www.iwm.org.uk/memorials/item/memorial/15957 (accessed 1 March 2017).

88. http://www.iwm.org.uk/memorials/item/memorial/27510 (accessed 1 March 2017).

89. Grieves, 'Common meeting places', pp. 180–1.

90. Gough and Morgan, 'Manipulating the metonymic'.

Chapter 8: Ain't Misbehavin'

1. *The Times*, 16 December 1918.
2. Quoted in Graves and Hodges, *The Long Week-End*, pp. 34–5.
3. The *Graphic*, 28 June 1919.
4. *Sheffield Evening Telegraph*, 27 June 1919.
5. John Montgomery, *The Twenties*, p. 243.
6. *Illustrated London News*, 7 December 1918.
7. *Illustrated London News*, 19 April 1919.
8. *The Times*, 12 April 1919.
9. Quoted in Graves and Hodges, *The Long Week-End*, pp. 34–5.
10. Kate E. Meyrick, *Secrets of the 43* (John Lang, London, 1933), p. 23.
11. The *Bystander*, 26 February 1919.
12. Still fondly remembered as the Hammersmith Palais, it finally closed in 2007.
13. *West London Observer*, 24 October 1919.
14. Nicholson, *The Great Silence*, pp. 153–4.
15. *Ibid.*, p. 154.
16. Quoted in John Montgomery, *The Twenties: An Informal Social History* (George Allen, London, 1957), p. 178.
17. *Manchester Guardian*, 16 October 1919.
18. *Manchester Guardian*, 25 September 1919.
19. Nicolson, *The Great Silence*, p. 158. Many more racist articles can be found in the press, yet there were few if any reported attacks, verbal or otherwise, on these musicians.
20. The *Bystander*, 8 January 1919.
21. Dave Haslam, *Life after Dark* (Simon & Schuster, London, 2015), pp. 38–9.
22. *Banbury Guardian*, 10 April 1919, p. 1. Webb's Quadrille Band was also for hire providing 'the latest music skilfully played by competent musicians'.
23. *Manchester Guardian*, 15 April 1919.
24. Nicolson, *The Great Silence*, p. 158.
25. Haslam, *Life after Dark*, p. 36.
26. *The Times*, 25 March 1919; 27 March 1919.
27. The *Bystander*, 26 February 1919.
28. For more about this see: Heather Shore, '"Constable dances with instructress": the Police and the Queen of the Nightclubs in inter-war London', *Social History* (2013) 38:2.
29. Nicolson, *The Great Silence*, p. 153. For the ladies 'powerfully sweet-smelling white face powder was piled into bowls'.
30. Collier and Lang, *Just the Other Day*, pp. 55–7.

31. Meyrick, *Secrets*, p. 23. In the 1911 census, Dalton Murray was a vocalist, presumably in the music hall. He was also known as Harry Dalton or Harry Simpson, under which name he was given when the Meyricks divorced in 1921.

32. Meyrick, *Secrets*, p. 20.

33. Collier and Lang, *Just the Other Day*, pp. 53–4.

34. Meyrick, *Secrets*, p. 23.

35. *Daily Herald*, 23 December 1919. Marek Kohn, *Dope Girls* (Lawrence & Wishart, London, 1992), p. 123.

36. *Daily Herald*, 23 December 1919, p. 2. See also *The Times*, 7 January, 29 January 1920. This the first of many times when Mrs Meyrick appeared before the bench.

37. Meyrick, *Secrets*, p. 33.

38. Lillian Wyles, *A Woman at Scotland Yard* (Faber & Faber, London, 1952), pp. 92–9.

39. *Ibid.*, pp. 91–2.

40. Annie Lai, Bob Little and Pippa Little, 'Chinatown Annie: the East End opium trade 1920–35: the story of a woman opium dealer', *Oral History Journal*, 14, 1, Spring 1986, p. 23.

41. Quoted in James McMillan, *The Way It Was 1914–1934* (William Kimber, London, 1979), p. 105. See also Collier and Lang, *Just the Other Day*, pp. 49–52.

42. *Daily Express*, 20 October 1920; *Evening News*, 5 October 1920 and *East End News*, 7 October 1920.

43. Martin Booth, *Cannabis: A History* (Doubleday, London, 2003), p. 183. Her story is told in detail in Kohn, 'Dope Girls'; *Daily Express*, 16 December 1918.

44. Sidney Felstead, *The Underworld of London* (John Murray, London, 1923), p. 284.

45. *Ibid.*, p. 285.

46. Philip Ziegler, *Diana Cooper* (Hamish Hamilton, London, 1981), p. 55.

47. TNA, MEPO 3/424, CID Report, June 1923.

48. TNA, MEPO 3/424; Kohn, 'Dope Girls', p. 154.

49. TNA, MEPO 3/424; Kohn, 'Dope Girls', p. 157.

50. Meyrick, *Secrets*, p. 55.

51. *Sunday Express*, 30 April 1922. Quoted in Kohn, 'Dope Girls', p. 128.

52. Kohn, 'Dope Girls', pp. 161–75; Meyrick, *Secrets*, p. 43; Lai, Little and Little, 'Chinatown Annie', p. 23.

53. This is discussed in some detail in Clive Emsley, 'Violent crime in England in 1919: post-war anxieties and press narratives', *Continuity and Change* (2008) 23:1.

54. *The Times*, 21 January 1920.

55. *The Times*, 21 January 1920. Neither the murders of Miss Shore and Mrs Buxton were solved.

56. *The Times*, 21 January 1920. The murder victim was 78-year-old Reuben Mort, a retired blacksmith who had £1,000 in a safe.

57. *Ibid.*, pp. 12–14.

58. Figures correlated on the British Executions website, www.britishexecutions. co.uk/chronology.php?time=1507194918. The average number of individuals hung annually between 1919 and 1939 was eleven. Twenty-four individuals were also hung in 1928.

59. *The Times*, 5 May 1919.

60. Taken from https://mickysix.wordpress.com/2014/06/20/henry-thomas-gas-kin (accessed 21 November 2017). The website contains several accounts of the murder. See also the *Staffordshire Advertiser*, 8 March 1919 and TNA, HO 144/1532/385637. Elizabeth had almost certainly taken to prostitution to supplement her Army allowance.

61. *Sunday Post*, 13 June 1920.

62. *Aberdeen Press and Journal*, 9 June 1920. See also *The Times*, 7 June 1920 and 23 August 1986 and Toplis' entry in the *Oxford Dictionary of National Biography*.

63. *Criminal Statistics for the Year 1922* (HMSO, London, 1924), Cmd2265, p. 6. See also Butler and Butler, *British Political Facts 1900–1994*, pp. 318–19.

64. *Criminal Statistics*, pp. 6–8. The greatest decrease over pre-war crime was for drunkenness, in part due to continued restrictions on pub opening hours and the weakness of postwar beer.

65. See Heather Shore, 'Criminality and Englishness in the Aftermath: the race-course wars of the 1920s', *Twentieth Century British History* (2011) 22:4.

66. *The Times*, 29 March 1919. The race was won by Poethlyn, the favourite.

67. *The Times*, 5 June 1919.

68. Brian Macdonald, *Elephant Boys: Tales of London and Los Angeles Underworlds* (Mainstream, Edinburgh, 2000), p. 9. The Elephant Gang was sometimes known as the Brummagen Boys because many members came from Birmingham. It was led by Billy Kimber, a leading character in the *Peaky Blinders* TV series.

69. Sabini was the model for the gangster Colleoni in Graham Greene's novel *Brighton Rock* (London, Heinemann, 1938).

70. Macdonald, *Elephant Boys*, p. 245.

71. Raphael Samuel, *East End Underworld. Chapters in the Life of Arthur Harding* (Routledge & Kegan Paul, London, 1981), p. 328, n. 15.

72. *Ibid.*, pp. 184–5.

73. *The Times*, 5 April 1921.

74. *Leeds Mercury*, 13 July 1920.

75. *Nottingham Journal*, 13 July 1920.

76. *Sussex Agricultural Examiner*, 13 August 1920; *The Times*, 10 August 1920.

77. For more about the 'Battle of Epsom' see www.epsomandewellhistoryexplorer. org.uk/RaceTrackGangs.html (accessed 23 November 2017).

78. Brittain, *Testament of Youth*, p. 469.

Chapter 9: Looking Forwards

1.   Matthew Richardson, *The Hunger Wars*, p. 128.

2.   *The Times*, 14 April 1919.

3.   *Daily Telegraph*, 14 July 2014. See also an ebook Steve Berry and Phil Norman, *A Brief History of Crisps*.

4.   *The Times*, 3 April 1919.

5.   *Times Literary Supplement*, 25 September 1919.

6.   Collier and Lang, *Just the Other Day*, p. 268.

7.   *Times Literary Supplement*, 11 September 1919, p. 484.

8.   Quoted in Bond, *Survivors of a Kind*, p. 26.

9.   *Ibid.*, p. 24.

10. Herbert Buckmaster, *Buck's Book: Ventures, Adventures and Misadventures* (Grayson & Grayson, London, 1933), p. 208.

11. For more about the house, which is still open, see www.talbothouse.be.

12. Lever, *Clayton of Toc H*, pp. 84–5.

13. *Ibid.*, p. 102.

14. Quoted at www.savethechildren.org.uk/about-us/our-history (accessed 9 November 2017).

15. *The Times*, 16 May 1919. The Council was fined £5 for not putting the printer's name on the leaflet.

16. The *Observer*, 9 June 1991.

17. *Manchester Guardian*, 31 May 1919.

18. *Manchester Guardian*, 16 August 1919.

19. *The Times*, 12 November 1920.

20. The Fund sought to become a limited company rather than a traditional non-incorporated charity, see TNA, BT 298/351.

21. Graves and Hodge, *The Long Week-End*, pp. 129–32.

22. *Birmingham Gazette*, 20 July 1920. The article was also addressed to home 'craftswomen'. See also www.researchpod.co.uk/pdf/get_a_grip_history_of_ rawlplug.pdf (accessed 6 January 2018).

23. Simon Fowler, *Tracing your First World War Ancestors* (Pen & Sword, Barnsley, 2013), pp. 104–6. The Royal Flying Corps had been founded in 1912.

24. Cecil Lewis, *Sagittarius Rising* (Penguin, [Harmondsworth, 1977), p. 212.

25. Graves and Hodge, *The Long Week-End*, pp. 80–1.

26. Quoted in *Ibid.*, p. 80.

27. *Ibid.*, pp. 81–2. It was not until just before the Second World War that the first commercial flights across the Atlantic took place.

28. Lewis, *Sagittarius Rising*, pp. 213–14.

29. *Flight*, 3 July 1919.

30. *Flight*, 16 January 1919.

31. Lewis, *Sagittarius Rising*, p. 211.

32. Robin Higham, *Britain's Imperial Air Routes 1918 to 1939* (G.T. Foulis & Co., London, 1960), pp. 29–30, 35.

33. *Ibid.*, p. 26.

34. *Ibid.*, pp. 26–8.

35. Butler and Butler, *British Political Facts 1900–1994*, p. 348; Peter Thorold, *The Motoring Age* (Profile, London, 2003), p. 88. In 1918, only 87,000 private cars were licensed. At the end of March 2017 there were 37.5 million vehicles on Britain's roads, www.gov.uk/government/uploads/system/uploads/attachment_data/file/620223/vehicle-licensing-january-to-march-2017.pdf (accessed 21 November 2017).

36. www.gracesguide.co.uk/Vauxhall (accessed 21 November 2017). Emphasis in the original.

37. *The Times*, 26 September 1919.

38. TNA, MUN 4/5774, Francis Tudsberry, Disposals Board to Brig Gen Sir H.P. Maybury, Roads Department, Ministry of Transport, 20 December 1919.

39. A list of manufacturers was published in *Autocar* in March 1919, see www.gracesguide.co.uk/1919_Car_Models (accessed 21 November 2017).

40. www.gracesguide.co.uk/File:Im19200117A-Wols.jpg (accessed 21 November 2017).

41. *The Times*, 2 October 1920.

42. Montgomery, *The Twenties*, pp. 175–6. The prices of Morris cars were cut dramatically in February 1921, which led to a boom in car ownership. Car ownership didn't become common until the 1950s.

43. *The Times*, 23 June 1920, 30 June 1921. Although flints and horseshoe nails were a greater cause of punctures than broken glass.

44. Mike Parker, *Mapping the Roads* (AA Publishing, Basingstoke, 2016), pp. 112–13.

45. Branson, *Britain in the Nineteen Twenties*, p. 226. Manchester and Wolverhampton were the first towns to introduce lights.

46. *The Times*, 29 November 1920; Branson, p. 226.

47. Branson, *Britain in the Nineteen Twenties*, pp. 220–7.

48. www.gracesguide.co.uk/File:Im19200103A-Vaux.jpg (accessed 21 November 2017).

49. Felstead, *The Underworld of London*, p. 50.

50. *Ibid.*, p. 51. Rolls-Royces apparently did not have locks at this time. Thorold, *The Motoring Age*, p. 116.
51. *The Times*, 21 January 1920, pp. 12, 14.
52. Butler and Butler, *British Political Facts 1900–1994*, p. 321.
53. *The Times*, 29 July 1920, p. 9.
54. Felstead, *The Underworld of London*, p. 34.
55. *Statistics of the Military Effort*, pp. 595, 852–7. Figures exclude vehicles used by the RAF and Royal Navy. On 30 November 1918, there were 735,000 horses and mules in the Army, p. 861.
56. Simon Bradley, *The Railways: Nation, Network and People* (Profile, London, 2016), p. 408. The new haulage companies were helped by the inflexible freight charges that the railway companies were forced to maintain (Butler and Butler, *British Political Facts 1900–1994*, p. 348).
57. Winter, *Sites of Memory*, p. 57.
58. Jennifer Hazelgrove, 'Spiritualism after the Great War', *Twentieth Century British History* (1999), 10:4, p. 430.
59. *The Times*, 1 March 1919. Lieutenant Peach's body was never found. He is commemorated on the Theipval Memorial to the Missing of the Somme.
60. *Lancashire Daily Post*, 6 November 191.
61. Collier and Lang, *Just the Other Day*, pp. 29–30.
62. Quoted in Winter, *Sites of Memory*, p. 59.
63. Quoted in Paxman, *Great Britain's Great War*, p. 275. Collier and Lang, *Just the Other Day*, p. 31.
64. Quoted in Suzie Grogan, '"A solace to a tortured world . . ." – The Growing Interest in Spiritualism during and after WW1', http://ww1centenary.oucs.ox.ac.uk/?p=3300 (accessed 21 December 2017).
65. Nicolson, *The Great Silence*, p. 97.
66. Van Emden and Humphries, *All Quiet*, p. 111.

Conclusion

1. www.1921census.org.uk (accessed 6 December 2017). No census was taken on the island of Ireland in 1921.
2. Taylor, *English History*, p. 600.

Select Bibliography

The book is based on the use of hundreds of different sources, books, archives and websites. The text is fully annotated so that readers can follow up anything that interests them. The books and other sources listed below are key texts for any study of the immediate inter-war period.

Arthur, Max, *We Will Remember Them: Voices from the Aftermath of the Great War* (Weidenfeld & Nicolson, 2009)

Branson, Noreen, *Britain in the Nineteen Twenties* (Weidenfeld & Nicolson, 1975)

Collier, John and Iain Lang, *Just the Other Day: An Informal History of Great Britain Since the War* (Hamish Hamilton, 1932)

DeGroot, Gerard, *Blighty: British Society in the Era of the Great War* (Longman, 1996)

van Emden, Richard and Steve Humphries, *All Quiet on the Home Front: An Oral History of Life in Britain During the First World War* (Headline, 2003)

Gerwarth, Robert, *The Vanquished: Why the First World War Failed to End, 1917–1923* (Allen Lane, 2016)

Gibbs, Philip, *The Realities of War* (Heinemann, 1920; online at: https://archive.org/details/realitiesofwar00gibbuoft)

Graves, Robert and Alan Hodge, *The Long Weekend* (Penguin, 1971)

Gregory, Adrian, *The Last Great War: British Society and the First World War* (Cambridge University Press, 2008)

McMillan, James, *The Way It Was 1914–1934* (William Kimber, 1979)

Montgomery, John, *The Twenties: An Informal Social History* (George Allen, 1957)

Nicolson, Juliet, *The Great Silence 1918–1920: Living in the Shadow of the Great War* (John Murray, 2009)

Paxman, Jeremy, *Great Britain's Great War* (Viking, 2013)

Mr. Punch's History of the Great War (Cassell, 1920)

Reynolds, David, *The Long Shadow: The Great War and the Twentieth Century* (Simon & Shuster, 2013)

Tooze, Adam, *The Deluge: The Great War, America and the Remaking of the Global Order, 1916–1931* (Allan Lane, 2014)

Webb, Simon, *1991: Britain's Year of Revolution* (Pen & Sword, 2017)

Websites

British Newspaper Archives – www.britishnewspaperarchives.co.uk
Cabinet Papers Online – www.nationalarchives.gov.uk/cabinetpapers
The Digital Times Online (via your local library)
Imperial War Museum Voices of the First World War Podcasts nos 47 'Armistice', 48 'homecoming', and 50 'legacy' – www.iwm.org.uk/history/podcasts/voices-of-the-first-world-war/podcast-48-homecoming
ProQuest Historical Newspapers: *Guardian* and *Observer* (via your local library)

Archives

Almost all of the original sources used in the book can be found at The National Archives of the United Kingdom (TNA) – www.nationalarchives.gov.uk

Index